In Praise of
STRONG WOMEN

In Praise of
STRONG WOMEN

A Psychiatrist's Memoir

DAVID KIRKPATRICK

GRANVILLE ISLAND
PUBLISHING

Library and Archives Canada Cataloguing in Publication

Kirkpatrick, David, 1939-
    In praise of strong women : a psychiatrist's memoir / David Kirkpatrick.

Includes bibliographical references and index.
ISBN 978-1-894694-70-4

1. Kirkpatrick, David, 1939-. 2. Kirkpatrick, David, 1939- — Family. 3. Kirkpatrick, David, 1939- — Relations with women.
4. Women — Psychology. 5. Psychiatrists — Canada — Biography.
I. Title.

RC438.6.K57A3 2009   616.890092   C2009-901369-X

Editors: Betty Keller and Wendy Bancroft
Text and cover design: Laura Kinder
Indexer: bookmark: editing & indexing
Proofreader: Renate Preuss

Cover image: *Woman in a Pink Sweater*, dry pastel, Sharon Hudson
www.sharonhudson.com

All photos taken by or in the collection of David Kirkpatrick and his family with the exception of the photo of Clair and David by Ross Powell

Granville Island Publishing
212–1656 Duranleau
Vancouver, BC V6H 3S4

www.granvilleislandpublishing.com

First published 2009
Printed on recycled paper in British Columbia, Canada

To strong and resilient girls
and women everywhere.

And to those who have collided with,
enjoyed and appreciated them,
and found the courage to love
and sometimes even to live with them.
Yesterday, today and tomorrow.
To them, I dedicate this book.

And especially to Betsy, Andy, Mindy and Clair.

Contents

Acknowledgements

MANY PEOPLE HELPED inspire this book. In addition to those whose stories appear in the book, several dozen come immediately to mind for their wit and wisdom, support, challenge, encouragement and expectations. Practicing what they preach, they model excellence, perhaps better than they know or appreciate.

Many others made a difference. High school teachers Olive Hammond (Latin), Charlotte Gorden (social studies), Joseph Elbert Schickedantz (mathematics), and the psychology professors who supported and encouraged me: Professors Jerome I. Berlin, Richard N. Carrera and L.E. (Pete) Cole. Writing teachers and early editors who started with me and urged me onward: Colleen Anderson, Terri Claflin, Linda Eckhardt, Clelie Rich, William Sellers and Glennis Zilm.

My brother Doug helped—and helps—keep me honest. Other family, all supportive, including Clair, Andy, Mindy, Sue, Edie, Bill, Suzanne, Fred, Carol, Christy, Stefan and Colleen. Office managers Joan McElligott and joy Fai who helped to balance and organize a busy office practice, and encouraged me to keep writing.

A number of physicians, nurses, psychologists, social workers and friends over the years who have taught me well. Psychotherapists who continued to believe in me: Molly, Virginia, Bob, Norm and Tom. Supervisors Lars and Randy. Good friends Bill, Dan, Darrell, Fraidie, Fran, Jay, Leonard, Maggie, Rob, Sara and Shmuel.

The staff of Strathcona Community Mental Health Team, reminders of why I enjoy practicing community mental health so much. The psychotherapy and psychiatric patients who taught me about resilient strength.

'The Group,' good UCLA nursing friends and strong women who Betsy shared with me: Betty, Cynthia, Henry Etta, Lee, Mary and Sylvia; because of them I am a better person. The many other strong women who taught me more than I taught them, including Annie, Aurelia, Beth, Britt, Christy, Deborah, Ellen, Ivy, Jan, Judy, Julie, Linda, Lukia, Mary and Nevenka.

Rabbi Shmuel Birnham who provided both religious and spiritual education and support.

My editor, Betty Keller, who saw what this book could and should be. She supported me, expected me to write my best, and reminded me that I was responsible not only for crossing my t's and dotting my i's, but also for writing a clear and readable book for the people who really matter: the readers. Wendy Bancroft then read and reviewed our manuscript. She refashioned the penultimate work into a story form that would not only continue to honor the reader, but also help make a good thing better. To Betty and her, I offer appreciative, humble, heartfelt thanks.

How is a good editor like a good therapist? They both tell you what you need to know. Not what you want to hear.

Foreword

DAVID KIRKPATRICK has written this book from his heart. He is a rare psychiatrist who is a humanist, interested in the importance, to us all, of the social world of relationships. He focuses here on his relationships with the women in his life and how they have affected his development as a man. This is a memoir full of love and admiration and thankfulness for the lessons he has learned from his female relatives, teachers and partners.

I knew a fellow once who stated, "Women rule the world and it's best that men acknowledge that and enjoy it!" Of course, women have not ruled the political world historically and still do not. But they do rule the emotional world of most of us and we can only hope that they do a good job. There is a phrase in psychology called "good-enough mothering" that has to do with infants getting at least their minimal needs met plus some degree of attachment. Men can do this mothering also but most often women are in this role. The author was fortunate enough to get this "good-enough mothering" from his mother and his aunts, and grandmothers. And he got so much more.

The women in his life showed him courage under adversity, hard work, warmth, encouragement, fortitude and a no-nonsense approach toward the children around them. Dr. Kirkpatrick makes a distinction between strong women and powerful women—the latter being individuals who use their power over children to bend them to their will. I believe this is a helpful distinction for readers because many people think power equals strength. When attempting to influence children or other adults, strength of character is what makes the difference in the lives of others. So much of what these women taught him throughout his life has been through their example, especially in how they handled the hard times.

But I must say something about a man who appreciates rather than fears the strong women he was born to, and those he picked to be in his life as an adult. He obviously relishes his relationships with them all and can sit back and enjoy what they do and say. I have experienced in my own life the disapproval of male relatives and colleagues when I asserted myself too much, or spoke out strongly, or expressed emotions that were near the surface. Their criticisms have always caught me off guard and have always hurt coming from ones so dear. There seems to be a need in many of them to control these strong behaviors.

Women are cautioned to show understanding and encouragement toward the men in their lives but I fear that those same cautions are not generally expected of men. Dr. Kirkpatrick seems to have learned this lesson from his earliest years and instead of attempting to bring the strong women in his life down a notch, he gets pleasure from the ways they approach life. It is a rare man and a rare psychiatrist who not only enjoys the women around him, but encourages them and learns what he can, and holds on for the ride!

Carolyn Crowder, Ph.D.
Tubac, Arizona
December, 2008

Introduction

IN SEPTEMBER 1985, following a long and miserable period of discomfort, my wife Betsy was diagnosed with cancer of the colon. Surgery was indicated and so, on a Friday evening that September, Betsy was taken to the operating room to have the tumor removed. While being rolled in, she was heard to say, "If anything happens to me, don't let David marry some geek!" Vintage Betsy. She enjoyed living in the here and now more than anything, but she could and would, simultaneously, look ahead when the moment, the hour or the day called for it.

We were lucky. The surgeon found no evidence of the cancer's extension. We all—Betsy, me and our two children, Andy who was then seven and Mindy who was three—breathed a sigh of relief. Betsy lived for the next four months with a temporary colostomy ("Mommy has a 'biper' [diaper]!" Mindy confided to a friend), but she gradually recovered.

Betsy lived those colostomy months pretty much the way she lived life: with humor, irony and wit. But not self-pity.

Ever. One weekend morning, while we were lying close to each other in bed reading, she spied me studying her stoma, the temporary opening to her colon created by her surgery.

"David, what are you doing there?" she challenged.

"Well, I'm . . . looking at your stoma, I guess," I responded, lamely if honestly.

"Well, is there a problem with it, dear?" she persisted, gently but firmly.

"Well, it's just that it—I don't know, Bets—it just seems to make me nervous, having an extra rectum in bed with us," I countered, totally off the top of my head.

"Well, don't worry about it, honey," she responded warmly. "Look at it this way . . . if you had had the colostomy instead of me, why, I'd be in bed right now with two extra assholes."

End of pillow talk.

With her colon cancer now behind us, we looked forward to a long, positive and contented future. Before Betsy's cancer, we had both been putting in long hours to establish the mental health clinic we had opened in Ashland, Oregon. This cancer scare made us take stock of what was important in our lives, and encouraged us to slow down some. Over the next years we began having breakfast together on Monday mornings, and even occasionally taking a half-day off to do things like go for long walks, in a manner quite different from our previous breakneck schedule and lifestyle. Both children were now in school, and life proceeded at a less hurried pace.

Then, on a spring day in March 1990, not suddenly or dramatically but softly, almost hesitantly, new symptoms began to appear, signaling that something was not right. Betsy experienced what seemed at first like mild indigestion: a twinge or a stitch, maybe a cramp, but nothing serious, I tried to assure myself. Don't go getting upset and bothering Betsy with your silly, stupid worries, David, I told myself. Then curious, spellbound, almost bewitched, we watched as the medical mystery slowly, almost lazily, began to uncoil itself. Like a yawning python awakening from a long nap.

When right lower-quadrant abdominal pains seized her more vigorously, Betsy went for blood tests and then for exploratory surgery. The surgeon found her uterus full of tumor. Midway through Mindy's second grade and Andy's sixth year of school, the lightning that was not supposed to strike twice struck Betsy, the highest, strongest branch on our family tree.

This cancer would prove to be far meaner and more advanced than the colon cancer had been, and an ill-starred but uncomplaining Betsy began chemotherapy and radiation treatments as the entire family faltered and hung on for dear life. What a vital, spirited life she had led, right up to the time this new milepost, milestone, millstone was given to her in such an unsolicited fashion!

Despite massive treatments of radiation and months of chemotherapy, Betsy's physical strength deteriorated. She became exhausted, bedridden and constipated. She was too tired to be cranky, yet very little escaped her attention; she watched and listened to the world unfold through her two children, her husband, her television and her telephone. She seemed to do better when she was being Betsy: complaining, pushy, a bit on the bossy side, controlling, or at least having some control over her life.

She was not happy about dying. On the other hand, she did not know self-pity and could still take one day, one hour, one minute of time and enjoy it to the fullest, with the energy and spirit that still persisted. After smelling some ribs I'd brought home for the kids and me one night from Safeway, she said, "Let me have one of those ribs." Chewing slowly and relishing what she knew she would vomit back up within the hour, she said, "M-m-m-m!" Live-in-the-moment ribs. Again, vintage Betsy. Aware of her own miserable condition, she was still more tuned into, and more interested in, her surroundings, especially her family. Her example helped keep me going, and probably kept our children going, as well. That much self-possessed yet selfless courage spilled out into our home, helping to feed and inspire us. If Betsy could continue being this way, in her desperate circumstances, how could we not?

Married to this tough, strong and determined woman who was fighting for her life, I struggled with two almost continuous fears. She would die. She wouldn't die.

In the end she did leave us, early in the morning of March 17th, 1991.

The next few years were difficult. Full of grief and loss for me and for our children. I turned inward, funneling much of this grief into my journal, writing about Betsy and what she meant to me, to her children and to her friends. I had always thought of her as a strong woman; now I began to think about what that actually meant. I thought about the kinds of things, events and experiences that had likely helped shape her strength. I thought about how the quality of her strength was in many ways different from that of a man's.

Slowly but surely, I began to realize and appreciate that I had more to say and more to write about this subject of women's strength, moving beyond my broken heart to profound appreciation, not just of Betsy, but also of the other strong women that I had known in my life. I thought, "My gosh, Betsy was strong, but so was your grandmother, David, and look at your mother, graduating from college when she was sixty-two." There was my first love, Jeanne, from grade three, and my next love, Jo, from college. There were teachers and friends.

I realized that these girls and women had shaped and reshaped me throughout my life, in a way that I don't think I had really appreciated; typical of strong women, they did what they had to do to get the job done, and didn't ask for any special recognition for their efforts or skill. Like strong women throughout history, they were unsung heroes. They had loved me, propped me up when I was weak and set me straight when I got out of line. They had taken care of me and moved on to myriad other tasks.

It struck me that, while they were often vulnerable, they were also tough, persistent, warm and courageous, frequently demonstrating moral strength by doing the right thing, regardless of the principle. They had integrity and they had resilience in the face of hard knocks. They were women who learned from their mistakes and from their successes. They knew when to act independently, but were not afraid to call on others for advice or support. While women are frequently givers to the point of self-detriment, the strong women I have known have also known how to take, when necessary.

As I thought about all these things, a book began to take shape, a book that would honor the girls and women in my life and, by extension, their sisters the world over. It would be a book that would thank strong women from the bottom of my heart and apologize to one or two from a similar place.

When you appreciate, you want to share.

As a psychiatrist and psychotherapist, I also had an interest in learning about strong women from a psychological and psychodynamic point of view. How do women become strong? Are some born that way? Do they gain strength as they grow and mature? I wondered how many men or women living with or attracted to a strong woman had mixed feelings about their situation, or were looking for ways to improve their relationships.

I wondered also why tough girls and strong women have not been honored, validated and celebrated more than they have been over centuries and millennia of recorded history. To some degree, that's a 'no-brainer.' History had been traditionally written for men, and by men. This was largely made possible by denying women an education, a denial justified by promulgating the idea that women do not have the mental capacity to absorb 'book learning.' This idea emerged from prehistoric times when men had time to discuss and debate between hunting animals and fighting off enemies. In time, these debates would crystallize into schools of thought. Women's chores were never-ending and, therefore, debates about them occurred while the women worked. These debates concerned the matters at hand: food and the welfare of their families. Ergo, it came to be accepted that they could not comprehend the larger issues, that they could not learn. This denial of women's mental capacity continues to this day in some parts of the world.

To be fair, in earlier and more primitive times, brute physical strength counted for much. In emergencies, the physically strongest and fastest individuals made decisions that could and would determine the survival of a family or village. These individuals were almost always boys or men. Thus, early primitive democracies were literally based on one man, one vote.

Second, and overlapping with that first reality, was the fact that cultures and societies became dependent on those physical realities, writing into the cultural fabric the societal roles that helped determine rules and codes of conduct. The value of those roles was directly related to their reliability, predictability, even their rigidity. Men hunted and fished and looked after their tribe by making the kinds of emergency decisions on which lives depended. Lives depended on women at least as much, but in perhaps less dramatic ways. Women cooked, gathered and foraged. They raised babies, looking after them in sickness and in wellness. They both watched over and also changed the accepted culture as medicine woman, mediator, custodian, midwife, and gardener and herbalist, curing salmon and seasoning food in the coldest winters and hottest summers, feeding their families and communities, thus helping ensure their species' survival. Women's contributions were often lost in the background, their contributions from day to day, as well as in times of family or community crisis, consigned sadly only to informal, oral history.

Women gradually and formally assumed even broader roles, and their communities began to further appreciate their intelligence and leadership skills. Egyptian women, for example, enjoyed considerable respect, opportunity and financial independence within their society. In ancient Egypt, the universe was seen as a duality of male and female, with the female deity known as Maat serving as the symbol of "cosmic harmony by whose rules the pharaoh must govern."[1]

In the Bible, Deborah stands out for her rich combination of judicial, religious, military and prophetic talents and influence. A judge and leader, she was commissioned by God to save the Israelites from their enemy, the Canaanites.[2] Few Biblical figures seemingly combined spiritual strength with such military competence and capability.

Through the ages there have been women who disguised themselves as ordinary soldiers or sailors in armies. There were knights in the Middle Ages who were women, as there were women warriors in Japan, Conquistadoras in Spain, women soldiers of the American Revolution and the Civil War, and women military pilots. In China, during the Shang Dynasty, noblewomen known as *fu* held office, paid tribute to the Emperor for the lands they controlled, led armies, regulated agriculture and supervised religious activities.[3] There have long been tales of the Amazon women warriors, and there are today matriarchal societies in places like New Guinea.[4] And in her excavations of *kurgans*—burial mounds of ancient Eurasian nomads—Jeannine Davis-Kimball uncovered artifacts supporting the routine importance of warrior women within those and other nomadic cultures. She reported that this new evidence "shows that women have always had a pretty prominent place in nomadic societies."[5]

According to Nicky Saunders, in *Women as Warriors in History*, women commonly took part in battles when their home, castle or town was attacked.[6] For example, a medieval lady would have expected to take charge of defense in her husband's absence. Joan of Arc, born in France during the Hundred Years War, fought heroically to defeat the English when they tried to destroy her village. Captured by the

English, she was condemned to die—not surprising in itself, but rather than being given a soldier's death she was convicted of witchcraft, and burned at the stake.

The Middle Ages saw both women and men gradually experience a regression of freedom, and by the eighteenth and nineteenth centuries women found themselves once again repressed, punished, even tortured and murdered for experiencing and expressing newfound freedoms.

Fanny Mendelssohn Hensel (1805–1847), for example, was an extraordinarily talented composer and pianist whose life, triumphs and defeats illustrate the challenges and difficulties experienced by gifted women 150 years ago. Fanny grew up in the shadow of her brother, Felix Mendelssohn, a composer known to all who love classical music. During a visit to England, Felix was given a private audience with Queen Victoria during which she (the Queen) sang her favorite aria from his Opus 8 for him. After the song, Felix confessed to the Queen that the composition was, in fact, not his, but his sister Fanny's. Felix is otherwise credited with supporting his sister's creative endeavors, but even he stopped short of helping Fanny get her music published "out of fear that she would not be able to maintain an active schedule of publication and thus be considered a failure."[7] In apparent frustration, Fanny is said to have once remarked, "You always remember . . . that you are a woman!"[8]

Only within the last one to two hundred years have technology and war begun to help level the playing field between women and men. Rosie the Riveter—in real life, Rose Will Monroe—was a vivacious icon, a woman who encouraged American women to leave home and assist in the United

States war effort. However, it was the shortage of men on the home front, combined with newer and lighter electrical tools and machinery, that would help create this opening for women to enter the work world in droves.[9] When World War II ended in 1945, most of the women who had followed Rosie's example returned to their homes or to more traditional jobs, but a barrier had been broken, and working outside the home would never again be so foreign and unacceptable for North American women.

We have come a long way in terms of recognizing women's rights and improved roles in society but that progress is uneven. There are still countries and cultures where women are devalued, where they continue to be suppressed, censored, imprisoned, unjustly punished, even murdered, for standing up or for speaking out. In December 2006, two female teachers were murdered in Afghanistan, along with their grandmother and two other family members. Their crime? Teaching children, specifically girls.[10] The Taliban's influence persists, and girls' schools in Afghanistan continue to be bombed.

Perhaps nothing illustrates women's strength more than the stories collected by Eve Ensler in her book *Insecure at Last*.[11] Traveling throughout the world, Ensler interviewed countless women warriors. For example, in Ciudad Juárez, Mexico, she spoke with women who had been brutalized, raped, exploited and whose friends were murdered; and the brave friends, sisters, mothers and women's groups who persisted in trying to stop the exploitation, the violence and the killing of their daughters, sisters and community. The daughter of a violent, abusive alcoholic father, Ensler herself has gone further than simply writing about her past: she has founded V-Day, the global movement to eradicate violence against women.

Thus, within these times and places many, if not most, girls learn early in their lives to protect and cover their force and vitality. They understand that their survival depends upon maintaining an outward mask of submission. However, stories like that told in the documentary *The Beauty Academy of Kabul*—about a group of women who open a beauticians' school in Kabul to provide women there with a means of earning a living and gaining some measure of independence and freedom—show that while the public face may show submission, the private space can still be one of strength.[12]

American suffragist leaders risked life and limb when working and speaking out for equal rights for women. Repeatedly bullied at meetings, Susan B. Anthony once spoke in upstate New York, overseen by a pistol-packing mayor to ensure her safety. Despite their frequent intimidations, however, women leaders persisted in their brave campaigns for women's suffrage, often working side by side with the abolitionist movements. We count ourselves as progressive here in North America, but women were not allowed to vote in the United States until 1920; they were not accorded status as a "person" in Canada until 1929.

History moves in cycles, sometimes in layers and levels. In the past, so-called primitive tribes developed roles suited to group survival, but these roles and rules relaxed with modernity and more civilized discourse. In many places, both women *and* men are now freer to exercise greater and wider behavioral options with less fear of retribution or backlash from their peer groups.

Still, few accounts celebrate the ubiquitous strong girls and women leading ordinary lives in every place throughout the world, without whose energy, strength, vitality and clever perspicacity the entire world would long ago have deteriorated and surely crumbled. Hence this book in which I pay tribute and say thank you to the strong girls and women in my own life and, in so doing, raise awareness of their presence everywhere and how we can best enjoy and appreciate their gifts.

Several years had passed since Betsy died and I first started thinking about writing this book. When I felt able to move on from Betsy, literally and figuratively, I relocated to Canada with my children, and married another strong woman. During this period of my life, the kids grew up and left home. My career as a psychotherapist has been rewarding but demanding, and I spent ten of those years as a psychiatrist at Strathcona, an exemplary community mental health clinic in Vancouver's notorious Downtown Eastside.

The book project got put aside while I tended to life's daily challenges, but the need to celebrate strong girls and women in text was always there and no more so than when I would see examples of this strength again and again, in my daughter, my wife, my friends and patients. I have a hunch that most of us have known one or more of these girls and women at some time in our lives.

Poet Sharon Barba's mystical paean, with reference to writer and diarist Anaïs Nin, suggests that it is time someone told their story.

A CYCLE OF WOMEN

It is that dream world Anaïs speaks of
that dark watery place
where everything is female
where you open the door of the house
and she waits upstairs
the way you knew she would
and her hair floats over the world.

Every woman has a history
mother and grandmother and the ones before that
the faces she sees in dreams or visions
and wonders Who? . . .

Each one is a queen, mother, huntress
though each remembers little of it
and some remember nothing at all,
resting in crazy houses
from the long spin of history
drinking the grief of their sex . . .
telling their daughters
the story of a sleeping princess
but knowing it takes more than a man's kiss
to wake one so bent on sleeping her life away:
. . . wake her up, as now,
using perhaps the kiss of a sister.

Let her go from there, start over,
live it again, until she knows who she is.

Until she rises as though from the sea . . .
not as delicate as he imagined her:
a woman big-hipped, beautiful and fierce.[13]

1 My Life With Strong Women Begins

I WAS BORN IN KANSAS CITY, Missouri, in 1939, at the outbreak of World War II in Europe and just two years before the United States would enter the war. And I have the receipt to prove it. Mother had either come back to the hospital as an outpatient after I was born to pay off the balance of her labor and delivery bill or, more likely, she had remained at Menorah Hospital for the better part of two weeks, as was the custom then.

> *Receipt A 25150 for $4.25*
> *($5 cash Received from Mrs. Elizabeth Kirkpatrick,*
> *Change Given $0.75) from the business office of*
> *Menorah Hospital, 4949 Rockhill Road, Kansas City,*
> *Missouri, 11-28-39.*

Telephone	*$. 25*
Bracelet	*$1.00*
For Circumcision	*$3.00.*

This time-out after a delivery was often the only rest most women enjoyed in those days. It would also be one of the few breaks from her hard-working busy life for the next forty-five years.

While war clouds already overshadowed Europe and much of the rest of the world, including Canada and Great Britain, the United States was experiencing relative isolation. My father joined the military service in 1942, shortly after the Japanese attacked Pearl Harbor; but for most of the rest of the war he was stationed at a base close to Yellow Springs, Ohio. We, my mom and I, lived in a small walk-up apartment in Yellow Springs. When I say small, I mean so small that when my brother was born in 1943, I was boarded out for part of a year because there was no room for a second child.

I've never doubted that my parents loved me, and I'm sure they hated the separation even if they saw me every day. But it was the end of the Great Depression years and money was tight all around. Not that long before, my mother's parents had lost their farm after years of financial struggle. It had both financially and emotionally devastated my grandfather, leading to bouts of deep depression, something that had plagued him throughout his life but was now heightened by the financial loss.

So, my parents did what they could. They made sure I was well looked after and worked toward reuniting our family as soon as possible. Strangely enough, it was the war that made that possible, at least for a short period.

Toward the end of the war, my father, an industrial engineer by training, was posted to Intelligence in the Army Air Corps and sent to Texas, where we joined him until he was sent overseas, first to Italy and then to Brazil. He was gone for two years, back only occasionally for visits.

In charge of the home front, our mother was the resin that would keep our family bonded together. She wrote to my father regularly, catching him up on how his two sons were faring and reassuring him in his isolation and insecurity before confessing her own aching loneliness for him. With no telephones to offer her the comfort of her loved one's voice, slow-going service mail was her only point of contact with him, but it helped to provide some continuity of experience between the war and our family's stateside existence.

Mother did well, shuttling the family between Texas and suburban Evanston, Illinois, north of Chicago, where we lived for a time with Aunt Elsie, her favorite sister, and her family of four older boys and two younger girls, Susan and Edith. But these were also the times when we would stay with Grandmother and Grandfather Kirkpatrick in the family farmhouse in rural DeKalb County.

At times we were joined at my grandparents' by my Aunt Joy, whose own husband—my father's brother, Tom—had been shipped to the Pacific theatre for a tour of army duty that would keep him apart from his family for thirty-seven continuous months. It is difficult to say exactly how long we spent with each family, because whenever Mom thought we had worn out our welcome in the place we were in, she moved us to the other; so we shuttled back and forth between homes during those years.

Mother and her sister Elsie were very close, so Mom may actually have preferred those times in Evanston. The downside was, however, that Aunt Elsie and Uncle Bill did not have a lot of money and had a hard enough time providing for their own family of six children, including my cousins Sue and Edie. Although I was not aware of it at the time, it would later became clear to us that Uncle Bill was probably unhappy as well as ineffective as a husband and a father.

For me though—outside of a time when my cousin Edie and I played doctor (she denies this)—it was the time we spent with Grandma that stands out most strongly in my memory. Grandma Kirkpatrick was the first woman, apart from my mother, who I loved and who showed me about strength in women. I can imagine me thinking in five-year-old language: "Oh, my gosh, there's another one: Grandma. She is different from my mom, but she is similar. I love her, I love Mom, too. Grandma is teaching me, and she's fun to be with." At the time I felt she actually was more fun to be with than my mother but, in hindsight, I know that's partly because she was the grandma. It is part of their job description.

I remember Grandpa Kirkpatrick, too, of course. Although my memories are positive—I remember, for instance, his Scottish humor and gentleness—he was nevertheless a background figure in this house for me. Grandpa Kirkpatrick was more involved with his cattle than his family. I do remember him getting grumpy in his retirement, several years later, and telling us to turn the black-and-white TV off because it was bothering him. But otherwise I don't remember too much about him. I know he adored Grandma, and I remember him proudly telling my father and mother after Grandma's funeral: "Look at all those cars in Pearl's funeral procession!" That was as close as Grandpa Kirkpatrick ever came to opening up a grieving heart to anyone, but he missed her profoundly and would follow her four years later.

A wartime home was a lot for Grandma to take on: two daughters-in-law and up to five children. And it was not just three adult women in the house, it was two mothers with a mother-in-law—three strong and dominant women. There was tension, at times, as the three of them fought for primacy. But it was my grandmother's house, and in her mind there was no question about this. She was the boss; the others were guests. And the others needed advice. In later years, talking about these times, Mom recalled Grandma scolding her for not taking better care of me, warning her: "Keep those little feet warm, Beth, if you want to keep that child well," and suggesting, "We could maybe lay him on the oven door or something." Once, I wondered out loud to her about how three strong-willed women had managed to live together during those war times. With characteristic humor, Mom replied, "Well, Grandma took lots of walks in the woods."

Aunt Joy remembered the first time she met Grandma Kirkpatrick. Apparently Grandma had been disappointed that her son Tom had passed up a girl more to her liking, and had greeted my Aunt Joy coolly and with characteristic bluntness, saying, "I was sure you were going to be a blonde." Thinking back about the person Grandma was, she was probably more comfortable with men than women, and the strain displayed in her relationships with her daughters-in-law suggested they were no exception. Fortunately it was a large farmhouse with lots of outdoor space, and also fortunately for my brother Doug, me and our Kirkpatrick cousins, Grandma seemed to thoroughly enjoy her grandchildren.

I remember her salt-and-pepper, pinned-up hair and simple gingham dresses together with the ubiquitous kitchen apron, tightly laced sturdy Oxford shoes, knee stockings and wire-frame spectacles. I can see her easy movements from the card table to her peonies, back inside to the kitchen where supper was cooking, and then back to our canasta game. Sometimes we would sit out in the warm Illinois afternoon sun looking for four-leaf clovers, her cotton apron draped over her folded legs. She would find four or five of those magic charms every time we looked for them. I never found a single one (but her). She neither pitied nor laughed at my luck, but modeled patience and perceptiveness by quiet example, whether we were searching for four-leaf clovers or playing croquinole, her favorite board game.

She was great with all of us kids. She laughed a lot and seemed to enjoy the time together as much as we did. I like to think, though, that I was a little bit special. I was, after all, the first of her grandchildren. There is a photo of her reading me a story; I'm looking at the book and she is looking down at me. There seems such warmth and love in her eyes.

These were unusual times for families. My uncle was gone so long that when he returned, my cousin Kirk, who had been born after my uncle's departure, hid in fear behind my aunt. There were, of course, many stories like this. During the war, although my mother was my primary caregiver, she shares space in my psyche with my grandmother in terms of very important and strong women. So, who to talk about first? After the war, my mother quickly became the most central woman in my life, but I think this story really has to begin with my Grandma Kirkpatrick.

2 Pearl Bernard Kirkpatrick

THERE IS A FAVORITE FAMILY STORY about Grandma that illustrates well her feisty character, and one of the traits that is a feature of strong women: to be able to take as well as give.

According to family lore, the incident took place in the spring of 1913, shortly after Grandma and Grandpa were married. Grandpa was outside plowing, while Grandma, inside tending the home, was also stewing about the size of the diamond in her wedding ring—a diamond she figured was so small as to be insulting. Agitated and steaming, she paced around her new farmhouse, then walked out onto the porch and pitched the ring far and deep into the flat, rich, black-soiled Illinois farmland.

When Grandpa returned, she told him: "Floyd, I lost my ring. Somewhere."

Grandpa was generous, smart and kind. He was also likely naïve about marital discourse and combat right down to the very floor of his quietly innocent, Scottish Presbyterian soul.

Much savvier about sizing up the market value of a Hereford steer bound for the Chicago stockyards than he was in appreciating or fathoming the behaviors of his headstrong bride, my grandfather promptly bought her a replacement ring—this time with a larger diamond, much more to her liking. One suspects he was aware of the discontent with the previous ring.

I remember Grandma's eyes. Bright and dark brown, they sparkled and gleamed with alert warmth. They also challenged in a way that suggests equal parts honesty, perspicacity and diffidence. She had tough, exacting eyes that hinted at an unguarded and world-weary frustration at . . . what? The foolish ways of the world? Or men? Perhaps just an Alsatian heart trying to find happiness within a more staid and somber Scottish-American, Protestant community.

Perhaps she experienced the lonely difficulties in starting out, as my mother did, eleventh of eleven children from a Midwestern farm family. There was a full generation difference in age between my mother and her oldest sibling. Her parents were already middle-aged by the time she was born.

I know little about my grandmother's first twenty years or so. According to family legend and history, however, my grandfather, Floyd Blair Kirkpatrick, first met Pearl Bernard on a hot and humid day in 1910 on the banks of the lazily flowing Fox River. She was diving for freshwater pearls—a story confirmed in our family photo album which features pictures of Grandma as a fetching nineteen- or twenty-year-old, her hair pulled up in a tousled bun, and her body covered neck to toe by body-length, early twentieth-century swimwear. She is immersed in the Fox River in these photographs, her clam tub floating nearby. "Floyd found his Pearl," family punsters and pundits would remark. Studio portraits taken shortly after their meeting suggest a breathtaking beauty with a swan-like neck, alabaster skin and a steady, even gaze.

It was her pearl money that helped pay my grandmother's way to attend the Oberlin Academy, a two-year school affiliated with Oberlin College, in Oberlin, Ohio. Oberlin was founded in 1833, the first coed college in the United States and also one of the very first in the United States to accept African-American students on a regular basis. Importantly for our family, both town and college were named after the eighteenth-century Alsatian minister, philanthropist and leader, Reverend Jean Frédéric Oberlin. Reverend Oberlin had officiated at the wedding of Grandma's grandmother and grandfather Bernard, in Alsace-Lorraine, some years earlier.

It says something about Grandma's strength and determination that, together with her sister, Maude, their school choice was not only the furthest from home that any of the eleven Bernard children had attended, it was also the most ambitious in terms of curriculum. Note the following description of a third year course in Latin Studies:

"Third Year: Latin VII – Cicero's Orations III and IV against Cataline. Manilian law begun. Review of Syntax of the Subjunctive and Infinitive. 4 hours a week."

It was a fiercely moral and protective climate in which students, especially women, were permitted to pursue their studies while being cautioned that:

"Young [Academy] people of bad morals are allowed to remain only until their character is ascertained. Reports

. . . will be made to parents at the end of each term, and in the middle of the [fall] term . . . it is the deliberate judgment of the Principal . . . that a liberal allowance of pocket money is a great curse to students. Those who have such an allowance, and still more those who are allowed to make any debts, are almost sure to fail in study and in conduct. Parents are . . . urged to look into this matter carefully . . . "

Oberlin's Conservatory of Music also reminded prospective students that:

"[The members of] this department are subject to the same regulations as other students in the institution, and its aim in furnishing a musical education under Christian auspices is similar to that of Christian colleges throughout the land . . . The young women are expected to consult the Dean of Conservatory Women before engaging their boarding places."[1]

Grandma and her sister Maude boarded at 103 North College Street in Oberlin. Where few women in the United States in 1905 continued beyond high school, these two girls distinguished themselves in their two years at the Academy. Grandma enjoyed a passion for music, both studying and teaching piano while there, and she would continue her love of teaching and music when she returned to rural Illinois.

She also learned to capture, simply, in soft pastels, the verdant springs and the melancholy mid-winter sunsets of the flat, west-central Illinois farmland that would be her home for the rest of her life. Two of her evocative landscapes brighten our home to this day; they are signed with a tiny PSB in a lower corner.

Eighteen miles southeast of the Bernard farm, in DeKalb County, Illinois, was the home established by the Kirkpatrick family. They called their home Woodside. My grandfather, Floyd Kirkpatrick, noted, "It was nice to have a horse and buggy because when I went to see [Pearl] when we were dating I could sleep on the way home except when the Bernard boys would get my horse drunk. Then I'd have to stay over until my nag had sobered up the next day." Their two-county courtship ended with an engagement and a country wedding, celebrated by the wedding ring with the unfortunately undersized diamond.

A farmer's daughter, Pearl took quickly to her new homemaking and farm responsibilities when she and my grandfather began farming at Woodside. Her years of being known as the Bernard baby—which allowed her to indulge in tantrums such as her peevish, ring-tossing episode—came to an end soon after marriage and two home births. Within the first five years of living as an adult with another adult, she grew into a poised woman, and perfected her ability to shuck peas, can and cook myriad meals on an old wood stove. She became well known for her "basted eggs" (my grandfather's favorite) and for her seven- and eight-course threshing dinners for the neighboring farmers, who worked together shocking and threshing wheat, in the days before the invention of combines.

I can almost taste the lusty cooking smells of her bustling and steamy noontime kitchen, though she would gently shunt me off to the side of her busy domain: her kitchen and the family dining room that overflowed with sweaty, soft-spoken Illinois farmers. A threshing dinner was a grownup event; children were welcome but only from a respectful distance away from the hot coffee, boiling potato water and the quiet companionship of the seasoned workers whose heavily bronzed forearms and faces contrasted sharply with the balance of their overall-protected chalky white skin.

My grandma helped out-of-doors as well, dispatching a chicken for Sunday dinner with one brisk and efficient chop of her hatchet. Once, as a ten-year-old city boy visiting my grandparents' retirement farmhouse, I watched as a crow that had been ravaging the chicken yard made its last mistake by landing on the top of a nearby pine tree. When it taunted Grandpa with its "caw . . . caw . . . " one time too many, he brought it down with his shotgun. But it was Grandma who delivered the coup-de-grace by wringing its neck after it landed hard on the grass.

Although my grandfather had a good sense of humor, the Kirkpatricks generally came from dour Presbyterian stock. It must have taken some adjusting for Grandma, whose own background was spirited and fiery Alsatian French. According to the Kirkpatrick side of the family, Grandma's own mother would occasionally drink too much homemade Alsatian wine and, when the local Presbyterian minister made home visits, would flirt and act inappropriately with him. Buttermilk and persistent Presbyterian devotion replaced the plentiful wine and less religious environment Grandma remembered from her childhood.

Grandpa was Scottish and seemingly subdued; nevertheless they complemented each other. She picked him up, while he probably helped keep her grounded. And as my father's brother, Uncle Tom, would remember years later, "Grandpa made the money, but it was Grandma who saved it."

In her middle fifties, what was probably a menopausal depression spilled over into her suspicious certainty that Grandpa was "seeing a floozy in Waterman!" Alarmed by her anger, and knowing the force she could be, my grandfather instructed my father and his brother to lock up the family's firearms, "... just for now." Grandma was not to be trifled with.

With a mind and moral character of her own, Grandma seemed to need the approval of others less than most of our family, another characteristic of strength, in my mind. This worked to my advantage when I visited, because she often chose to stay home on Sunday mornings and make egg noodles to go with her stewed chicken dinner, rather than endure what she perceived to be another boring sermon from the Presbyterian minister. On these occasions, I got to stay home with her. These were very special times in my memory, as we worked and played together: me helping her prepare the Sunday dinner, she teaching me to play canasta or gin rummy.

Overall I think she was kinder to—and maybe less abrupt with—my brother, Douglas, and me and our four Kirkpatrick cousins than she had been with my father and his brother, our Uncle Tom. Grandchildren you could love and leave. They were more fun and less, much less, responsibility.

As a parent herself, she could be not only unflappable but clever and courageous. Once, on seeing that my Uncle Tom, then only three years old, had climbed to the very top of the seven-storey feed silo and was walking on the silo roof, she thought as quickly as her tart tongue could wag. Not wanting to startle him, she went back into the farmhouse, quickly returning wearing a hat, purse and glasses. In a quiet and calm voice she called up, "Come on, Tom, it's time for our visit with Aunt Jennie." It worked. Tom climbed down safely from that dangerously high perch, and off to town they went. The woman Tom would marry two decades later, my Aunt Joy, noted, "I think that was wonderfully quick thinking on her part." Quietly resourceful, Grandma Kirkpatrick problem-solved in a no less effective way than her equally strong sisters of subsequent feminist generations, perhaps more quietly, and maybe, just maybe, with slightly less panache.

Grandma was a good parent, but could be bluntly critical as well as overly protective of her sons. Her tough and anxious ways probably helped mold my father into the anxious person that he became. My father would get anxious when things were disorganized or, in his mind at least, out of control. Memories of him relapsing into suspicious thoughts and interpretations, especially when under stress, persist for me today. He could be anxious when less than two hours early for an appointment.

Although it was never diagnosed, what I observed and what I know now, suggest to me that he had Obsessive Compulsive Disorder, moderately severe. He worried obsessively, and was compulsive about the need for cleanliness and organization around the house. You could see it in the way his tools were organized in the basement and in his attention to order in the yard. Mom noticed it first when they were courting and his car was always spotless, a plus for her.

But Grandma Kirkpatrick's anxious pushiness was an important part of who she was, and it was also part of the strength that she modeled, a strength that would see my father drawn one day to my mother. It was probably no accident that my father, David Easton Kirkpatrick, would be attracted to such a strong and resilient go-getter as my mother, Elizabeth Ann Cowan.

My mother probably shared more openly and more warmly with her husband and children than did her mother-in-law, but both produced anxious sons. My grandmother's first-born, my father, became an anxious engineer. My mother's first-born became an anxious psychiatrist. It's perhaps noteworthy that neither my father's younger brother, nor my own, were so afflicted. Parents tend to make more of their mistakes on their first-born, when they are themselves more anxious and less confident.

Be that as it may, my own memories of time with Grandma are not about anxiety, but rather about her warmth. It was both a sensation and an experience that would see me hunger for this particular and all-too-rare quality for the rest of my life. It would make me into a 'warmth' fanatic and admirer, a connection connoisseur. I have treasured it in friends and acquaintances, and even perceived it in enemies, over the years since those quiet, lazy Illinois summer days when my grandmother and I enjoyed time together.

What is warmth? I can best describe it as a person's ability to connect with another in an unhurried, un-anxious way. Not all warm women are strong, but most strong women are warm. It is a difficult, but not impossible trait to learn. One cannot read about warmth in a book and expect to acquire it, but one can appreciate it—as in a beautiful, summer Illinois- farm sunset—when it occurs and while it happens and from whom it emanates. Some people have warmth they share with everyone, and some perhaps with just a few. Unlike moonbeams and falling stars, warmth cannot be saved in a jar for rainy days or for special occasions. Thank goodness.

From Grandma, I quickly learned to love all things warm, including water, weather, scenery, paintings and other art forms, homes and their exterior and interior ambience, fabric, color and sounds. More than any of these, I learned to love and enjoy and appreciate warm people.

Perhaps it does not seem significant today, more than fifty years after I last saw Grandma Kirkpatrick, that I was cheated out of a chance to say goodbye to her. But the memory still hurts and disappoints, and so it was important, after all. One weekend in the spring of 1954, after making only the vaguest references to my grandmother's health, my parents climbed into their 1952 wood-paneled Ford station wagon, and drove west from Ohio through Indiana to Illinois. Shortly after arriving at my grandparents' home, they phoned back to tell our house sitter and family friend, Mary Dykstra, that, "Grandma . . . didn't make it." I do not know to this day why my brother, Douglas, and I were excluded from this trip. I would have appreciated a chance to say goodbye.

It was probably a mixture of practicalities combined with my father's shyness about bodily functions, including but not limited to urination, defecation, sex, death and dying. This was somewhat unusual for a farm boy. I remember when our much-loved Springer Spaniel bitch, Cocoa, was aging, she was shipped to a farm near Springfield to die; sent away from the family who loved her dearly to spend her last days with strangers, to do something quite natural that people and animals do every day: to die. Whose decision was this? My father's? My mother's? Or both? They explained this to neither my brother nor me. Death was a distant experience, something that happened to other people and other dogs in other states, with other diseases and disguises than any I'd ever been exposed to or taught about. It didn't have much to do with Douglas or me, I guessed.

I still miss my grandmother and her quiet but persistent sense of who she was and was not. Sometimes when I'm in my office with an older woman patient, I am reminded of her, and I remember what I loved so much about her: her warmth, her kindness and her bluntness, in equal parts. A quiet, never resting perceptiveness that screened and sifted the world for hypocrisy, schemes and superficiality, and missed very little.

Time alone with her, just she and I. And those dark Alsatian eyes.

Goodbye, Grandma.

3 Reuniting

HAVING MY FATHER AWAY was hard on my mother in ways apart from having to live in other women's houses and act as single parent to her children. There were all the unknowns and the fear of what might happen to Dad.

Dearest—

Sometimes this living like this makes me ache inside. The problems mount up so high with no one to share them, and I wonder how Joy managed so long. Why did you say the Army changes people? Do I know about that or is it something you don't know how to explain?

Your very lonely
With love in her heart—
Beth

Like women all over the world, Mom longed for Dad's return and for life to return to normal. Looking after two children, probably both homesick as well as anxious for their father in ways that would follow them for years—especially me, the anxious son—her style was to take charge, unilaterally, with neither objection nor self-pity. It was a farm girl's shoulder-to-the-wheel approach; being a single parent during those years probably only enhanced her lonely decisiveness.

On Friday, August 31, 1945, twenty-five days after the first nuclear attack on Hiroshima, and twenty-two days after the second nuclear spear thrust into the heart of Japan would officially end World War II, my mother wrote the following letter to my father.

Dearest—

We have so much to tell you—first of all—the big box came and not one thing was damaged. The vase is beautiful—I love the color & shape and it is sitting on the window this minute . . .

David's talking to Julie on the porch right beside my window.

"Don't you wish we had a real aeroplane—then we could go to Brazil and see my Daddy!"

Julie—"What if something happened to the plane?"

David—"We could have a parachute and jump out a little bit when we come down low and unsnap our parachute. You have to bend your knees when you get down real low."

Suffice it to say,
I love you—Beloved Beth

Her relief and joy were evident in these lines, interwoven with her focus on her children and their latest behaviors and changes. With the war over, the issue burning continuously in the back of her mind was: When was her husband coming home? When, in fact, would the family, her family, be physically together?

The answer came within two months. My father returned to Wright Patterson Air Force Base, in nearby Dayton, Ohio. At last he was back in the United States and living somewhere where we would be with him again. Mother packed up our belongings, thanked Aunt Elsie and Grandma and Grandpa Kirkpatrick for their support, and moved us to a one-storey brick bungalow on Phillips Street, in Yellow Springs, Ohio, just twenty miles from Dayton. Dad could commute back and forth. We could be a family again. Mom and Dad were both ecstatic.

Mother held our family together over the war years but like women were doing with soldiers returning all over the country, turned more and more to taking care of her own. She still wanted to complete her education; like Aunt Isabel and several other Cowans, she wanted to be a teacher. For now, though, she set those goals aside to focus on us. (Within a few years our two cousins would move in, enlarging our team by fifty percent.) For his part, Dad was just glad that the war was finally over and he was really home. We were all ready to settle into regular American family life.

The first order of business was for Dad to get a job, and he soon found one at Marshall Fields, in Chicago. I remember the morning we were about to leave Yellow Springs for Chicago. The moving van was outside and the movers were loading up our furniture and taking it out. In the midst of all this, Dad announced he had changed his mind, that we were not going to move to Chicago. Instead, he was going to work for Rikes, a high-quality department store in Dayton. It came as a shock to my brother and me, although Dad would most certainly have discussed it with Mom before making any final decision. I'm still not sure why he made the decision to stay in Dayton, but, to be fair, children were not included in family decisions in those days to the degree they are now. Dad would work for Rikes Department Store for the next thirty-five years, until he retired.

We stayed in Yellow Springs, moving in 1949 to a larger home on President Street, which overlooked the Antioch College golf course. Except for some short journeys back to rural Illinois for rest and comfort with Grandma and Grandpa Kirkpatrick, Doug and I remained in Yellow Springs with our parents until we left for college.

Now that I think about it, my father and mother were about as well matched as Illinois bacon and Minnesota eggs. Typical of couples at that time, he went to work while Mother tended the home and made the decisions around children and schooling. Dad was not very involved in our lives—never, for example, going to my basketball games. I'm not sure that my mother did either, but it seemed to matter more to me that he did not.

There were times when Mom was anxious, and sometimes she spread herself too thin trying to take care of as many people as she could while also taking care of all the housekeeping tasks. She would delegate tasks but, in her anxiety that things be done right, she micromanaged. In this sense, because she could sometimes be scattered, my father performed the balancing role, his own need for order and organization helping her organize her life more effectively.

Overall, my father's compulsive ways of organizing his life complemented Mother's somewhat scattered, yet competent style of homemaking. When frustrated, Dad would curse loudly; Mother would pray quietly, then get on with her business. It was a close match, but Dad probably needed Mother more than she needed him, especially after the war, when his anxiety level seemed to increase.

He became hyper-aware of the need for security, constantly checking the locks and making comments like, "Things aren't safe" and "Let's watch out" and "You can't be too careful" and "Has anybody been in the house since we've been gone?" When does suspicion become paranoia? When is it appropriate and when is it overdone? When his anxiety was low, he would relax and be jovial and fun to be with. When it ratcheted up, he'd get cranky and irritable. That was probably when Mother treated him, comforted him, was there for him in ways that they wouldn't talk about to us. She was the one to settle him down, and this helped to bond their marriage.

He was a five-hundred horsepower engine operating on ninety-five percent efficiency; she was a thousand horsepower engine operating on about seventy-five percent efficiency. The net result was compatibility.

Family therapist Dr. Carl Whitaker has noted dryly that, "We marry one of four people: Our Mom. Our Dad. Our not-Mom. Our not-Dad." My father had probably chosen to marry his Mom, and if he was ever aware of any irony—or happy correlation—in his choice, he never discussed it.

Also not discussed by either of them was the fact that Mom was six years older than Dad. In fact, my brother and I would never have known this if we hadn't, many years later, been rummaging around in some of the boxes in the attic of our house in Yellow Springs and, coming across marriage documents, did the arithmetic.

We found many family documents in those boxes, including a journal kept by my mother, which detailed her interests and activities in the years leading up to meeting and marrying our dad. From these, and the stories she told me about her youth, I've been able to piece together her story before I came along.

4 Elizabeth Ann Cowan and Isabel Cowan

BEING BORN INTO A BUSY FAMILY that eked out an existence on a hardscrabble Minnesota farmland means you are facing some big challenges in life. Being born the youngest of eleven on this vital acreage likely leaves an indelible mark of vulnerability. By the time Mom came along, her own mother was exhausted from having and caring for her many children; she had little energy left for much more than love. Mom was pretty much raised by her older sisters, especially by the twins, Elsie and Edith. She was closest to Elsie, but Mom's memories of growing up are of her feeling hungry, needy and a bit lonely.

She adored her father, a gentle man whom she idealized and described as a "saint." In the absence of a strong mother role model, she looked to him but it was loving from a distance because he was a cattle-breeder and busy with that work. He was also a man who suffered from periodic depression, and had dropped out of law school because of it. Still, he was more available than her mother, and he was less tired and thus a bit sharper. It was kind of like, if you're not getting much from your mother, then focus your energy on your father—a perfect father from a distance is better than no father at all.

Mom had a loving but distant mother, and a loving and only slightly more available father, and she had sisters and brothers. All had their influence, but one of the greatest influences in Mom's life was her Aunt Isabel, her father's sister, who took Mom under her wing and helped set her on the path to become the strong and resilient woman she was. I never knew Aunt Bell, as she came to be called, but she was such a force in the family—so much a part of the lore—that I *feel* like I know her. She was such a strong influence on my mother that no story about my mother can be told without including a description of Aunt Bell.

Aunt Bell, and her sister, Agnes, never married; they were my mother's "spinster aunts." As maiden aunts, Isabel and Agnes were frequently called upon to assist their married siblings during times of crisis. Hence, Isabel came to spend a lot of time with her brother, Hector Cowan, and his family after my mother's birth.

It was Isabel who marched my Grandfather Cowan out behind the dairy barn the day grandmother's eleventh child was born. "Now, Hector," she said, "there'll be no more of that!" Did he think he needed more than eleven children? He got the message. My grandmother was too tired to go on. He knew Isabel was telling him that he risked losing the necessary closeness traditionally preceding the conception of babies.

Isabel had, without the encumbrance of a family and needing an income, pursued education beyond that of most women of that time, which was fortunate for my mother. After completing both her undergraduate studies and a year of post graduate work, she taught and administered schools before becoming a superintendent of schools in Iowa's O'Brien County. Eight years after graduating, at the age of twenty-nine, ill health forced her to give up her career. Then, after being defeated for re-election to the post of school superintendent, she traveled to Europe with her sister Jean, came home and resumed teaching for nineteen more years.

Did her college education mean that she was greatly advantaged over other women of that time? What advantage it conferred, she had achieved through hard work, grit and determination, and delayed gratification. Was she disadvantaged in not having the support of a husband and children? While it is tempting to try to envision the family of an earlier time through today's prism and perspective, it is more probable that people did what they had to do at that time, facing a mixture of advantage and difficulty or privilege and hardship, just as they do today.

No Susan B. Anthony nor Emmeline Pankhurst, and born almost sixty years before Betty Friedan, Aunt Isabel was neither an early feminist nor a trailblazing pioneer in women's rights. Although neither a wife nor a mother, she apparently did not see herself as a martyr or a victim subject à la Betty Friedan's *Feminine Mystique*.[1] I doubt that she ever felt unfairly pressured to fulfill an idealized, traditional woman's role in order to be somebody important, valued and recognized.

My guess is that she neither chose a life of childless spinsterhood nor avoided it once it became apparent that this was to be her experience for the balance of her life. While accepting her childlessness, she persisted admirably in her loving devotion and satisfying enjoyment of children. Some of this may have been due to her position as first-born daughter in a large Scottish-Canadian family; she probably experienced a more powerful combination of caretaking, nurturing and responsibility in looking after her many nieces and nephews, than did her younger sisters.

Aunt Isabel Cowan would have been in her early forties by the time Mom was born, but she looked younger than her age. A physically strong woman, she was tall and thin, not beautiful but handsome. One of my cousins described her as "kind of a beanpole person," with bobbed hair cut to earlobe length. She was thought of as precise and extremely intelligent, as someone who could ruffle people's feathers and who could be firm to the point of unyielding. Cousin Sue remembers:

When the old phone back in Windom [Minnesota] signaled that Aunt Bell was coming for a visit to the farm place, you never saw such a scurrying! Cleaning. Dusting. Washing! With her penetrating eyes, she would look over all the grandchildren who happened to be there that afternoon, one at a time. Usually, but not always, followed by an understated snort of satisfaction. She was not the sort of grownup a child trifled with!

She may not have been someone to trifle with, but Aunt Isabel loved children and she loved teaching; she encouraged children to have a respect for learning, enquiry and hard work. One of my mother's cousins, recalling a time when Isabel and Agnes had lived with her family when her own mother had been ill, said of Aunt Bell's tutelage:

I have not imagination enough to describe the atmosphere of dignity, intelligence, and loving Christian character we girls were privileged to finish our development in. Newspapers were read from front to back, many and most new books from the Library were read and commented on by all three. There was never any doubt that people were to use their brains and their bodies for useful work.

Spirited herself, she preferred children to show spirit as well, even though they could be more difficult to handle. On a trip to England, she noted how obedient English boys were in the classroom, and then observed:

Still, notwithstanding the surface docility of the English school children, I have observed that the Adamic spirit is only kept under for the time being, not exorcised nor even latent. At a discreet distance from the school den, this spirit of mischief is given full scope. I must say, I was glad to see this evidence that "the boy" is universal and all prevailing. I think I have spent as much time and energy as the average woman in trying to make the small man behave himself as is becoming a person of his position, but I have yet to learn to prefer the model, conventional good boy to the turbulent, restless, rollicking fellow who does not need Satan to "find mischief for his idle hands to do."

I have lived long enough to see a goodly number of the latter class fairly started in the battle of life, and have good hopes that their surplus energy will in most cases be directed upon the "good" and not the "evil" side.[2]

It was Aunt Bell who walked my mother into the elementary school on her first day, insisting that she be promoted immediately to second grade. Not only could her young niece read, Aunt Bell explained, but early promotion would mean "one less year her little legs will have to carry her to school." An interested aunt and a respected educator, her words carried weight in that Minnesota classroom, and her manner likely sealed the deal.

The benefits for my mother were clear: she had a caring and attentive adult role model who encouraged her to think for herself, express her opinions and pursue her dreams.

Thank God Mother had an aunt like Isabel who took a special interest in her life beyond what her parents could offer! Where she would have been without this tough and battle-hardened field sergeant overseeing her progress, both in and out of school, I hesitate to guess.

Aunt Isabel influenced my mother's development in many important ways, not least of which was passing on her own views about the importance of education. It was no surprise that when Mom finished high school, she wanted to pursue higher education herself. However, by then the country was deep into the Great Depression; her dad had lost the farm and there was no money to spare for their daughter's education.

Mom left home and worked her way through a year at tiny Buena Vista College, in Iowa. Unfortunately she was unable to earn enough to keep herself in school, and had to drop out. Very discouraged, she later told us that she had found emotional support and a second home in Kansas City, Missouri, where her slightly older and wise-to-the-world brother, Andy, had already established a Cowan beachhead.

As it turned out, this was not quite the way it happened, as we learned at my parents' fortieth wedding anniversary celebration. At that event, my mother's sister, Aunt Edith, inadvertently handed out two sets of Cowan family records, one of which, more classified than the other, revealed that Mother had been married before.

After leaving college, Mom went to Chicago, where she taught piano and attended Northwestern University. There she met and married a smooth-talking rounder named Joe. The marriage had gone horribly, and Mother had exited it as quickly as she could, divorcing Joe around 1935—a time when mostly only movie actresses dared indulge in such scandalous behavior. Mother had grown up adventurous, taking occasional social and personal risks and making random, albeit infrequent, mistakes. But when mistakes happened, she could and would cut her losses quickly. An intuitive card player, she rarely if ever followed good money after bad.

We guessed that this first disastrous marriage had a lot to do with why her closest brother, our Uncle Andy, had encouraged her to come to Kansas City to heal. Once there, she quickly found work at Montgomery Ward's as a stenographer and settled into life in Kansas City, which included striking up a relationship with a new beau named Greg.

Working down the hall from Mother was a busy and vigorous young industrial engineer, David Kirkpatrick, newly minted from the University of Illinois. Family legend has it that Greg returned from a week out of town to hear that a rival was pursuing his girlfriend with organization, energy and focus. Mother and her newest beau began going out occasionally, then regularly. David gradually replaced Greg.

With brief and vivid entries in her diary, Mother recorded the breadth of her interests and activities that first year in Kansas City, entries referring to lost jobs, politics, war threats, family bereavements, church, choir, picnics and parties, and the transition from Greg to David. The entries are notable not only for giving us an insight to her life, but for their attention to world events—surely a touch of Isabel.

February 1, 1938: Went to church to hear Greg sing. Met his brother for first time.

Feb. 15: Tried on my turquoise formal. Benny Goodman on the air imitating Ted Lewis' "When my Baby Smiles at Me". Practiced [piano] like a good girl.

March 12: Income tax 5.00. Presbyterian Board 5.00. Shopped for picnic hamburger. Hitler "annexes" Austria.

March 16: Letter from Aunt Belle. She misses Elmira + Aunt Della so much: "I like to imagine the cheery greeting Della would give Elmira in the Promised Land."

March 29: Attended Public Speaking Class first time. Kirkpatrick brought Floss and me home. Election returns coming in on radio.

April 5: Public Speaking Class. Kirkpatrick brought me home.

Sixty years later at my father's memorial service, she would recall a single, proud memory of the courtship that followed: "I remember he had this car he kept so clean. And he would drive all of us without cars home. I was always the one he would drop off last!"

May 5: David's [Kirkpatrick] birthday. Moved to 409 E. Armour . . . a little let-down because apartment wasn't ready.

May 22: To church in morning. Walked both ways. Rode to Excelsior Springs with Kirk. Home in time for a date with Greg. Emporia Choir.

June 19: To church, practice and then Kirk came over about 3:00. To Excelsior Springs with Him [sic] to swim. Long, lazy ride in the country, beautiful scenery. Fun.

June 24: Stayed home and packed to go to Manhattan. Kirk called.

June 27: Back to work feeling sleepy. Caught up on odds + ends. Drove golf balls with Kirk. (Sent Dad $25.00.)

July 1: Phil called for date. Asked him to call back Saturday night when I knew more about David's plans.

July 3: Up at 4:45 to get picnic lunch ready. Started about 7:30 —and drove down to Big Bagnell Dam in Ozarks with David. Drove almost 500 miles. Tired but happy.

July 4: Slept late. David came over at 12:00 for waffles. We waited until 6:15 + saw Test Pilot + Mr Deeds Goes to Town. He's swell.

July 14: Letter from Greg. Listened to Bing. Greg met Floss at the boat and saw her off to Hawaii. Hughes landed in New York. 91 hours around the world!

July 15: Phil came over and we went swimming. He's very juvenile.

July 16: Dave came over and we thought of going to a show but went for a ride instead in the rain. He loves me, and I love him and we're going to be together forever.

July 17: Couldn't sleep last night. I was so thrilled. David Easton Kirkpatrick—isn't that a wonderful name and it's going to be mine.

July 21: We talked about budgets. Dave played golf. I had a bad time getting a ride home, but he came over after he cleaned up. He's awfully sweet.

*July 25 [her birthday]: Edith had oiled silk umbrella . . . [and]
   compact waiting for me. The girls at the office gave me
   slip. Wrote and told Greg we were all through.*

*Aug. 17: David came over and we talked + planned and just felt
   happy about being together.*

*Aug. 31: I brought home my diamond. This is the big news
   of the month. It is beautiful + David + I both love it.
   Chuck + Dave for dinner. Greg came over and I told
   him it was too late.*

When Mother saw what she liked, her excitement and enthusiasm were exceeded only by her sense of focus and importance. *Carpe Diem.* Seize the Moment. And seize she did, empowered by and acting with her Aunt Isabel's sense of what is important. If you know what you want to do and must do, why . . . do it! Family history has it that Mother's disappointed suitor Greg could only protest helplessly, "Where's the fire, Beth?"

A letter from Aunt Isabel's arrived after Mother had returned from her trip to Minnesota to introduce David to her family. Written in the difficult scrawl of one who has written with increasing haste with each decade, it reads as follows:

Dear Bessie—

. . . I hope I do not need to tell you that I am living with you these days and praying that your present happiness is a symbol of the new life that is waiting you. Since I have seen David, I feel assured for you . . . It was pleasing to me to hear your relatives express so kind an opinion of David, and your father's emphatic approval of him settled that matter for me.

You are a fortunate woman to have found such a man, & I think he's not faring badly in the bargain. God be willing for both, that you may make the most of your prospects.

Wedding gifts are beyond me now-a-days, but when you see something that a dollar will buy, spend the bill I am enclosing and let it represent to you all the love that the most cherished gift would imply.

Give David my kindest greeting and tell him I am looking forward to the real friendship that will grow up between us. I have come to the end of my paper. Add to what I have written, all you can imagine of my affectionate concern for you.

With much love,
Isabel Cowan

There it was, that warm and authentic seal of approval from one who had helped raise my mother, as much as her own mother had. Now Mom could go ahead with her life. Sadly, just after Christmas, 1940, my mother's "almost mother," Isabel Cowan, died in Windom, Minnesota. It was a very sad time for my mother.

In November 1938, my mother and father married in a small ceremony at a friend's house in Kansas City, Missouri; the prenuptial anxieties and reveries were duly recorded on my father's 8-mm movie camera. Beth Cowan was, according to my father, the woman he had dreamed of, and by the end of the year they sounded both content and blissfully happy to have found each other.

5 Mom and Dad and Dayton, Ohio

Let's sing a song of long ago
When things were green and movin' slow
And people'd stop to say hello
Or they'd say hi to you
"Would you like to come over for tea
With the missus and me?"
It's a real nice way
To spend the day
In Dayton Ohio
On a lazy Sunday afternoon in 1903[1]

RANDY NEWMAN S SONG MADE DAYTON, OHIO, synonymous with average American family life, and in many ways that's what the Kirkpatrick family was: an average American family, albeit a rather anxious one. We didn't actually live in Dayton, we lived twenty miles away, in Yellow Springs. We did live a kind of *Father Knows Best* existence, in that my dad went away to work every day, while my mother stayed home and took care of my brother and me. We went to school and became immersed in the things that boys do, my brother always a bit easier about life than I. Like any family, if you look under the surface, all is not perfect.

My father, as I've already mentioned, was an anxious person. He came back from the war exhibiting probably more anxiety than he did before he went. This anxiety would not diminish over the years; at times, when worried or under stress, it would worsen to a paranoid or inappropriately suspicious degree. He did go briefly to the Fels Institute in Yellow Springs, to discuss his problem in counseling, but out of shame and/or anxiety he never shared the experience with my brother or me. Nor did we know how much he told our mother. It would be decades before I began to appreciate that not all dads—indeed, very few dads— struggled with anxiety of such proportion.

Mother would worry, but never to the same degree nor with the frequency that our father did, and while praying seemed to soothe Mom, it never appealed much to our fretful dad; if it did, he never shared that information. Mother could laugh at the world, but she rarely laughed at Dad, except anxiously, when his anxiety reached paranoid proportions. Dad could laugh with my brother and me, but less often than mother did. He became flustered, whereas Mom remained calm and tranquil, almost all of the time.

Ironically, although Mom's strength had been one of the most compelling and attractive things about her when they first met, this same strength was something that Dad struggled with throughout their marriage. In Kansas City, he could wrap his arms around her vigor, power and vitality, yet when he married her, he seemed unaware of the original source of much of that attraction. I still remember him sputtering in frustration in the middle of a skirmish with her over who knew what. "Oh—Beth! Damn it! Dadblame it! Oh, the Hell with it! Oh, BETH!" The good thing about them was that neither held a grudge. They would fight, my father would sputter and then Mom would say, "Now David, let's talk about this." Likely, that would be the last we would hear of it.

I don't remember them actually fighting more than three times in the twenty-five years I lived at home. Perhaps she did state her case when my brother and I weren't around, but she never directly disagreed with him in front of us. There were times I wish she had, because I inherited my family's anxiety. And it wasn't just that they didn't fight in front of us; my cousin Edie, who became like a sister to me, once said, "There was a lighter feeling about life that came from the Kirks." While anxiety was a running theme in the family, so was laughter.

Mom's way of arguing tended to take the form of quiet resistance. She figured actions spoke louder than words. When, for instance, she had enough of my father's rigid, compulsive engineer's style of relating to her, she would go and buy a Sunday dress or two off the rack at the Salvation Army, and then brag about her bargains when she arrived home. By then my father was working in upper-level management at Rikes, a store that offered some of the finest clothing in Southwestern Ohio, and where Mother would get a twenty percent employee discount. Her buying clothes at the Salvation Army store rankled him.

I was influenced both by a stronger but at times changeable mother, and a less forceful but more consistent father. There were days when I enjoyed the best of both my parents, when Mother's strength combined with Father's organized, consistent way of operating. On the worst days, though, I experienced my father's anxious weaknesses and my mother's uneven manner.

My own anxiety was first formally identified by my nursery school teacher, Miss Forster, when I was three years of age. Miss Forster seems to have understood my combination of alert curiosity and scattered restlessness. The Antioch College Nursery School and Day Care Center became a safe place for me to take my first steps away from home and Mother.

In December 1942, Miss Forster noted in her second Antioch College Nursery School Semester Report:

> *Language Development: David still has a babyish way of talking. On the mental test he passed the vocabulary test at the four-year level and could define words at the five-year level.*
>
> *Characteristic habits and attitudes: Interested in everything, asking many questions . . . impulsive . . . apt not to stick long at any one kind of play. Needs encouragement to 'concentrate' in his play and opportunity to play for uninterrupted periods.*
>
> *Characteristic emotional behavior: Some signs of some insecurity, especially in the repetitive questions he asks to which he knows the answers . . . a means of getting adult attention.*
>
> *Characteristic social behavior: He also tends to be . . . resistant to suggestion. David is older mentally than his age. Resents any semblance of being 'pushed around'.*
>
> *Place in group: Is happy with other children most of the time . . . He frequently assumes the role of leader, and can stand up for his rights . . . tends to worry about things.*

(Signed) Miriam Forster

In those unevenly typed but perceptive reports, Miriam Forster drew clear-sighted and sharp-witted conclusions that were based on her nursery school observations of me at three years of age. An anxious child struggling with the interwoven problems of the uncertainties of World War II, impulsivity, attention difficulties and a sort of righteous insecurity that found me asking questions to which I frequently already knew the answers. I would wrestle with this particular admixture of intelligent advantage, anxiety and attention problems for the next half-century. My parents were warm and loving, but they didn't say things like, "We're proud of you, David. You're a good kid." It just wasn't in their vocabulary. As a boy, I was very unsure of my worth and frequently deterred by these traits.

I remember one time I was delivering newspapers and had just dropped off a paper at a house up the street from ours. A small black girl followed me into the yard of this house so, when I left the yard, I waited for her to come out and then closed the gate. She walked back over to her house and I went home. Her insecure father had watched this and thought that I had taken her out of the yard because she was black. He called the police who, later that evening, called my dad.

The next morning, my dad, who was extremely anxious around authority figures, chewed me out, telling me I was in trouble. He said, "The police are calling us, David." I just sat there in my pajamas, tearful, before going to school. I was very hurt because he never stopped to say, "What is your side of the story? Do you want to tell me what happened?" It would have made such a difference.

To make matters worse, Mom didn't follow up much better—at least not when I was there. She said something like,

"Oh honey, it will probably be okay," and patted or kissed me on the head. I was overwhelmed by the injustice of it, and just cried.

This is what often happens when an anxious family stumbles and temporarily does not function well. The family implodes and people get pulled into it. And I—the anxious child of an anxious father and an occasionally inconsistent mother—did not have the confidence or the security to speak up and say, "Hey, there is another side to the story, folks. Hello! Does anybody want to hear it? David here." That just wasn't how I was wired, not as a twelve-year-old newspaper boy.

Mother was a loving, bright, impulsive and kind woman whose somewhat scattered ways suggested an uncertain waif, much more comfortable at giving love than in receiving it—almost certainly a better giver than taker.

I remember when Mother would receive a Christmas present from someone she hadn't expected to receive a gift from. She was very unsettled by receiving one more gift than she had planned, and she had one, almost predictable, response: she would go into the kitchen and bake another coffee cake to give to the person who had given her a gift. My dad would say, in frustration, "Beth we're in here opening presents!" "Oh honey," she'd call back, "I'll be right there." That was a theme for years when we were growing up.

Did I mention that my mother was impulsive? Let me tell you about the time I was thirteen and she yanked down my pants after my brother said, "David has hair everywhere." Mom just said, "Well let's see, honey." And yank, down they came. I was mortified. Of course, my brother enjoyed it even more, seeing me exposed that way. My mother, ever the farm girl, just said, "Oh that's not a big deal, David. That happens. Now you kids gotta get to school."

Douglas and I were not the only children our mother raised. On a cool spring evening in 1949, a late-night phone call knifed its way through the stillness of our home with the devastating news that my mother's most cherished sibling, Elsie, had died of breast cancer.

I remember lying in bed and having my mother tip toe into the room my brother and I shared, and crawling into bed with me—the smell and taste of her deep and sudden grief covering my bed like a warm and heavy blanket. I was puzzled about it at the time, but now I know that she was heartbroken and needed comforting. I imagine my father was out, but whatever the reason, that night I was probably her source of solace. It was as if I were Mother's mother. I didn't mind. My mother and I were always close and these moments of mutual nurturance would help me grow into the kind and caring person that I am on a good day, and likely contributed to those other moments when caring for others was all I seemed to be able to do. I am, like my mother, a better giver than taker, especially when under stress.

Just forty-three years of age, Aunt Elsie had left behind six children, the youngest of whom were my cousins Edie and Sue, both of whom my brother and I had gotten to know well when we'd stayed with their family during the war. The boys had all been older and seemed not too interested in spending time with us younger cousins.

When Aunt Elsie died, Edie was nine and Sue was thirteen. They had already spent some pretty tough years while their mother was ill with cancer. In later years, Edie told me of a time she'd had to find her own way to kindergarten because her mother was in the hospital and there was no one else to help her. It had taken her several hours to find it, and no one in her family thought to comfort her in her distress. She seemed to have spent much time alone.

She'd been ill since I was four. The treatments had been horrendous—the skin was actually burned from the radiation. No one seemed to think about encouraging me to talk about the loss. I don't know if my siblings were ever taken under a wing; my father was not communicative.

Sue's experience of her mother's illness was quite different.

At first, I did not know that she was dying, even though she was in and out of the hospital with many surgeries. Because I caught chicken pox, a broken arm and rheumatic fever in that same year, she and I had the experience of traveling on the elevated train to Chicago weekly to see Dr. Harry Scott, a great-uncle who supervised cancer treatments for her and helped me with my own problems. Trained as a nurse, Mother had already spent the year nursing me at home in spite of her own condition, and I also learned how to take care of her in small ways.

She must have known that God would have to take care of the rest of the mothering in the long haul for we built into the city trips visits to museums and special, quaint restaurants where we talked about life, and she dared me to dream big dreams. We were like two ships floundering in a stormy sea, and shared time with poems she wrote and little stories I wrote or questions that would surface from the Book of Knowledge Encyclopedia where I filled the days, since school was not possible that year. She reminded me that I was a Cowan woman and Cowan women got an education so that they could take care of themselves. We shared visions for life and how to let God use the tough times to make us strong in Him . . .

After her death, the family seemed to break apart. The older boys left home and moved on in their lives, Uncle Bill turned to his work, which demanded much of his time, and Sue went to live with neighbors, who were apparently well off—she was treated to such things as having a chauffeur pick her up from school. She recalled that the family's welcome and the stability of their home were a relief after all the sadness she had experienced. "Their life of horses and country clubs was never dull." They offered to send her to college if she would let them adopt her. An offer turned down.

Uncle Bill sold the family home and, with Edie and Dan, moved to an apartment located over his business. Our Aunt Agnes, a very religious woman, came to take care of them. Edie writes:

Saturdays, she took me to the Moody Bible Institute, Sunday mornings and Sunday evenings church meetings and Wednesday evenings prayer meeting. She suggested that my brothers who smoked and drank were going to "hell." She was a most unappealing person and didn't make me want to follow her lead. What she exposed me to was not joyful.

After this, Edie went to stay with another aunt, but remembers it as a "distant relationship." She also recalls that, "All the moves isolated me from my family and others, too.

I felt deserted as my four brothers were living elsewhere and starting college. I was very lonely."

Their father remarried and the three youngest children, Sue, Dan and Edie, moved in with their dad and his new wife. Edie recalls the woman: "She loved her cat more than kids." Sue's recollections are not any more positive: "Dreams faded. Thoughts of college dimmed. My father did not think women needed an education."

It was not a happy arrangement. That summer, 1952, when the girls were twelve and sixteen, their brother Jack, who was kind of the family caretaker, brought them to our Ohio home for a visit. He explained to my mother that the girls "needed some time away from Chicago." He added, "Two weeks or so. Maybe three. Okay, Beth?" I remember that they stayed for that period of time, went away, and when they returned they stayed forever. Before I knew it, they were enrolling in my school!

Sue remembers that her brother Jack had asked my mother if the girls could stay a few months, but it took less time than that to convince Sue that this was where they belonged:

We fell in love with normal family life in the semi-rural college town of Yellow Springs, Ohio. We learned more about what it meant to be part of a family and we liked it.

Representing a committee of two, I asked Aunt Beth if we could stay, to which both she and Uncle David replied, "Yes." I learned how to make soufflés, home made bread and the value of good compost for healthy tomatoes. Family parties where dads square-danced with their daughters made the circle complete. Instead of being the fifth of six children, I was now first of four, a new placement in the family totem pole.

Yet I did not have to be responsible for family events. Just feeling like a normal teenager was a relief.

Edie had similar memories:

Aunt Beth and Uncle Dave, David and Doug and Sue became my family. Sue and I were truly accepted into the family and into the whole family of friends. I was never completely rid of the loss I had experienced but I saw examples of what life can be and those examples were compelling. I had fallen into life with loving, giving, caring people. I was so fortunate to become a part of this wonderful family at this point in my life. The kernel of healing began in the Kirkpatrick household although I didn't know it then.

They really did become a part of our family. Suddenly I had sisters! Just as suddenly, I went from being the first-born of two boys to being the second in a gang of four siblings, two of whom were female. The downside was losing my trail-blazing number one position; the upside was that I now was able to observe girls up close. I had much to learn.

Edie was just three months younger than me and became a seventh grader at Bryan Junior High School, where I was an eighth grader. Sue was more than three years older than Edie and me, and that fall started out as a tenth grader at Bryan High School. Douglas was in the fourth grade at Dayton Street Elementary.

The girls were socially advanced, well beyond Douglas and myself, and we became accustomed to an increasing number of phone calls from young men with deeper voices than either Doug or I enjoyed. We were curious and envious, but, at the same time, we experienced our own social circles widening.

Even as we taunted and teased, we were learning about dating and courtship rituals, makeup, and even something of teenage female dress and sexuality. The first and second Halloweens after the girls arrived, our house seemed to be bombarded with more rotten watermelons than usual, and our windows were soaped more than in the previous five years put together. All this drove my anxious, vigilante father into vigorous night-time surveillance forays, complete with a high-powered flashlight and Cocoa, our Springer Spaniel, at his side.

My parents quietly pulled together as they assumed the new pressures of bringing up an unexpectedly larger family. Sue and Edie shared an antique double bed in what had been the guest room. It was next to the room my brother and I occupied on the second floor of our home. They needed more time before going to bed: they washed, scrubbed, rinsed and polished their faces with a variety of cold creams, soaps and astringents, all of which was quite new to Douglas and me who were used to getting ready for bed in two to four minutes. We watched these nighttime rituals from a discreet distance with a mixture of incredulity and curiosity.

We also watched, with a combination of disgust, amusement and envy, as Edie and Sue softly massaged our uncomplaining father's head, while simultaneously crooning the McGuire Sisters' hit parade song, "Sentimental Journey." Or as we listened to one or both girls read their English assignments to our mother, while snuggling in Mom's bed, receiving the warmth long denied them. A mother's touch and presence, delivered—in the family tradition—by a loving aunt. Both Doug and I would grumble at times about these Illinois interlopers. We rarely admitted the truth to ourselves, though, or to each other, but we were the better for this unforeseen change in the quantity—and quality—of our new family.

I did not appreciate it at the time, but over the years I have come to see both Sue and Edie as strong, resilient and hardy survivors. As bereaved, essentially orphaned pre-teens. They had been shopped out in part-time arrangements with various Illinois relatives and friends, and the only shelter from their father's put-upon, whining and complaining sense of incompetence. Sue would bravely face more hardship in the years to come, losing her first-born, Michelle, to crib death, that grief compounded by an unfortunate marriage. I have known several people who have experienced very difficult lives, but I've not known a person who has been through as much as Sue and still landed on his or her feet with so little self-pity. She remained poised, with equanimity and a smile, ready and eager to enjoy each moment.

Neither Sue nor Edie ever quit fighting for a better life; they persisted and each, in different but admirable ways, prevailed. Sue was able to pursue the college education she so badly wanted, including a year of study in France. A spunky Edie grew way beyond her childhood losses, and today makes a big, positive difference within her community.

Our family was given a showcase gift of strong survivorship when these two cousins arrived. It would take me a while to contemplate, then appreciate the strength they modeled and shared with us. I am pleased that our family provided a haven for them, knowing that it was my mother who made it possible. As Sue said: "Throughout this Aunt Beth added the touch of graciousness and spiritual strength that spurred us to stretch our vision for our lives."

Mom was always there to look after all of us. If she had one weakness, it was that she erred on the side of being too giving. To be strong, you need to be able to take as well as give. Mom looked after herself, but she made sure she looked after everyone else first. For example—and it's a big one—she never lost her desire to complete her post-secondary education. She did eventually complete it, but only after my brother and I and our sister-cousins completed our own educations. Eventually, she enrolled in night classes at Dayton's Wright State University. Dad would arrive home from his work at about the time Mother was taking off for her night courses. This happened night after night, year after year. My father and my mother's best friends encouraged her, though I'm not sure how much she needed encouragement.

Mother married Dad at a time in US and Canadian history when society was just beginning to encourage women to push the limits of traditional societal structure, including staying in school and returning to school. Mother married a husband with a university education, a man who empathized with and fully supported her dream to return to school one day and to graduate with a bachelor's degree. The middle-class suburban lifestyle that they had worked for thirty years to build and maintain, while not one of wealth, was certainly comfortably prosperous. All this made the pursuit of her dream more affordable and thus more realistic than for many women of that period. Mother also enjoyed sterling role models, women in her extended family and in her community who had gone beyond women's traditional educational and professional roles.

Something else assisted Mother in her quest for higher education. The small Midwest college community in which our family lived was known for Antioch's role-bending examples, including cooperative education. It offered Mother powerful paradigms for doing things differently, for exceeding the conventional norms of even the mid-American 1950s.

While Aunt Isabel had enjoyed nieces, nephews and students, and Grandma Kirkpatrick had taken loving, if anxious, care of two children and a husband in her busy farm household, Mother wanted to do more: to raise her children and to teach in the schools, to teach beyond the piano students she had taught in the 1950s. Or at least to acquire the ability and the qualifications to teach school and earn the respect and distinction that rightfully went with educational achievement.

Whatever the motivation, her drive to complete her college degree at this point in her life was focused and demanding. She had waited long enough.

In 1970, a week before I graduated from the Medical College of Georgia, Mother, six weeks shy of her sixty-second birthday, graduated from Wright State University with a baccalaureate degree in primary education. A week later she attended my graduation. Unfortunately, involved in my own final exams and exercises, I had missed hers. Highly intelligent and intuitive long before she received her bachelor's degree in teaching, this was nevertheless a great achievement and a moment of public recognition. I brag about her and this achievement to this day. Quietly and with shy pride, she had taken her place beside her husband, her four children and a large group of friends, an officially educated person.

She did some substitute teaching after her graduation, then she and my father bought an Airstream trailer and joined

Wally Byam's cadre of "Blue Berets," a troop of retired couples, whose navy blazers, gray dress-pants or skirts and sporty berets signaled their adventurous spirits. Postcards arrived from North and Central America, even Europe, before our parents sold their Yellow Springs home, and settled in southern California. Mother did a little more teaching but slowed down, her goals met, her life circle approaching completion.

For Mom, getting there was more than half the fun. It was probably almost all the fun. She spent most of her life in the present, a little less in the future, and the least of her time in the past. She never carried a grudge; experiencing a reversal, she would trade up, going on to more mature, richer and more rewarding relationships.

Like her Aunt Isabel, she persisted in her goal-directedness. Graduating from college more than forty years after she had begun never seemed to her like such a big deal. She did what she had to do at the appropriate time. Start college. Drop out during the Depression to help her sister continue in college. Return to university part-time. Work. Marry. Divorce. Date. Narrow the field. Marry David. Have two babies and raise them while David was off at war for four years. Put her own children through school. Take in two more children, the two youngest of her much loved late sister Elsie, and raise them too. Maintain her household. Look after her bright but anxious husband, nursing him through a major heart attack that almost killed him, followed by a protracted period of cardiac recovery. Help put all four kids through college, including two and a half years of study abroad, Sue and Edie a year each, and Doug for a summer. Help send one to graduate school and two through medical school. Return to college, commuting twenty miles each way, at night. Graduate in 1970, at age sixty-two. What's all the fuss about?

I got much from my mother, though much of what I learned from her I would not appreciate for decades. Much was given to me without words, by model and example. She taught me sensitivity through her behavior. And she also helped make me sensitive in the course of the sixty-one-year relationship we would build together before she died in 2001. She was both a powerful teaching figure—stronger than my father in most situations—while simultaneously a somewhat needy, occasionally diffident and almost always moving and affecting mother; probably in great part because she was the youngest of eleven siblings and never too far away from that responsive, receptive and perceptive youngest child's position. She was somewhat vulnerable, as one who was raised principally by older sisters and maiden aunts. But she combined that position and those features with an inquisitive and extremely alert intelligence, the curiosity of one eager to learn anew each day, and eager to pass on those daily lessons to her loved ones.

Children learn a great deal by watching a strong mother perform in family crises: bereavement, serious illnesses, home accidents, neighbors needing help. I remember, for example, an early summer evening in Yellow Springs, probably 1953 or 1954, when I was still stumbling through the growing-up process. It was raining and Mom was driving our Mercury station wagon when she spotted a neighbor, a poor boy we called Sing-Ding, in the middle of the street. I can still see the street light reflecting off the tears streaming down his charcoal face as he pulled the carcass of his freshly killed mongrel dog off the busy and slippery Ohio State Route 68.

Mother immediately stopped our large and bulky vehicle, in the process slowing traffic and embarrassing me with her so public display of altruism. She got out of the car, but not before I made some kind of protest. I don't know what I did or said, but I certainly remember her response. After determining there was probably nothing more we could do for Sing-Ding, she returned to the station wagon and sat quietly for a minute.

Then she smacked me with eighteen quiet but clearly punctuated words:

"Don't you ever forget to stop and help those who need you. No matter who they are. Ever!"

And on a good day, I don't.

6 Jeanne Revoir
and Early Lessons in Love

SHE PHONED ME one Saturday afternoon, in 1947, when
I was vacuuming the living room floor of our small family
bungalow on Phillips Street. Jeanne Revoir hadn't called me
on the phone before, and I was pleased to hear from her on
a weekend, as we saw each other only at school. She came
right to the point: she wanted to see me, soon. Could we meet
somewhere? Maybe at her place, "to play and do stuff." From
the moment I hung up the telephone, I began experiencing
anticipatory fantasies with my eight-year-old curiosity.

Jeanne Revoir viewed the world through sparkling,
almond-shaped, greenish-blue eyes. Fine-boned, she had a
small but endearing—to me—overbite which, when combined
with her high cheekbones, lightly olive-colored skin, dark
brown hair suggested—to me—a young Egyptian princess. I
remember her, now, as charming, assertive and spunky, and
know, now, that when she saw something or someone she
wanted, she went after it, or them.

Jeanne was eight and a half years old, three months older than I. Together with her younger sister, Janice, the family had just moved back to Yellow Springs, from nearby Dayton. I was excited and pleased to be invited to her house, but told my mother only that I was "embarrassed." I had never had a chance to use that word before; it was an eight-year-old code word for "I'm so excited!"

My mother drove me over to Jeanne's in our dirty, white '46 Buick, and dropped me off in front of her white frame house on Pleasant Street. What followed after an afternoon of talking and laughing together was a whirlwind prepubescent courtship of maybe six weeks' duration. She was quick to remind me in about the second or third week of that heady experience that we "could never marry because you're Protestant, David, and I'm Catholic. See?" I could not figure that one out, but I knew enough not to look a gift horse—or filly—in the mouth.

This, for me, was so novel an experience that I had no words to describe it—unusual for a verbal kid, though not that bizarre for a shy and cautious boy, and I was both. I liked what I was feeling, like ginger ale bubbles going right up to tickle my nose, only better. Despite the likely ridicule of my classmates, each day I knew I wanted more of it. This was even more astounding considering my sharp need for approval from others, that was just then beginning to emerge. I wanted to be with her, to have more time with her on the playground or on the slide or pushing her on the swing. We would spend extra time together on the playground. I can still remember how good it felt being near her. Days would also go by when we wouldn't see much of each other, and then there would be an occasion that would make my heart skip a beat or two, anchored in memories that stay with me to the present.

As I type these words, I realize that psychologists, psychiatrists, social workers and other so-called experts would say I had a crush. That it was infatuation or puppy love. That it was a pre-Oedipal cathexis with a love object, important only in how it anticipated or perhaps mirrored the "more important" relationships to come and helped bridge the distance between the family relationships of the past and the important ones awaiting me in the future with the person with whom I would one day build my own new family.

Whatever it was, it was the first time in my life that I had experienced that wonderful, warm-all-over, wanting-to-be-with-her and no-need-to-talk-or-even-think-about-it feeling. A fish doesn't know it's in water, and a dreamy, somewhat sensitive third-grade boy didn't know that others, almost everyone in the world for that matter, either had or would have this feeling, several times in their lives.

After Jeanne's phone call came ringing its way through my tousle-headed existence, she would share more of herself. And I would learn more. She clearly spelled out the limitations of our relationship—sort of an eight-year-old's prenuptial contract and a prescient one at that—as we continued to see each other. And despite the fact that there were these religious problems in our relationship, not to mention the unspoken fact that both of us were barely eight, it was not surprising that there would be more to come for us.

One day after school, a small group of us, including Jeanne's sister, Janice, walked south on Xenia Avenue, away from Jeanne's house on Pleasant Street, but not exactly towards my house on Phillips either. Walking past the Presbyterian Church, we decided to go inside; I suspect it was more Jeanne's doing than mine, but I was in full agreement.

The solemn Presbyterian narthex was slightly gloomy and absolutely private on that weekday afternoon. We let ourselves into the silent sanctuary, every footstep and spoken word muffled. I remember thinking, "This is sure different. This is not like when I come here with my family, trying to sit still in my scratchy wool pants on Sunday mornings. This is fun. I like this!"

Jeanne quickly organized us into a wedding party, and as we stood facing the altar, she prompted Janice on how to proceed with the service. And then we were married. Pretty heady stuff for a third-grader from rural southwestern Ohio. But there was more to come. If memory serves me right, Jeanne then suggested that we might have a honeymoon of sorts. We scooted under the hard, Protestant pews in the second or third row and snuggled, maybe sharing a hug and one or two awkward kisses. An ever-so-brief moment of private, ecumenical enjoyment followed, below where my family usually sat on Sundays. The few members of the wedding party remained at a respectful, giggling distance while my bride and I briefly cuddled. We left the church as quickly as we had arrived, and we all went home. I walked back on cloud nine-and-a-half to our single-storey brick bungalow on Phillips Street.

Shortly after that, the honeymoon was over. Our class had gone to a parent-approved movie at the Little Theatre, I think it was a *Flicka* film. Emboldened by the events of the recent weeks, I put my arm around Jeanne. She made it comfortable for me to do that, and we warmed up to each other easily and naturally, and as *Flicka* faded into the background, I felt warm and good all over. And affectionate.

The next day at recess, I was greeted by hoots and hollers of teasing derision, accompanied by the shaming index finger brushing its counterpart at right angles in rapid fire. The playground was full of pint-sized preachers, scrawny scolds and grade school gossips. I can't remember how Jeanne took this morning-after punishment and rebuke, but I think it bothered her less than me. It took a lot to get her upset about anything, at least that is how I remember her.

In six weeks I had experienced my first love, helped immensely by my diminutive partner's natural skills in liking and loving, and reaching out to an other. In my oversensitivity, however, I went from bliss to shame, overreacting to the envious and childish playground gossip and teasing. It was my loss.

I was only a third-grader, but I wasn't stupid, I knew that the feeling had been good. It would, of course, not be my last experience of love outside my family. I would have this wonderful, don't-even-try-to-describe-it feeling many more times in my life. But this was the first time.

And what have I learned about love since that I hadn't already learned from this strong girl? First, whether it is early affection or love experienced thirty or forty years later, being loved is somewhat easier than the loving experience. You know when love is being offered. It is palpable and wonderful. But loving the other person is slightly more problematical, especially for a third-grader. It calls for imagination, courage, initiative and more—qualities more obvious in Jeanne than in myself. It has its own learning curve that beckons ever so quietly: "C'mon in! The water's fine!"

Being loved by someone outside my family of origin for the first time called for skills as yet unpracticed.

But, like any learning experience, you get better if you stay with it. You need to keep learning and practicing the skills involved in loving the other person back. We assimilate and absorb these skills in our family of origin, assisted by the gift of time, when there's no hurry and no pressure. Loving a new, unrelated person back, responding to her gifts of love was a whole new experience and an opportunity, to boot. I learned, for example, that you don't love back because you've been loved. Or love more when you've been loved more, or love less when you've been loved a little bit less.

Loving is its own reward, and I had a great teacher my own age. My memories of Jeanne Revoir would help me grapple with that, help me learn and understand this fact long before I could put it in words. A strong girl falls for a not-so-strong shyer boy, or maybe she just wants to enjoy an afternoon of play with him. Jeanne was also more assertive, proactive and verbal when it came to setting up a play date with someone she would like to get to know a little better. She took the initiative in making this happen, something that this third-grade boy would not have thought of doing during a hundred third-grade years. But he responded to Jeanne's offer with elation and pleasure.

The problems and challenges of being with a strong woman in the decades to come would not surface during those memorable six weeks. I did not dwell on the significance or importance of her being the one to initiate the wedding ceremony, complete with honeymoon. I was living in the here and now and having too much fun to worry about the implications of dependency today and being a married third-grader tomorrow.

Jeanne Revoir was the first of many strong and competent girls and women I would find myself drawn to, and often in love with, throughout my life. Almost all of them were verbal, intelligent, competent and usually slightly bossy people, who resembled my grandmother and mother in their forthright and frank abilities to do many things well, including loving and connecting.

Why did Jeanne choose me to share her energy and her bounce, her social and romantic courage? Perhaps it was a combination of classroom proximity combined with the lure of my own intelligence and/or third-grade likeability. Maybe she recognized some of her own spunk and spine in a latent form within me. But she did choose me, however briefly, and in reaching out, offered me the opportunity of liking and loving her back.

We must have stayed in warm contact for a while longer, as I noticed that two years later she and I were sitting together for our fifth grade portrait with Mr. Shaw overseeing his minions. And Jack, a sixty-five-pound, sandy-haired tough guy, confronted me on the fire escape one afternoon that same year, warning me, "Kirkpatrick—I don't want you messin' with my woman!" That was my first experience with the complications that sometimes ensue in loving a strong girl or woman.

It would be years before I would become that comfortable again in loving someone simply and naturally. Throughout high school, my shy and—on my worst days—timid and anxious personality would somehow make it easier for me to be loved than to love proactively and with appreciation. That gift from, and memories of, Jeanne would help sustain me through long years of frustration and loneliness, years of liking people from a distance. It would remain with me from the third grade to my junior year in high school to my second year in college, and beyond.

7 Strong Teachers and Early Learning

ANOTHER, COMPLETELY DIFFERENT set of memories of my years at Dayton Street Elementary, the two-storey block building with its tired brick exterior and rusty wrought-iron fire escapes, also remains with me. I had several exceptional teachers. For example, my second grade teacher, from 1946 to 1947, Mrs. Amalje B. Esterline.

Mrs. Esterline

A large and imposing woman, whose bespectacled head was topped by a generous crown of salt-and-pepper braids, Mrs. Esterline appeared even larger in her two-piece business suits with their ample shoulder pads. An old pro, probably in her fourth decade of teaching, she was coolly efficient, unflappably tough, warm and kind. It took a lot to get her rattled, because I never saw her that way. She was quietly and firmly wise, to a degree that stopped just two feet short of cynical.

She was perceptive, like Miss Forster, my nursery teacher. Mrs. Esterline recognized that my level of anxiety and restlessness was above average; if unaware of the label, Attention Deficit Disorder, I think she appreciated the symptoms. I was disruptive and scattered. I teased my schoolmates and didn't pay attention in class. I was mentally drifting. Attention Deficit Disorder, or ADD, is basically five things: being scattered, restless, impulsive, unfocused and distractible, presenting in various combinations. I certainly exhibited several of these traits, possibly inheriting the scattered restlessness from my mother and/or the anxious qualities often accompanying ADD from my father.

A practical and sensitive woman, Mrs. Esterline knew how to deal with my symptoms in a way that distracted and focused me while preserving my dignity. And I think it was she who gave me a dime-store loom and a bag of elastics, encouraging me to make potholders when I was bored and/or ahead of my classmates. "When you're finished with your assignments, just make some of these, David . . . it might be fun, you know." In time, she would just say, "David, it's time for a potholder." I would say, "Yes, Mrs. Esterline," and go to work. An hour later I'd be back with the other students working on assignments. I struggled with ADD pretty much all my life. When I got to college I had problems concentrating on assignments and listening to lectures. I was unfocused, and I knew that no matter how hard I tried, I wasn't doing as well as I should have been. Nobody besides her—no psychiatrist, psychotherapist, teacher or counselor—would diagnose this until just over ten years ago. But Mrs. Esterline saw it, and she dealt with it appropriately.

I started slowly in second grade, but finished the year well, with the exception of handwriting (never to be my strong suit), in which I was awarded a gentleman's C+. But my second grade memories stand out because I received my first and only paddling. I had waded out in the swampy reaches of Dayton Street's playground searching for tadpoles, and returned to the classroom after recess, soaked to my knees. Mrs. Esterline delivered her ping-pong paddle punishment—with hindsight, a badge of honor—so matter-of-factly, so quickly and efficiently, that it was over almost before it began, and I was back at my spelling and arithmetic.

No one ever said that Mrs. Esterline overreacted. For a sensitive but not stupid seven-year-old, the lesson was clear: You did it, David. Take your punishment.

Mrs. Esterline was tough, but never rough. The paddling only hurt once. The gain was long-term: the knowledge that strong women are okay, that I could trust Mrs. Esterline to enforce school rules fairly. Life promised to be impartial. I could trust her. It was, in hindsight, an enormously comforting experience. On a strong woman scale, Mrs. Esterline was medium strong. Bright, warm, tough, but not rough, she was the inexperienced second-grader's ideal teacher. Very different from my fourth grade teacher, Mrs. Finley.

Mrs. Finley

The memories of my fourth grade, particularly of Mrs. Lilly Finley, are powerful; they cast a shadow over most of my years at Dayton Street. She seemed just like any other teacher at the beginning of the year. Not that I'd had much experience with evaluating teachers, but the first years with Mrs. Waite, Mrs. Esterline and Mrs. Dillon had gone reasonably well, in the mind of a naïve beginner. I soon learned Mrs. Finley was not the same as the other teachers.

I still remember her walk. Compared to that of my previous teachers, it was a more forceful, more determined, slightly bow-legged and graceless stride.

A walk with a purpose, someone who had places to go, things to do, and was impatient with anyone who was in the way. She smiled the way she walked, purposefully and powerfully. It was not so much a warm smile as the grimace of someone who preferred the upper hand and fancied few surprises in her life. Served up with a sort of opportunistic charm, it said, "I'm smiling at you. I'm in charge, so relax and don't cross me. Or you'll regret it. Do you understand?" Much of the analysis is hindsight, but I remember the details.

Fourth grade began auspiciously enough on a midwestern Indian-summer day in 1948. Located on the second floor, our classroom faced west, towards Dayton, and allowed for five rows of six wooden desks in each row. Each desk had a pine seat with a well-marred desktop, a grimy groove for a pencil and a one-and-one-quarter-inch hole for the inkbottle.

I remember my own desk: middle row, third or fourth desk back—a secure place in which to seat my small fourth-grade bottom. The wall behind me featured a bookshelf with simple age-appropriate books. Posters on one wall adorned an otherwise barren classroom. The school and that room were probably fifty years old by the time our class started there.

There were about twenty-eight of us. I remember the rough-cut McMann brothers, Harold and Ronnie. My first Jewish friend, Donnie Katz, who had just arrived in Yellow Springs. Barbara and Jay Bradley, whose dad had been promoted to chief of police. And cousins Gerry Partee and Viola Shook, whose mother and father were sister and brother respectively.

Mrs. Finley was new to the school that year. She never referred to Mr. Finley. No one asked her where she came from, nor did she volunteer that information. Unlike most of our teachers, who were part of our village and even our past, Mrs. Finley seemed to have arrived without an identifiable network or community.

Without knowing her, we had no markers or clues with which to fit her into our box of understanding, our framework of relative comfort. She appeared to be in her early fifties, with graying hair, ample energy and a body still supple enough to precipitate occasional classroom fun. She liked to play games, her way. That was part of who she was. I remember her bringing in a rose brooch made of a new and seemingly indestructible plastic material. She informed us it was called "Plexiglas," and smashed it with a hammer in an enthusiastic classroom demonstration.

At least once we played charades, and I remember correctly guessing the nature of her mini-drama, in which she played a father refusing his daughter's plans to run away with her boyfriend. ("You can't elope!" In other words, 'cantaloupe'.) The absolute control she demonstrated in that charade was a harbinger of the worst experience of my life to that time.

One late winter day, we were playing out behind the school on the large expanse of mud, sand, gravel and the occasional patch of grass that passed for a schoolyard. There was a poor man's merry-go-round, a few dilapidated swings and some seesaws. Mrs. Finley joined us on the playground, and I must have mouthed off or been slow in understanding her instructions. In any case, something provoked her because she grabbed me roughly by the neck, scratching me with her long fingernails, and pushed me into a group of classmates. I was scared and shaken at the time, but afterwards I thought little of it. After all, I had proudly experienced my first and only paddling long ago, in grade two.

My mother wasn't as good at denial as I was, and the perceptive farm girl could spot a needle in a haystack. When I arrived home that night, she greeted me as usual, although I sensed trouble coming from somewhere.

"David, come here." She paused, inspecting me close up. "What's that mark on your neck, honey?"

"Uh, nothing . . . really."

"Let me see it better, over here in the light by the window, David. Hm-m-m-m. Well, my goodness! What is it, dear?"

"Well, it's nothing . . . it's . . . uh . . . Mrs. Finley . . . uh . . . she just pushed me a bit, that's all. What's for dinner?"

It was no use trying to change the subject, and Mrs. Finley's roughness was no match for my mother's concerns. She may have avoided open confrontation with my father, but Mom had no such qualms where her children and others were concerned.

She was on the phone immediately to the school principal, Henry Halchin. It made no difference to her that it was after school or that I would suffer mortal embarrassment if she went further with this. Like an angry grizzly sow protecting her cubs, she charged ahead, heading off further danger to her young. Mr. Halchin agreed to meet my mother in two days' time. Time dragged by as slowly as the nearby, muddy Little Miami River on its sludgiest days.

Henry Halchin—called "Henshit" by Miss Ella Abbey, our town wag and senior oracle—was said to have been weaned on a pickle and had the cadaverous skin color to prove it. He betrayed only two moods: sour and bitter. I knew him from the Presbyterian Church, and he was one of a group of residents who could do twice as much damage to you because of having status and clout. I worried about them (the way the president of a small-town bank might worry about an inside job).

On the day of our meeting, Mr. Halchin appeared obviously well briefed by the other side. He questioned me again about my version of the events, skeptical in tone and regarding me with slate-colored eyes that penetrated to the core of my vulnerable fourth-grade heart. When I answered, he looked down at the floor. He paid some superficial attention to my mother's concerns, looked at me once or twice briefly and dismissively.

He clearly read me for a liar and my mother as an over-protective busybody fussing over her helpless brood. But my mother wasn't a busybody, she was a bear, and I wanted to go through the floor. I walked out of Mr. Halchin's office that morning avoiding his noxious gaze, consoling myself with the thought that things could not possibly get any worse. I was wrong.

The following morning, Mrs. Finley's class started with the usual Lord's Prayer, led by a classmate, and some brief announcements. Then Mrs. Finley intoned, "Now class . . . ," and began a general homily about loyalty, as she moved to center front of the classroom. She followed this with a short moral discourse about how we must all tell the truth and look after each other. She began to walk around the desks, her voice becoming louder. She picked up the tempo as she took an ominous left turn between the second and third row and began slowly walking down the aisle that separated me from my friend Donnie Katz. With measured steps, she circled, then stopped suddenly in front of my desk.

With the ease and suddenness of a woman who had almost certainly grown up on a farm and was highly experienced at killing animals, she reached over the student in front of me and, in one continuous move, grabbed my hair, snapped my head back sharply and banged it down hard on the pine desktop behind me.

"We've got tattletales in this room, class!" she trumpeted. "It's too bad they don't get their facts straight before they get everyone upset, isn't that right? Isn't that right, class?" Her question was clearly and acidly rhetorical. "Isn't that right, class!" There was no answer. The entire class sat mute on their hinged, contoured seats as she hyper-extended my head and exposed my neck as if I was a defenseless barnyard rooster about to meet his maker on the chopping block.

"I don't see any scratch marks, do you, class? If you do, tell me now, so we can have the truth out. Don't be afraid. It's okay to tell the truth now, class. Does anybody see any marks—I mean, any marks at all, on David, our little tattletale?"

In silent loyalty, not one of my classmates spoke. After what felt like an eternity, she released her death grip on my hair, walked back to the front of the classroom, and changed the subject.

My shame and humiliation were exceeded only by the strain on my neck. I walked slowly home that night, by myself. My mother greeted me at the door and, with seeming innocence, asked me, "How were things at school today, honey?"

"Um. Okay, I guess." I wasn't going to take any more chances. I quickly headed for my bedroom before my mother could corner me, inspect me and set me up for an even worse fate. Sometimes enough is enough.

I never did get on Mrs. Finley's good side again, even though I tried. Not with her directly, but with her identical twin sister whom I discovered worked seasonally at Rikes Department Store, where my father had worked since mustering out of the Army Air Corps. Whenever I saw her sister in Toys or Women's Fashions, I tried to get her attention. She might have had only the vaguest idea who I was, and must have wondered why a co-worker's son would walk by more than once and smile at her as if he actually knew her.

I was like the Stone Age people who made sacrifices to the frightening and unpredictable forces of nature by constructing dolls and totems that were meant to be identical to those terrifying forces. They probably learned, as I did, that no matter how much it looks like those dolls or totems, it's never the same as the real thing. No matter what I did, I made no headway with Mrs. Finley.

Mrs. Grote

Teresa Grote (pronounced Grow-tee) was my last elementary school teacher, and the last to fuss over, scold and pound some rules of mid-western Roman Catholic common sense and decency into those twenty-nine sixth-graders. She had more than a few miles on her by the time our class reached her, and I can still picture her looking tired-out. She had a bit of Aunt Isabel in her: she was a no-gimmicks teacher, and an austerely chiseled monument to the Midwest plains that had spawned her. She wore poplin print dresses that hung on her generous avoirdupois more or less like a shopping bag, and sturdy lace-up oxfords with generously wide heels. Her brown hair was streaked with a growing number of silver threads and plastered unimaginatively to her head, giving her the appearance of a tired flapper who had arrived in an open-air flivver and just taken off her helmet. She surveyed her restive students through rimless bifocals that magnified the dark bags under her eyes.

What was slightly sinister about her was her Roman Catholicism. Mrs. Grote wasn't just a Roman Catholic, she was a Roman Catholic in a position of considerable authority, even though the closest thing to a sermon I can ever remember her preaching was on the importance of putting a swatch of a brown paper grocery bag on your abdomen: "It works for stomach aches. Don't ask me why. Just do it, class!" This would not have reassured my father, whose distrust of all things papal and Catholic hung in the air of our home like a badly mutated virus.

In our grade school years, we had heard frightening and amazing rumors about St. Mary's Catholic Church at the north end of Phillips Street, suggesting that Protestant children were at risk every time they walked by it. Someone had heard that some Protestant kids who snooped around there and went in during a Confession, or something like that, were never seen again, by God and by golly. A friend's cousin had a neighbor who swore his brother-in-law heard it from his barber, or something like that. Obviously, these rumors were true, or almost true, and had to be taken seriously. Or did they? After my warm and positive experience with Jeanne, I wasn't sure.

Combining this with my father's anxious, unconditionally insecure view of life, I asked myself, "Why take chances?"

When we walked to our elementary school, we almost always transferred over to the east side of Phillips Street, to leave as much room between ourselves and St. Mary's tired red brick façade as possible. The priests might catch and enslave us. Or make us do a Eucharist, or something. Why, indeed, take chances? But we could not avoid Mrs. Grote, who combined all the qualities of a grade school principal, teacher and inspector on our last stop before junior high school, with the mysterious and sinister aura of the holy Roman Catholic Church.

I was on the receiving end of her verbal wrath at least twice. Once I brought a garter snake into our classroom; we had caught it in the swamp out behind the school, and wanted to show off a little bit to the girls. "Out of here! Now, David!" Mrs. Grote said. Another time, I returned from recess wearing only my undershirt and jeans, a sixty-two-pound Stanley Kowalski showing off once again for Stella, Jeanne and several of their friends. Mrs. Grote let me know that she would have no truck with this kind of foolishness. *A Streetcar Named Desire* did not run down Dayton Street in front of our school. End of talk.

She was a fair person, though she ruled with a largely humorless attitude. "Fools' names and fools' faces are often seen in public places," she would cluck, when learning of the latest graffiti printed by unknown pre-adolescent artists on the brick side of the school. To my shame, when I announced, "Ditto," to indicate the same grade given by another student during a project report, she intoned gravely, "There's a smart aleck in every crowd!" She was never mean, and was honest to a fault. What you saw was what you got, each and every time, with no surprises.

Mrs. Grote was our first ethics coach and teacher, informing us about particular situations involving applied morality in terms and words that sixth-graders could understand. She would preach common decency, honesty and other basic values time and again to the point where it became boring, so we had no idea that her lessons in values would lay the groundwork for principles, values and moral decisions we would have to confront many years downstream.

Two of the worst sins, she reminded us, were pride and dishonesty. I remember the lesson she drew for us regarding the *Titanic*, which had sunk off Newfoundland's Grand Banks about forty years previously. "Remember this, class," she said. "Before this so-called great ship sailed for North America, it had a banner around its ballroom that proclaimed . . . do you know what it said, class? It said, 'Not even God can sink this ship.'"

She stopped talking. She let the parable speak for itself.

On another occasion, she told a story about a service station attendant who had tried to cheat her much-loved son, Jack, by reporting a false oil reading on his car engine's oil dipstick. "Let's go all the way down this time, mister," said her son, "and see how much oil I've really got!" In life, one had to "go all the way down," take a deep scoop of a problem, make a serious assessment of a confusing or difficult situation. Avoid the temptation to cut corners, to take the easy way out or in. These were not hollow clichés, but metaphors that would last us for life.

Her rules of life were simple, and there were only five:

1. Keep it simple, buster!
2. Be honest.
3. Be kind, if you have any energy left over after being honest.

4. Be quiet.

5. Be serious. The world has no place for smart alecks.

How fortunate I was that my very impressionable junior school years ended with Mrs. Grote and her solid and decent values—values rooted in a kind of hard-nosed practicality, evidenced on the day of our annual class picnic (Chapter 8) when, after ever-so-brief reflection, she refused to let other students sacrifice themselves in a perilous situation.

Forgiving

I consider myself fortunate to have had these teachers, even Mrs. Finley. From her, I learned for the first time that the world can be unfair. I learned it's not always safe to share secrets with others, a lesson that would haunt me for decades to come. It would be fifteen years before I would risk sharing a secret with anyone and decades more before I would again experience anger so ugly and destructive. She taught me about people, but it would be fifty years before I would consciously appreciate it.

It was Saturday, December 2, 2000, and I was sitting at my desk in West Vancouver, British Columbia, reorganizing some parts of this book, rethinking where I wanted chapters to go and reminding myself that I had wanted to take a completed first draft to my editor before Christmas, when the phone rang. A warm and friendly mid-western drawl announced, "I'm not sure to whom I'm speaking here, but I'm phoning from Ohio after my sister-in-law told me you've been searching for information on a Lilly Finley in Ohio. She was my aunt . . ."

Before listening to what the man had to say, I offered by way of explanation that I was writing a book on strong women, prompting a soft chuckle from my caller, "Well, my aunts fit that description—tough," he said, and added, "Of course, in a good way, you know." I took a deep breath, held the telephone tightly to keep from dropping it as I reached for a pencil and began scrawling notes on a scrap of paper as fast as I could write.

I learned that Lilly Finley and her identical twin with whom she was extremely close were born in the late 1890s, the fourth and fifth children in a family of eight. Their parents, a southern Ohio farmer and his wife, were, like mine, Scottish-American. Lilly's father believed deeply in education and passed up real estate and farmland investment opportunities in order to send his many children for as much higher education as he and his wife could afford. He therefore farmed on a sharecropping basis, south of Yellow Springs, on a Greene County farm belonging to a Xenia doctor. Like my grandfather, he would bring feeder calves home from Chicago to fatten them up before slaughter.

During the first part of the twentieth century, students interested in teaching careers would attend college for two years, qualifying them to teach elementary and high school after they passed a certification test known as the Boxwell Examination. And it was for this purpose that a number of Mrs. Finley's family, including nieces and nephews, had attended tiny Cedarville College, about eight miles from Yellow Springs.

It turned out there had been a Mr. Finley, to whom my teacher had been married. He died from a heart attack when the couple was living in Florida; Mrs. Finley returned to Ohio to be near her twin Millie, whom she had never stopped missing during their times apart. Though Mrs. Finley remarried after that memorable 1948–49 year at the Dayton Street Elementary School, she lived out her remaining time close by her sister, who predeceased her by just a few years.

I often remind my psychotherapy patients of the importance of forgiveness. You do it not so much for religious or moral reasons, although these are important; you do it mainly so that you can get on with your life. You do it for selfish reasons or, as I would now say, out of enlightened self-interest. When you forgive this way, you stop holding someone else's behaviors responsible for your life—including its current ups and downs, highs and lows, victories and defeats. Don't wait to forgive. Do it now. Even putting it off for fifty years, as I did, is not as bad as putting it off forever.

I thanked my kind caller, again, silently—about twenty-four hours after his phone call. I didn't realize how much I'd learned from Mrs. Finley until I began writing this book. In that fourth grade setting, especially in those two dramatic, traumatic showdowns with her that had reinforced my inaccurate impression of her as a strong woman, she had been stronger than me. But she was not a strong person. Compared to me and my classmates she was powerful but she was more rough than tough. She was expedient, outspoken and reactive when she felt vulnerable—or more than likely when she experienced her professional status being threatened. Probably feeling not so good in herself and about herself, she subjugated her classroom and her kids to allow herself to feel better about herself. And perhaps against those smaller yardsticks, she did feel better about herself, sometimes. Probably lacking in kindness, warmth, fundamental integrity or a clear sense of the ethical rules of the grade school teaching rod that she used—and misused depending on the situation facing her—she was not a strong woman. But boy, she sure felt like it at the time.

A strong woman stands on her own, and her strength and integrity and values have a mind of their own as well. They are absolute and unconditional. Mrs. Finley's strength was mainly relative, and it fades as I wrestle with my narrative, recalling it, turning it over in my head, in my heart, in my typing fingers, still trying to make some sense out of that awful experience over fifty years later. What doesn't destroy us makes us stronger.

8 The Reunion

ON JULY 3, 1982, Bryan High School's tiny 1957 graduating class returned to Yellow Springs, Ohio, for our twenty-fifth-year class reunion. It was held in the banquet room of The Shadows, a supper club with nylon curtains and vinyl dinner tables, in Xenia, about eight miles south of Yellow Springs. It was the first serious attempt at reuniting the scattered members of our class, and many of us had not seen each other since graduation. Jeanne Revoir Galliger was there, looking tanned and svelte; in fact, all seven of the graduating girls had returned for this reunion, but only six of the fifteen graduating boys had found their way back. Most of those returning had come with husbands or wives; a few came alone.

A banner on the wall proclaimed:

We Are Surpassed in Numbers
But Not in Courage

My tanned and beautiful wife, Betsy, sat at my side, observing the activities and enjoying herself, while quietly monitoring my dancing with Jeanne. We had just moved to Ashland, Oregon, from Vancouver, eight months prior to the reunion, and could hardly afford this trip. But I didn't want to miss it, and so we had come with our three-year-old tow-headed son, Andy, now safely stowed with an old friend.

My classmates looked much as I remembered them from a quarter of a century before, only a little grayer, fatter, balder, older. Perhaps some of us were also wiser. We enjoyed catching up on each other's lives, quickly dismissing those who wouldn't come back and remembering those who couldn't. David Blackwood, a gifted athlete and a generous, genuine friend to many of us, had been killed in a fiery car crash while speeding in a Los Angeles freeway tunnel. Barbara Bradley was there, but not her brother Jay, who had committed suicide less than ten years after graduation. Gerry Partee wasn't there, either. Gerry had drowned at our grade six school picnic.

Gerry's story is important to share, not just because I want to pay tribute to this generous young person but because she exemplifies something I've observed in many strong women; that is, they do what is right regardless of the circumstances, regardless of the principle, or threat.

―――

"You don't really know the story of what happened that day, do you?" Jay's sister Barbara quietly said to three or four of us sitting in a dimly lit area on the second floor of the supper club that night. Her question came out of the blue, between dance sets. A few more people gathered and prepared to listen; we hoped the band would not start playing again until we had heard. Barbara seemed to need to talk, and the six of us sure as hell needed to listen.

———

Gerry Lee Partee was shy and soft-spoken, I remember her that way back in Mrs. Grote's sixth grade class, in 1950–51. Her hair was the color and texture of rusty steel wool and crowned her lightly freckled, round face. She had the closest thing I would ever see to a Mona Lisa smile. She spent most of her time at school in the background.

Gerry was the only girl, with five younger brothers, in the hard-working blue-collar Partee family. Someone said that Gerry's dad, Lewis Partee, had moved to our part of southwestern Ohio in the Great Depression to enroll as a cook in one of President Roosevelt's Depression era work programs, the Civil Conservation Corps where he met Gerry's mother. He and his wife and family lived across town in a large home that had been built onto more than once. When I knew him, he was doing hauling, masonry and stone work, a variety of handyman jobs. Years later he helped my father install a flagstone sidewalk next to our President Street house.

It was May, 1951; soon we would be rubbing elbows with junior high school peers. It was heady stuff, and the annual spring picnic for fifth- and sixth-graders traditionally helped celebrate this transition. It was to be the last event of the last month of our last year at Dayton Street Elementary School, that tired brick building with its wrought-iron fire escapes.

John Bryan State Park, where the event was held, was about five miles south of Yellow Springs. Its acres of beautiful rolling timberland were bisected by the Little Miami River, usually only twice as wide as a country creek, but now slightly swollen from the annual spring run-off. It was a peaceful place, the silence broken only by the occasional B-47 bomber from nearby Wright-Patterson Air Force Base carrying their practice payloads of nuclear weapons to the distant Cold War. I remember the park had an enormous barn used for storage and park maintenance. It was said to be the largest barn in the world, although someone in Yellow Springs had heard that the Russians had built a bigger one.

By the time we arrived at John Bryan on our bicycles the morning of the picnic, hamburgers and hotdogs with mustard, ketchup, relish and all the fixin's were laid out on picnic tables in the upper level of the park. We broke naturally into groups, some playing games on the grassy field above, others dipping their feet into the river below. The moment that remains frozen in time for me is playing catch in the warm sunshine. Jane Dykstra, an old friend going back to nursery school years, Mr. Shaw, our fifth grade teacher, and I lobbed a softball back and forth in a sun-soaked triangle.

It was about 1:30 p.m. when Carl Douglas, a classmate, came charging up the hill, screaming as loud as his breath and running would allow, his panicked words slurred together:

"Mr.Shawcomequick!GerryPartee'sunderwaterdown belowintheriver! Hurry! HURRY!"

Victor Shaw spun and bolted down the hill. We followed as fast as we could. Down the hill! Down the winding access road! Get there any way you can, but hurry! By the time I reached the river, four or five clusters of fifth- and sixth-graders had gathered. Adult picnic volunteers stood on the bank staring helplessly into the slow-moving waters of the Little Miami. Gerry's friend, Barbara Bradley, was softly moaning, "Gerry! Gerry! Gerry!"

Peter and Charles Abbott, probably the best swimmers in the entire grade school, begged Mrs. Grote to let them dive in, to search for their classmate. Our sixth grade teacher looked ahead to the right where Gerry was last seen. Never turning to the Abbott brothers on her left, she continued her pitched gaze. Her face contorted with anguish and horror, she never took her eyes off the water. After what seemed like an hour, but was probably no more than eight to ten seconds, she began to shake her head sadly and slowly from side to side. Enough was enough. She didn't want any more of her students endangered.

Fierce and rapid whispering surged around the water's edge. It seemed Gerry and Barbara had been wading together, when Gerry stepped over a shelf or drop-off and went down over her head. Neither she nor Barbara were swimmers. Barbara had somehow made it back to shore. Gerry had not. Urged away from the water by Mrs. Grote and Mr. Shaw, we trudged back up the hill, reluctantly and resentfully. Still there was no Gerry.

Alerted by passersby, five older students suddenly appeared on their bicycles with their heads bent downwards, focused, racing downwards to the bend in the Little Miami, their well-muscled legs pumping like sets of twin pistons. We cheered as they approached, high school students from nearby Wilmington, also attending a spring school picnic. Anyone bigger than us represented hope. Surely they might know what to do, when our own teachers seemed completely helpless. One or two of these older students did find Gerry, brought her to the surface and helped place her in the waiting ambulance that would rush her to the Yellow Springs Clinic. As the ambulance sped back up the hill and roared past us, a figure could be seen inside, moving up and down, performing artificial respiration, we guessed, the way it was taught then. It seemed like a surreal movie that we were both watching and participating in. She would probably be fine, we thought and hoped. Hooray for the older students, whoever they were!

About an hour and a quarter had elapsed since Barbara's first cries of distress and Carl's shouts for help. The picnic was forgotten, but that event seared our minds forever. We packed up our things, a few of us plodded over to our bicycles to begin the ride home, to await further news. I straddled my Monarch bicycle, with its balloon tires, battery-operated horn and rusty maroon paint, and pedaled my way back into town, more or less on autopilot. Pulling into our driveway, I threw my bike up against a tree and walked slowly into the hallway of our President Street home.

"Hi, honey! How was the picnic?" my mother inquired.

Silence.

"David . . . ?" Silence.

"Mom . . . uh . . . let's sit down."

My mother patiently waited.

"Mother..." and the words still wouldn't come. I averted my gaze, looked across our well-worn walnut family dining table. "Mom . . . uh . . . the picnic was okay and everything, and then Gerry Partee, she fell in the water, or something happened. I still don't know what yet, but you . . . um . . . you know the creek, that little one that runs by the picnic shelter? In the lower level of the park? And some guys, they had to dive down to try and . . . try and get . . . you know. . .to get her or find her.

And we . . . uh . . . couldn't see everything by then . . . we were up above . . . but . . . then an ambulance drove away, but we couldn't really see her. And . . . I don't know if she's okay . . . or anything!"

A lump had formed in the back of my throat. My mother quietly went into her emergency behavior, doing what she always did when faced with a crisis or important rumor. She phoned her best friend, Mary Dykstra, Jane Dykstra's mother.

Mary Dykstra had assisted at the picnic. And, having been born about seven miles south of Yellow Springs, in Goes Station on the Little Miami River, knew everyone and everything in town and practically all of Greene County. Or so it seemed. It was about an hour before our phone rang back. It had to be Mary. What was the news?

Gerry Partee had drowned. She was dead.

I couldn't believe it. Nor could my mother. Dead? Drowned? I had no idea what these words meant. Really meant. I could hear my mother softly moaning and sighing in the study near the telephone. I didn't need any more details. I had heard enough and seen enough for one day to last a lifetime. Numb and dumb, I went to bed soon after that. What was there to stay up for, anyway?

Next day, the morning paper, *The Dayton Journal Herald*, carried a one-column front-page story headed by a picture of Gerry. The headline shattered the silence of our small village with its loud and clanging typeset: "Girl Drowned, Friend Saved By Brother."[1] The story explained how Gerry and her friend, Barbara, had been wading in the Little Miami when both had stepped off a shelf into water over their heads. Barbara's brother Jay had pulled Barbara ashore, but he could not reach Gerry.

"He'll be rewarded, that's for sure," announced Jay's proud father, Yellow Springs Police Chief Russell Bradley.

The next morning we returned to our school one more time, to clean out our desks, return books to the school library and close up for the year. There we learned that we would visit Littleton's Funeral Home to pay our last respects to Gerry. No prayers, no explanations. The entire sixth grade class walked over to Littleton's Funeral Home in one silent and homogeneous mass.

Mr. Littleton greeted us at the door and showed us in. I numbly followed the classmate in front of me into the medium-sized viewing room. Gerry's body lay upon a simple, satin-covered catafalque, resting higher up than any of us, so that we had to look up to see her. She was laid out in a dress of layered white tulle bunched up around her shoulders, creating a sort of shawl. For all that she been through in the last eighteen hours, she appeared calm and peaceful. She wasn't sleeping, and she wasn't awake. I couldn't grasp that she was dead, whatever that was. I had never seen a dead person before, but they certainly couldn't look like this. Her eyes were closed. She was unusually clean, much more than the rest of us on any given school day. Her rusty steel-wool hair had been carefully brushed to encourage it to lie down.

The sixth-graders took brief peeks, looked away, looked again. We mumbled and whispered to each other. Then we all left, not quite the unified group that arrived ten or so minutes before. I didn't say a word, just headed robot-like back to school to finish cleaning out my school materials. In a morning filled with shock and sadness, I walked out of Dayton Street Elementary, leaving the innocence of those grade school years behind forever.

Old people die. Soldiers and sailors die. Now even one of our own had died. And nothing would ever be totally safe or comfortable again. If it could happen to one of our own, a sixty-five-pound, red-haired, freckle-faced twelve-year-old girl in small-town Ohio, why, it could happen to anyone. At any time. Gerry's death told us that we *would* grow up and learn about dying, like we were doing today.

———

Thirty-one years later, at The Shadows reunion, Barbara Bradley took a deep breath, as those of us gathered around her held ours. "Well," she said, "what happened at the picnic, it . . . it wasn't really like the way the newspapers had it, okay? What really happened was . . . well, Gerry was on the shore down there in the lower level of the park with Jay and me, you know? Near the shelter down there, remember? She was on or almost on shore when it all started. I was wading offshore, I mean away from the shore just five or six feet or so, when I stepped off a ledge there in the water and went down real fast. I thrashed around, couldn't really swim, but got maybe halfway back to shore. It was hard." She paused before continuing. "Then Gerry reached out to give me a hand to pull me into shallow water. And when she did that, well, what happened was I guess she just got . . . she just sorta got pulled in, you know? And then . . . that was . . . that was it, you know, and Jay and I couldn't find her and that—that was it! That's all there was to it. That was it . . ."

Her voice dropped as she looked at one or two of us briefly, then at the spaces between us, and wiped away tears. The music started up again, getting louder. Each of us stayed with Barbara for a short while, torn by her story and our respective memories. Then we all drifted away. I returned to sit next to Betsy. The truth wrestled with the myth I had believed and hung onto for over three decades. Barbara had been the wader in distress. Gerry had reached out to pull her ashore, and was pulled into the water herself. The two had traded places. Barbara lived and Gerry died.

And I realized, at that moment, how close we had been that day to courage. To a strong girl. Gerry Lee wouldn't have used those words. She just did what she had to do.

We will never know exactly the agony and guilt that Barbara and Jay Bradley experienced following this tragedy. The year after our reunion, Barbara was killed in a motor vehicle accident near Dayton. She outlived her brother Jay by about sixteen years.

I knew I would have to get back to Gerry's family one day, and on Sunday, February 6, 2000, I decided I'd put it off long enough. Why was I anxious? I was anxious because I wanted to talk about the accident, tell the truth, talk about Gerry. A strong woman. If people back in Yellow Springs didn't want to talk with me, well, that would be okay, I reassured myself.

I called ninety-three-year-old Mary Dykstra, archivist, historian and friend, who half suggested, half insisted I talk to Gerry's brother, Mark Partee. Not finding his name in the phone directory, I chose Diana Partee instead.

"Hello?"

"Hi. Is this the Partee residence?"

"It is."

"I'm calling from out of town for a Mark Partee and . . ."

"Yes, this is his home. That's my husband."

And we began to talk.

Diana Partee was a sensitive and encouraging listener. With her permission to continue, I pushed ahead, shared the story of the way in which we thought Gerry had died almost fifty years ago and how thirty-one more years elapsed after her drowning death before we learned the truth, from Barbara Bradley. I thanked her for listening. Between her tears, she thanked me for phoning and promised to ask her husband to phone back.

Mark Partee called within two hours of returning home from a Sunday shift at his plumbing and heating store. We talked easily and freely for almost forty-five minutes. He remembered the Kirkpatricks, though in his words, "As you know, seven years difference in age when you're that young is a lot, so I didn't really know you and your brother. But I have always known of your people, and your friend Darrell's dad, JD . . . he just died, you know . . .

"And Gerry . . . let's see, '51, wasn't it. I was only four at the time. I cried at her funeral. The other vivid memory I have of her was her falling down once on the way to church and pulling a pocket off the jumper my mother had sewn. Gerry was upset. I cried."

We seemed to agree that memories are unfathomable places into which we tuck certain special pieces of our past. Why those particular bits? Or why do we especially recall those pieces? We decided to leave the mystery alone. I asked him if he thought his mother would talk to me about Gerry, about the drowning.

"She's been in bad health for a while," he said. "She's eighty-two, I think, and has congestive heart failure and collects fluid. But I'll talk to her, and I think it'd be fine if you phoned next week. It's under my dad's name in the phone book, even though he's been gone for several years now. And send us your questions or fax them to me at my office if you're in a hurry to get some answers."

I signed off, thanked him and told him I'd be in touch with his mom, Dorothy or "Dodie" Shook Partee. When I hung up, I wondered if I'd done the right thing. The family had its own understanding of what happened. Was it right to come in a half-century later and disturb their equilibrium? Sometimes you're better off leaving things as they are.

A week later, with some anxiety, I called Gerry Partee's mother. Even though Mark had reassured me that it was a fine idea and that his mother would probably have no trouble with it, I still felt like an intruder. I needn't have worried. After I talked with a grandson, she came on another line and put me at ease. She was warm, friendly and talked easily, with scarcely any prompting. Today she lived quietly on a small farm on the outskirts of Yellow Springs, surrounded by four sons and eleven grandchildren.

"Oh yes, David. I remember you . . . your family. I think I remember the girls better, though," she admitted candidly, in reference to Susan and Edie, my sister-cousins.

After she finished a brief but comprehensive overview of her family tree, Dodie Shook Partee shifted to her daughter, her kindness, her strength, with ease and without tears.

"I . . . had all these boys. Phillip, he died about six years ago, Mark, Jimmy, Pat and Terry. Gerry . . . she was the oldest.

She was a kind girl . . . always ready to help somebody. . .to run errands, she'd take things all over for different old ladies in town. She was scared of water . . . wouldn't go in anything over her ankles . . . so I couldn't figure it out when I heard about her and Barbara in that swimming hole." Her voice trailed off slightly then continued steadily. "It's the same one we used to swim in out there in the park, when we were kids."

How had she heard the news then? "Well, [Patrolman Estel] Boggs drove up and down our street. He never did have the nerve to come and tell me, I guess."

Dodie Partee continued, "Well, who called was Mickey [Viola Shook, Gerry's cousin and a classmate of ours]. She phoned, shouting and shouting, 'Gerry's dead! Gerry's dead!' Finally, she turned the phone over to her mother and the two of them came over pretty soon."

I took this moment to ask her if she'd heard Barbara Bradley's high school reunion story, from Mark or Diana, after I'd talked to them last week.

"I really can't express the feelings . . . I can't believe it, you know? I didn't understand it before with Gerry being afraid of the water and everything. I thought . . . well, it must've been a spur of the moment kind of thing with her and Barbara wading. We didn't know until last week—I can't believe it. My sister Patty [Shook] . . . she knew the story all along!"

I had heard that she'd given up on God and religion, and asked her if that was true. "Not really, but I'll tell you, my husband Lewis– when she died, he couldn't get over it for the longest time. 'If that's all God thinks of me, why then forget it!' That was pretty much how he felt about losing her, and he pretty much never went back to church. And Phillip too.

"Church was important for Gerry. She used to drag Phillip out to it. They both walked.

"I went for a long time, but when the kids got older, I went less often. You don't have to go to church to believe in God and be a Christian, you know? I asked Dr. Menino why they [her husband and son] had such a hard time with it. He just said, 'Well, you know some people can talk about these things. And some can't.' And that's pretty much how it was."

If Gerry was like other first-born girls, she would have been the super-responsible daughter, likely doing that job naturally, and more by choice than because it was foisted on her. Her mother's words led me to the conclusion that three factors shaped her personality: she was the Partee family's first-born girl; she was their first-born of either sex; and she was their *only* girl, followed by five younger brothers. True to form, she was unfailingly kind and helpful, strong and responsible, traits which helped lead her to her death.

So this twelve-year-old, remembered by her mother as a kind girl who was always ready to help somebody, would die doing what she did best throughout her brief and memorable life, doing what she loved to do: looking after and taking care of others. With her initiative and courage, she wasn't just being responsible that tragic day in 1951, she was brave, tough and strong, probably without thinking for a second of the risk she was taking. This young girl acted quickly, saved a friend's life, and lost her own in the process.

9 Zaiga

ZAIGA FOLKMANIS sits just below me in our fifth grade photo, between Carl Douglas and Sigurd Knemeyer, and down one row from Gerry and Jeanne and me. She wears a waistcoat on top of her short-sleeved blouse with its Peter Pan collar. Her head is topped with a luxuriant crown of dark braids. She has a warm smile and dark brown Baltic eyes and appears more relaxed and less cautious than most of the kids in the class photo. She lights up much of our half of it. She arrived in town just months before the photo was taken.

The Folkmanis family lived in Cesis, Latvia, where Zaiga's father was president of the state bank. Latvia, which had been dominated since the thirteenth century first by Germany, then Poland and Russia, gained its independence following the 1917 Russian Revolution. It enjoyed autonomy from 1920 to 1940, when it was annexed by the Soviet Union. Occupied a year later by Nazi Germany, it again became part of the USSR at the end of World War II. It achieved full independence again in 1991.

Caught between warring Russians and Germans, the uprooted Folkmanis family left their homeland. After living in a series of refugee camps during the war, they found their way to Miami Valley, where they were unofficially adopted by the citizenry of Yellow Springs. The picture in the *Dayton Daily News* is captioned, "Konstantin Folkmanis, his wife and three children leave their war-torn roots to start a new life in Yellow Springs, Ohio."[1] In the picture, our Presbyterian Church minister, Herbert Schroeder, extends a welcome to first-born Zaiga, her younger siblings—brother Atis and sister Baiba—and to her parents.

Work was found for Zaiga's father in the local Morris Bean Foundry, casting aluminum tire molds. The bank manager in him must have swallowed hard, if briefly, when he began working with his hands. He managed a gruffly cheerful exterior, as when he welcomed his children's school friends to their apartment on Xenia Avenue.

Zaiga and I became good friends. Our bond was based on our interest in delivering newspapers, and also on mutual need. I was a shy, anxious kid and she was new to the community, and hadn't made many friends. I remember her tagging along with me on my afternoon paper route in the sixth and seventh grades. I had around sixty customers—I delivered the weekly and Sunday editions of the *Dayton Daily News* on my Monarch bike—and she was welcome company. I enjoyed the attention, and I liked her, and her warm and responsible personality.

She had a soft, faintly accented alto voice. She chatted with me, asked me questions about paper routes, about some of my customers, about Yellow Springs and its people, and I told her stories about some of the dangerous dogs on my route. She told me

Latvian words, phrases or expressions, including those for body parts that my prepubescent mind and body wanted to know more about. She could be a friend without worrying about the sexuality and all the stuff you worry about when you're a teenager. She helped me deliver papers and we laughed. The closest we came to anything sexual was her patiently teaching me the Latvian names for those different body parts.

So we walked around delivering papers, and talking. If the irony of a small town kid trying to explain a small part of the world to a world traveler and survivor of World II ever struck her funny or bothered her, she never let on. The afternoons delivering the *Dayton Daily News* with her at my side always seemed to go faster.

I gave up my *News* route sometime during the seventh grade year, and so saw less of Zaiga. One evening around that time, at our new home on President Street, I remember my parents discussing something, or someone, in hushed tones. I wasn't really interested. We three were still at the dinner table—Doug had gone upstairs, I think—and I was lingering over my dessert. They didn't want me there listening, but they needed to talk right then, and so they did.

Someone was seriously ill. They—he, she, whoever it was—had a disease with a name to it. Something like Hampton's Disease. I began to listen carefully. Hodgkin's Disease, that was it. Whoever had it was in big trouble, I could tell that. My mother and father had never talked like this before around me, and their tones suggested something forbidden, even shameful. The more I tried to listen, the quieter my parents became, until the entire conversation seemed to shut down under its own weight.

I remember the fear in the air in our dining room that night. My parents had a secret they wanted to keep from me, though deep down, they knew they could not keep it from me forever. They had already failed in this once. The secret was that life sometimes stops much sooner than parents and families hope for.

It was Zaiga. She hadn't been feeling well, and a doctor's examination and subsequent tests confirmed the worst. Oncology, the treatment of cancer, has made astounding advances in the decades that have followed, especially in the treatment of leukemias and the related soft tissue tumors like Hodgkin's disease. In 1951 a young person diagnosed with Hodgkin's disease faced a terrifying and life-threatening experience.

My memories blur for the next fifteen months. Zaiga still came to class, looking pale but okay, and then she would disappear again for a week or two, for treatments, we guessed, at a nearby hospital, in Springfield.

"She's gone for some kind of treatment."

"How's she doing?"

"I heard she'll be back!"

"Does anybody know when?"

It had not been long since Gerry Partee had died, and we weren't ready to be sad again. Though nobody talked much about Zaiga's health, everyone listened.

Then she would reappear, with wizening weight loss, but seemingly light-hearted, without an ounce of self-pity. Somehow she managed to continue her seventh and eighth grade studies with good cheer and a resilience she wore lightly and gracefully. And if grace is the ability to maintain poise under pressure, Zaiga had it with plenty to spare. She also had enough poise, dignity and courage to make up for the rest of her seventh- and eighth-grade peers, who were careening back and forth among hormone disturbances, early rock-and-roll music and an occasional interest in their studies.

Her achievements were honored when she received Bryan Junior High's Citizenship Award in the eighth grade, which recognized her continuing good grades, academic responsibility and upbeat faith and courage under the most disheartening conditions. We began to see less and less of Zaiga, as if maybe it was okay for her to fall back, now, and let the rest of her peers take over.

In the spring of 1953, as we were about to graduate from Bryan Junior High School to Bryan Senior High School, I heard the news about Zaiga's death, probably from my mother. After a long and brave effort, Zaiga Folkmanis had succumbed to Hodgkin's disease.

Growing up in war-torn Europe and living in camps for displaced persons, Zaiga had surely experienced more horror and discomfort than her Yellow Springs classmates could ever imagine. Sadly, less than three years after achieving the safety of America, she had gone from being a plucky young girl to an exhausted and emaciated, only slightly older young woman.

I remember going to school the following Monday and awkwardly dropping a borrowed quarter on her brother Atis's desk. I didn't really know how to say I was sorry, I didn't even know how to say, "I don't know how to say I'm sorry." I guess that quarter came as close to words as I could muster. He received it in good spirits with a wan smile from one eighth-grader to another. Today, more than fifty years later, I would tell him how much his sister meant to me, and still does.

I regret that she and I didn't get to grow up together, were not able to keep in touch, to share news about our children, careers, families and ourselves.

For years afterwards, Zaiga's mother and father were a familiar sight as they walked up and down the sidewalks bordering Xenia Avenue, the north-south street that passed for a main thoroughfare in Yellow Springs. They walked when it was windy and sunny, when it was cold. Spring, summer, fall and winter. They had lost their country, their careers and their roots; perhaps also their pride. And then they had lost their first-born.

I remember Zaiga's resilience and quiet courage. She had lived through so much. She had traveled to a new life in a new town in a new country and then faced a new enemy, Hodgkin's disease, all before she turned fifteen. She was born of strong DNA—her mother and father had survived, brought their family to America. Zaiga graduated from the School of Hard Knocks, *summa cum laude*. I miss her still. And her dark brown Baltic eyes.

10 Set in Concrete

IT WAS TO BE ELEVEN YEARS between my dalliance with Jeanne in the third grade and my next romantic adventure, but when it happened it was powerful. Josephine Jacobson captured my heart more than I had known was possible.

Part of the reason I hadn't known it would be possible is that I think I'd kind of given up hope. After all, eleven years without a girlfriend? Well, I did have one girlfriend, Mickey Shook, for about six or eight weeks in my senior year, and I had a crush on a girl in grade seven. I was a late starter and high school years were no exception. I was anxious, isolated, cautious, careful.

I filled up my high school years with study and basketball. Basketball is huge in the Ohio, Indiana, Kentucky triangle. I was always good enough to be on the team but never good enough to play very much. But it was fun. You shoot hoops after school. You hang around with the guys. Atis, Zaiga's brother, was one of my friends. You're caught between basketball and girls, and apart from memories of Jeanne, girls were still mostly fantasies for me.

The best contact I had with girls was in junior high school, when I and many of my friends took dancing lessons on Saturday morning with Professor Barbulesco, an engineering professor at a nearby college. Barby, that's what we called him when he wasn't listening, was a tiny guy with a goatee; his wife was even tinier. I think he was five foot one and she was maybe four foot eleven. He would remind me, "David, you have ze movements of ze caveman." As if I needed reminding!

We learned the basic moves of the fox trot, the tango and the waltz, but it was really just an excuse to hold a girl. We'd put a quarter in the jar Barby kept, and for a quarter you got to hold a girl close for an hour or so, sometimes several girls. Our parents likely encouraged us to go for dance lessons, but we needed little encouragement. We would play basketball on Friday night and go to Barby's house the next morning— more courage in the group, I guess, than in individuals. It was good fun. Good memories. It was an escape from my anxious loneliness, which saw me being very hesitant about reaching out to others.

Edie would say, "You know, David, Janet Blackwood kind of likes you." "Okay, what do I do now?" "Well, you know, what boys and girls do?" "No, Edie, why don't you tell me."

I really didn't know. Edie may have been three months younger than me but she was about four years ahead in terms of sophistication. She had been dating for a while. My cousins gave me permission and encouragement. They did everything but say "All right, put your right arm around her left shoulder." Everything but the concrete map that a boy like me needed.

So I put my energy into basketball, into doing things with my chums and into my studies. I really enjoyed my courses, and I did well in school. I loved Latin—which nobody studies any more—and math: trigonometry, geometry, algebra, I loved it all. I was president of the senior class—all twenty-three of us. The biggest honor went to the top three students, they got to be on the Students' Council. Fourth runner-up, me, got to be president of the senior class. But I didn't look a gift horse in the mouth!

As class president, I had to give the toast at our fiftieth reunion, in 2007. Many of us showed up for that reunion. Not surprising, because the school was small and we had been pretty close. We may have felt bonded, too, because of Gerry's death, and Zaiga's. "To Yellow Springs, Ohio," I said in my toast. "The town that confused uniqueness with importance." Locals knew what I was talking about; there were a lot of heads nodding in that audience.

Once famous and infamous for the presence of Antioch College, Yellow Springs is, or was, an unusual place. Antioch was a center of radicalism: it encouraged innovation and creative thinking. I think one of the factors spurring my mother on to complete her education was working in the work-study program at Antioch while she attended night school. Several of my classmates went on to study at Antioch, and many people from other places came to Antioch to study. Friends were taught by Coretta Scott King when she was a student teacher there. Rod Serling, a post-WWII Antioch student later famous for writing the TV series *The Twilight Zone,* was one of our babysitters. Until, that is, he wouldn't let my brother Doug out of bed to go to the bathroom.

I went to Oberlin College, in Oberlin, Ohio, because it was time for me to leave Yellow Springs. It was important, also, that my Grandmother Kirkpatrick had gone there, that it had an excellent reputation, and that I received a small scholarship to go there. I started school at Oberlin in the fall of 1957, in forestry.

Why did I choose forestry? I didn't choose it; my father chose it for me. My favorite course in high school was social studies, which should have been a clue, but I missed it at the time. I had no idea what I wanted to be, so my father had me assessed by the psychologist in his workplace. She looked at my score on the aptitude test, and concluded: "David likes science and he's a loner: he should be a forester."

It didn't take long before I knew it was a case of mistaken identity. I liked people more than trees. I flirted with the idea of becoming a minister, then in my second year in college, I switched to a liberal arts program with a focus on psychology and sociology. I didn't understand this stuff, but something in this area beckoned to me. I knew from my very first psychology course that I had come home—at least in an academic context.

I was much happier after switching my study program, but I was still anxious, still had undiagnosed ADD. My marks went down—I was just getting through with Bs and Cs. The college workload was wider, deeper, broader and more demanding, but the demands on my undeveloped abstract intelligence were more complex. No longer could I get away with memorizing facts and spewing them out in an examination. I was faced with problem solving, and I had problems following the instructor as he led us through complex thinking—like telling us about retroactive inhibition in rats' learning, and challenging us to explain their behavior.

I worried that I wasn't intelligent enough, but I know now that it was more about being anxious, about concrete thinking and about ADD. I couldn't concentrate, I had trouble completing assignments and I had trouble with abstract thinking.

What exactly is concrete thinking? A story comes to mind about a guy and a girl who meet at a singles bar. They hit it off—great chemistry. They're schmoozing and drinking, and he says, "You're a lot of fun, Barb." And she says, "Well, I like you too, George." And he says, "Well, shoot, how about coming home with me tonight?" She says, "I would just love to . . . but I'm on my menstrual cycle." He says, "Well, that's great, I'll get on my Harley and follow you!"

I identify with that guy in the singles bar. For me, it was not always being aware when a girl was interested in me—or when she wasn't. Not being able to connect the dots. Accepting the psychologist's advice that I should be a forester is an example of concrete and overly trusting thinking. "Oh, okay. You know more than I do, so . . . I'll study forestry!"

It was a pattern beginning in my high school years that would continue on into college. Josephine Jacobson began to help bring me out of that mode of thinking. We never went 'all the way,' but she introduced me to sex, petting, necking and love.

Jo and I met on a fall day, in Professor Michel Fujole's second-year French class. The irony totally escaped me at the time: me stumbling like a clumsy rube through second year French, the language of my forebears, in an institution of higher learning named after the pastor who had married my Alsatian French ancestors. I should have been doing well! What did not escape me was the powerful attraction I felt for my classmate. I began taking second looks at her, this beautiful blonde with oh-so-large and expressive blue eyes, tawny Florida skin and a generous mouth that suggested a warm, inviting and kind woman. Our first conversation, after a French class, came more easily and comfortably than any I had experienced with a girl or woman since Jeanne. Jo reached out to me without being aggressive, made it comfortable for us to be together and looked straight at me without being obviously flirtatious. Wow.

Getting my courage up, I invited her to a movie that was showing downtown the next weekend: *Some Like it Hot*, a funny, Billy Wilder jazz-age farce about two musicians hightailing it to Florida to escape avenging 1920s mobsters. It featured Tony Curtis and Jack Lemmon hiding in drag inside a Pullman car carrying an all-women's band that included Marilyn Monroe playing a woman of uncertain strength behind her ingénue façade.

It was a funny movie and an even more wonderful date. The first time in a long while that I'd gone out with a woman because I wanted to. During the movie, I fell quickly and comfortably in love with this lovely young woman from Florida. As I walked her back to her residence in Johnson Cottage, a small house for second-year coeds, an emotional and sexual undertow began within me that would push and pull at me for the next twenty-four months, and then for the rest of my life.

I walked Jo to her door, which was illuminated by a bright light—and always under the watchful eye of the housemother—and started to return to my dorm. Then, spinning around, I returned to the threshold where Jo had remained, watching my awkward efforts. I said something like, "I just wanted to . . ." And suddenly, without planning, found myself kissing her tenderly, full on her soft and receptive lips. No pulling back and no games. It was the most wonderful kiss of my life to that time. She made it safe for me to respond to my feelings about her, emotional and physical. I waltzed back to Wilder Hall three feet off the broken sidewalk. I was exhausted and alive, energized, happy and tingling. I had joined Tony Curtis and Jack Lemmon on that train to Florida, to Jo. I was a lucky man and could not wait to see her again.

The next year and a half was a passionate, whirlwind dating relationship: numerous dates and lots and lots of kissing, necking and petting—all of which were new for me.

I had never experienced anything that powerful nor that captivating. It was as if I were a mine that contained precious, magnetic ore and then, one day, a love-geologist burrowed deep inside me and showed me what riches lay within: the ability to love deeply. I didn't know how to handle any part of that strong and powerful experience. I only knew that when I was with Jo I wanted more. I loved being with her when we flirted, even when she was teasing me about my numerous nervous tics. I remember writing a poem for her that ended with the following lines:

Yes. Jo. I love that name so.

My Jo.

We talked about anything and everything. She spoke slowly, coming from the South. She was a warm person and connected with others in an unhurried and un-anxious way. In terms of life, she was a lot smarter than me. She taught me about unconditional love, sensual pleasures and sexual warmth, kindness and honesty. Once I asked her, "Jo, a penny for your thoughts."

Pearl Savoie Bernard, 1905

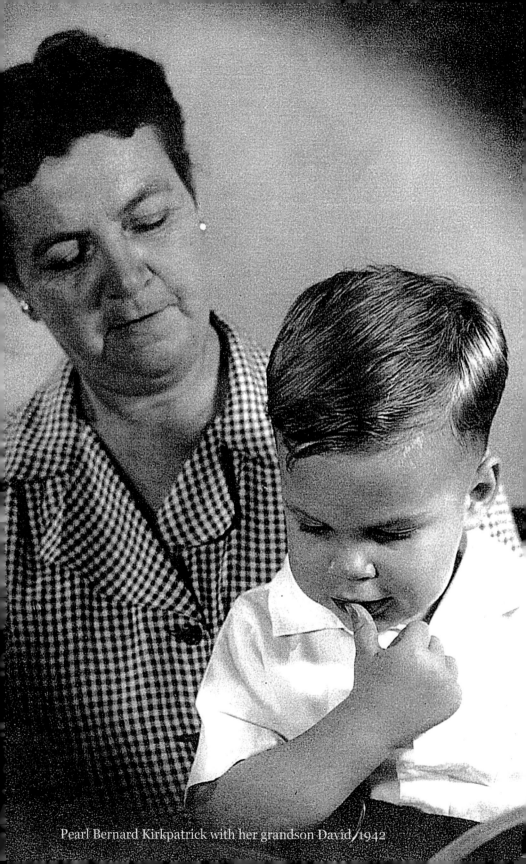

Pearl Bernard Kirkpatrick with her grandson David, 1942

Great Aunts
Agnes and Isabel
Cowan, 1895

Illinois Landscape by Pearl Bernard

Elizabeth Ann Cowan, 12–15 months

Elizabeth Ann Cowan, 1936

Elizabeth Cowan Kirkpatrick, with sons (l–r) David and Douglas

Dayton Street Elementary School Fifth Grade Class, 1949 – 1950, Yellow Springs, Ohio. **Bottom Row**, (l–r): Atis Folkmanis, Barbara Bradley, Pat Payton, Teacher Mr. Victor Shaw, Patty Bridgett, Tommy Miller, Donnie Katz. **Second Row**: Peter Abbott, Roxianne Owen, Jimmy Amundson, Viola (Mickey) Shook, Maryellen Calvert, Ronnie Rankin, David Blackwood, Ollie Jay Bradley. **Third Row**: Carl Douglas,

Zaiga Folkmanis, Sigurd Knemeyer, Linda Anderson, Ronnie Hamilton, Rita Hammond, Billy Cornell, Marilyn Holsworth. **Top Row**: Harold McMann, Ronnie McMann, Ruth Martin, David Kirkpatrick, Jeanne Revoir, Tom Yeakley, Cheryl Lampkin, Freddy Miller, Gerry Lee Partee, Dick Fisher

Betsy and Andy sharing a bath, 1978

The Kirkpatricks, 1985
in Ashland, Oregon

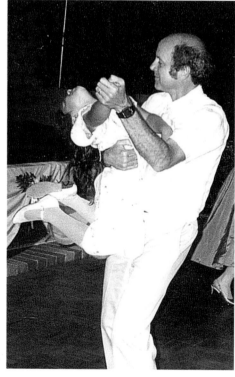

Mindy dancing with Dad, 1987

She responded:

I was thinking of the many, many
      times the shores, the waves caressed,
And of the many, many times your lips to mine
      have pressed.
I was thinking that of all the boys I love you most of any.
Now tell me: Were my thoughts worth a penny?

At the end of our first year together at Oberlin, in June 1959, Jo discarded an earlier plan to transfer to the University of Florida and prepared to return to Oberlin in the fall. We said goodbye and I headed home to Yellow Springs where I had found work at the Morris Bean Foundry, doing the dirty work of preparing molding mud, securing casting forms and making tire castings. She went to Door County, Wisconsin, to work as a social worker intern in a summer work program known as the Migrant Ministry.

I missed her a lot. So, in July, on the way to visit relatives in Chicago and Minneapolis, in my parents' 1958 wood-paneled Mercury station wagon, I stopped, unannounced, at the migrant fruit-picking camp where she worked. I should have warned her I was coming.

I walked into the building where she was supervising a dance for migrant kids. She was sitting on a table and sitting beside her was a guy who, Jo later told me, was a Migrant Ministry peer, a handsome Mexican lad. There was a mix of emotions on her face. She was delighted to see me, flabbergasted to see me, guilt-ridden to see me because she was also having a relationship with the young Mexican. She almost fell off the table, and looked like she didn't know whether to laugh or to cry.

I didn't either. I had neither the maturity nor the social expertise to come up with a reasonable hypothesis about why there was so much tension in the cool Wisconsin air. Too much was going on too suddenly, and neither of us was able to talk about it. I spent eighteen uncomfortable hours there, and left for Minneapolis the next morning.

When we reconnected that fall, back at Oberlin, Jo told me that she'd had a brief relationship, and that she felt pretty awful about it. I remember she made me a batch of cookies, as if to say, "I'm sorry. It was a mistake. It won't happen again. I promise. Okay?" The cookies were delicious, but ninety-five percent of what she meant by those cookies went over my head. I was struggling more and more with attention deficit disorder, and I never delved too deeply into any conversation. I completely missed the depth and breadth of what she was trying to communicate to me. I was happy to be back together with her, and didn't think about the summer events any further. But underneath this rather shallow thinking was a growing desire to smooch, talk, walk and hold hands—with other girls. My appetite was awakened, I wanted more.

Later that year, I broke up with Jo. She was in her practice room in the conservatory where she was studying her piano lessons. To my knowledge, I had never hurt anyone before, and I felt awful about how sad and tearful and hurting Jo was—but that didn't stop me from breaking up. It took me many years to realize how much she meant to me, and how much she still means to me. I love her—in ways that surprise me—although until this year, I hadn't seen her in almost fifty years. Jo got over her heartbreak and got on with her life. We kept in touch and about every five years one of us calls.

I have the ability to appreciate relationships, if not at that moment, then as time goes by and the dust settles. I appreciate and value what people have given me. I appreciate Jo. She had beauty, warmth and kindness, and not a mean bone in her body. She had the courage to vigorously pursue a relationship that was important to her. This was a kind of strength I had not experienced before: the strength to refuse to live in the past. She was too busy, too strong and too healthy to spend any time in the past. It is a moral strength. She balanced her responsibility to herself and her commitment to others with comfortable competence. She avoided bitterness and resentment against clumsy, youthful and inexperienced lovers such as myself. She preferred the high road of the present.

Jo was one of my brightest teachers. She modeled courage and taught me about self-respect and appreciation. How to love and be loved. Her strength lay in appreciating another's values and worth, and in valuing, validating and mirroring those positive qualities back to that person. She reified, that is, she was able to both see and enjoy the abstract in concrete terms, and allowed me to glimpse, through my low, moody self-esteem, a better, more worthwhile person. If I could not envision my own worth and potential strength, I could at least appreciate them through Jo and her appreciation of them. She helped pull me into the here and now.

Someone observed that "mental health is growing up before we grow old."

> *If we only knew then*
> *As foolish young men,*
> *(Is there any other kind?*

You're out of your mind.)
what we now know, today . . .
Why, we'd avoid more disaster,
and grow up much faster.
And sooner.
Amen.[1]

In 1986, Jo and I talked on the telephone. She told me that she and her husband were helping people less well-off, both locally and internationally. Few people lead lives with such meaning; the world is a better place for Jo's place in it. She sounded much like the twenty-year-old Oberlin College student I remembered, and whose life and personhood I appreciated even more twenty-five years later.

In December 2004, a Christmas letter arrived in which she shared the achievements of her children and her husband. Almost as a postscript, she volunteered that she "went to Fort Benning, Georgia, in November to join the movement to close the School of the Americas. I am becoming more radical with age." Indeed. The US Army School of the Americas was established to help train Latin American security personnel in combat, narcotics control and counter-insurgency, but its graduates are perceived by its critics to be involved in widespread human rights violations throughout Latin America, including torture, extortion and execution.

If the word radical comes from the Latin word radix meaning root, then Jo has been experiencing the roots of what and who she is. She is warm and caring, but she is also a fierce and strong warrior with an intense sense of social justice.

Of all the learning I did at Oberlin, my relationship with Jo Jacobson was by far the most valuable. All the psychology classes put together were nothing compared to the time I spent with her, in my sophomore and junior years.

A half-century since I had seen Jo, my wife Clair and I visited her in Kirkland, Washington, on November 7, 2008. She was visiting her son, daughter-in-law and grandchildren following the loss of her beloved husband, just two months earlier. After some anxiety—what would it be like visiting her with Clair, and after so much time had passed between us?—I settled down.

She and Clair did well together, and the three of us chatted, almost singing in musical warmth, laughter and comfortable harmony. Much came into focus for me during those five hours with Clair, Jo and her family. And I tried to put it into words in a short missive I penned.

Hi Dear Jo,

I so enjoyed the time with you on Friday, sharing you with Clair, Clair with you, and me with both of you. What came into sharper focus as Clair and I returned to Vancouver was a lucid sense of what you gave me in our second and third years at Oberlin. Wow.

In loving me, you taught me about love at its most vital and essential. Unconditional, brave, unselfish. Your love of me pulsed through those cold, wet Oberlin winters, and in those hot spring days. Independent of my love for you, I know now that you deeply and happily loved me for some . . . twenty months, was it? With laughter and occasional tears you taught me that loving is indeed its own reward. I experienced a sense of awe at what we had created together.

I regret only that it would be years, decades before I would appreciate what a gift of learning, loving and learning about loving that you tendered. I know now that I was extraordinarily privileged to have been the recipient of your loving gifts. And I appreciate you now, more than ever, for loving me as you did. And teaching me.

Thank you,
David.

11   Post-Graduate Studies from Atlanta to Anchorage

I GRADUATED FROM OBERLIN in 1961, not with honors, but at least with my class. I still wasn't sure of my career path, but I thought, "Well, I guess I'm going to be a psychologist." I applied to several graduate schools, and was accepted by Atlanta's Emory University for a master's level program. It was a good school, although I didn't know it at the time—I was just glad they accepted me. At age twenty-one, I left Ohio and headed south, to Atlanta, Georgia.

At Emory, I encountered a teacher, Dr. Jerry Berlin, whose vigor and charismatic energy reminded me what it was about clinical psychology and mental health studies that had beckoned me—and that three years in undergraduate rat-and-pigeon learning laboratories had almost made me forget. Jerry had studied with Dr. Carl Rogers, and was teaching clinical psychology in our graduate curriculum, turning kids on to psychology and psychotherapy. If Jerry Berlin didn't get you excited about clinical psychology, you were destined for forestry.

It was through Jerry that I became friends with Dan and Maggie, two of his senior students, and two people who remain strong and loyal friends to this day. (How do you thank someone for the gift of people they've shared with you?)

I had a lot to learn from Maggie, Margaret Ann North. She was an undergraduate biology major taking a graduate level psychology course, in large part because she had been drawn to Jerry Berlin, the same as me. She was and is one of the brightest people I have ever met.

My fantasies of having a close relationship with Maggie—and her late model Thunderbird—quickly evaporated when Dan Mermin arrived at a party held in Jerry's old and spacious house. Bored, mildly depressed and drifting at Yale, Dan responded to Jerry's promise that if he came south, to Georgia, he would "get him laid"—an offer more compelling than any Yale could offer. Dan took one look at Maggie and told her he would soon marry her.

Maggie's story is of a searching, tough, extremely intelligent girl, and one who would become a strong and wise woman. I had liked, loved, been in awe of the female species in the past. But Maggie brought the word 'respect' to mind. As I write, I am aware of how much I respect women, partly due to Maggie. Maggie continues to model it, practice it, demand it. She, in turn, respects all people: women and men, black and white, yellow, red and brown, gay and straight, Jew, gentile, Muslim and Christian, occidental and oriental. She has little time for buzzwords like feminism and lesbianism and integration. People, she says, are more important than groups, trends, slogans and causes.

And she should know.

For thirty or so years, our lives and dreams intersected and overlapped. Dan and Maggie returned to Yale so Dan could finish his schooling there, then moved back to Georgia, where he replaced Jerry Berlin as president of the Human Development Institute (a psychological company teaching marriage, family and office communication skills using programmed learning materials). Eventually they moved into Atlanta's inner city, where Maggie took a teaching job at a new and progressive private school, Paideia, while raising their two boys. Dan then returned to graduate school in psychology, and Maggie entered medical school two or three years later. They graduated within days of each other. Dan was awarded his Ph.D. on May 11, Maggie, her MD on May 13, 1977, with distinction, at the top of her class.

Maggie thrust forward into the 1970s, '80s and '90s, knowing pretty much what she wanted. Raising two boys with the devotion and focus of a Zen mistress, she was a logistical genius who organized her family at home and abroad, anticipating her three guys' needs in highly instructive ways. She was a model for parenting excellence, and while I probably never quite lived up to her standards, her example and my memories of how she, and Dan, raised their children helped keep me going during times of family crisis and tragedy.

Her expectations of her children, her partner and her friends reflected what she wanted from herself, and she carried this set of standards into relationships and moral combat. Until my daughter came along, I had never known such a bossy person as Maggie Mermin. It has taken me a while to appreciate that her bossiness is the external manifestation of her inner conviction that we must all do our best. Until I met and married Betsy, I never knew anyone who understood loyalty the way Maggie does. Maggie exemplifies the saying that "a good friend is 100 percent loyal, maybe 70 percent agreeable; a bad friend is 100 percent agreeable and 70 percent loyal." Partnerships are not about thinking alike as much as they are about thinking together. I learned that from her too.

Maggie and Dan packed their marriage in after thirty-something years. Before their marriage gave out, they fought and made up. Laughed and cried. Cross-pollinated each other with humor, challenge, exhortation, sexual interchange, love and anger. With liberal amounts of forgiveness, but rarely hatred. If mental health has to do with growing up before we grow old, each of them grew into more mature, healthier and stronger people than when they started out together. Their growth was not always interwoven, however, and their personal avenues of emotional evolution diverged, at first slowly, then more dramatically, toward separate and independent lives.

Today Maggie is happily remarried to Susan, also a strong woman, in a quieter and more understated way. With Susan, Maggie seems content. She has never begrudged Dan his new life, nor blamed him for any of their past problems, and she has deeply appreciated his support and encouragement during her long and demanding years in medical school and residency in internal medicine. She left a past life with a partner and found peace and tenderness with a new partner, with whom she enjoys a deep sense of mutuality, contentment and happiness.

I have observed the dynamics between Maggie and Susan, and I have talked with many women in therapy, and I sense that strong women in a relationship with another woman experience fewer power struggles than do heterosexual couples that include a strong woman. There is less ego-involvement and less of the prideful, often self-destructive conflict that often characterize heterosexual marriages. Two strong women will tend to be practical and more concerned about living with and meeting their partners' needs than about winning. Maggie and Susan enjoy at least one more emotion common to all happy and contented couples: appreciation of the other.

I continue to marvel at Maggie's toughness, competence, integrity, and her commitment to balance the needs of her patients with her desire to have time with loved ones and with her own self. She uses the same yardstick on others with which she measures herself. She is existentially strong and gifted, not only with rich intelligence but also inspiring courage. I suspect that she worries less about missing out on an afterlife than about not having lived this one fully and deeply, together and apart from Susan.

It was said of Rose Kennedy that she could wipe away a tear close up as easily as she could spot a hole in a sock at 100 yards. This same alertness and sharp-eyed perceptiveness was and is Maggie Mermin. She would approach cynicism, but hit the brakes before she got there. "I dunno . . . ," she would say and follow those innocent opening words with a soft-spoken but hard-hitting attack on phonies, charlatans and demagogues.

She is brave. Once she chased a purse-snatcher down the street in urban Atlanta, all the while shouting fairly graphic comments about the nature of the criminal's family relationships. She didn't catch the villain, but I don't think she regretted the chase.

Maggie still models that courage and integrity and has difficulty understanding why the rest of us don't follow her basic rules of excellence. She would scold me for my worst and grubbiest behaviors, but that would be the end of it. Constitutionally incapable of carrying a grudge, she might sharply confront you, then enjoy a glass of iced tea with you five minutes later.

Maggie encounters the weak-hearted and comforts the burned out, she lives life with courage and gusto and appreciates the importance of detail, the nails that help to hold us together.

———

Jerry Berlin was a strong believer in the injunction: "Doctor, heal thyself." He could see that most of us were neither very sick nor very well, but that we had work to do on our personalities. One day he said, "David, you need therapy. We're going to find a psychotherapist for you." Jerry Berlin brought me together with Tom Malone, the man who would become not only my therapist but also my mentor.

Tom had credentials as both a psychotherapist and as a physician. Only about a third of psychologists, or psychiatrists for that matter, are actually psychotherapists. It is a particular approach to treatment.

Psychotherapy is me operating as my client's research assistant, bringing into focus what's troubling them, sharpening the questions rather than providing easy answers. The idea is the better the questions you ask, the more easily the answers will follow.

Today I write medications and I do a small amount of

biological psychiatry, but I see myself as a psychotherapist. That's what and who Tom Malone was. His late-starting background in medicine likely helps account for my later decision to follow the same path. He had an enormous effect on my life, including my life with women.

He was an older, wiser, stronger man than the father I'd known—he was the kind of father I hadn't had. Irish-American, pipe-smoking, warm sense of humor, tough. Tom let me know when I was doing well—when I was moving toward my potential, making a good thing better—and when I wasn't doing well—when I was regressing, falling back on my old habits and defenses, focusing on yesterday rather than today and tomorrow.

Today, I am a psychotherapist myself, and I recognize that most of us don't grow much beyond what and who we are at twenty-five or thirty. We have more experiences, but our personal growth is pretty well static after that. This may be truer of men than of women. Men say, "I don't need help, I'm not sick." Women say, "Well, Bob, I'm going for help because I'm not well, or not as well as I want to be, or could be." My bias as a therapist is that psychotherapy, while not the only way to strength, is one of the more verbal, more explicit ones.

I still see a therapist because I want to make a good thing better. I have room to grow, places of strength that I have not yet experienced. I have things to do, and one of those things is to develop unexplored areas, parts of myself that I am continuously learning about. Becoming stronger. Not just being who I am, but being more of who I am and who I could be.

It took years of therapy for me to appreciate the full pipe-smoking impact of Tom Malone, psychotherapist and teacher. Tom's influence on me during the years I visited him for psychotherapy sessions, when we traded pipe tobacco and raunchy jokes, transformed my life.

Tom taught me that sex was important, and at the same time pushed me to think about life in larger, lustier and more unreserved terms: "People need each other and need to be honest with each other" and "David, you're a better giver than a taker, so let's start balancing the account" and "Why aren't you screwing?" and "Are you going to be a doctor or aren't you?" and "Where are you going with your life?" He did a fair amount of self-disclosure, and then he would come back to me. He was challenging and confrontational, and also supportive.

I remember the first time I slept with a woman. It was in the summer of 1963. I was twenty-three years old, a late starter—but better late than never.

I came into Tom's office the next week, and he asked, "Well Kirk, are you seeing anybody?" And I said, "Yeah, Jan." And he said, "What about sex? What's stopping you?" And I said, "Well . . . nothing." And he smiled and said: "You bastard, you were getting some and you weren't telling me about it!" With a mixture of paternal and avuncular pride, he then said, "All right. Let's get back to work." We would drink our coffees and smoke our pipes. That was the day when everybody smoked indoors: cigarettes, pipes, whatever.

My time with Tom Malone was a classroom wherein I would grow emotionally, socially, intellectually and sexually. "Where is your next girlfriend?" and "What happened to that last relationship? What did you learn, David?"

He was the father that gave me permission to grow up sexually, emotionally, intellectually and socially. He showed me how I needed to take better care of myself and be kind to myself. He taught me about success anxiety—about which I wrote in an article published in the *Canadian Journal of Psychiatry,*[1] "What often ties people up is not a fear of failure, but fear of success. I see this with the women I work with in psychotherapy who are struggling with the issue of strength, and help them to understand what it means and how it affects them. I suggest that they ask themselves: How much is it okay for you to grow, how far beyond, how many of your friends and family, in how many different ways, how soon and how comfortably?"

In retrospect, I think I suffered from success anxiety myself at times.

Tom gave me all that combined with that most valuable of all classroom currency: humor. When I moved away from the area, I continued to have sessions with him over the next several years.

Thanks to Tom Malone and to Jerry Berlin, I finished my master's degree—with a thesis in the area of social psychology in conformity—more grounded and centered than when I had started. I had no idea, previously, of who I was, nor had I known that I didn't know this.

So, there I was with a master's degree, and the thought that perhaps I should get a doctorate. With this in mind, I interviewed at Boston University and at Brandeis, in Waltham, Massachusetts, with Dr. Abraham Maslow, a hero of mine, a man with a dry sense of humor. At the end of our interview, he said, "Do you have any questions?" I said, "Well, this Hierarchy of Needs, this is great stuff. We need more of this." He replied warmly, "Well, if you think so, David, we'll work on it."

Returning to Atlanta, I decided that I was probably not ready for more graduate school and that I would take some time out. Then Dr. Eric Lincoln, an impressive scholar from Clark College, also in Georgia, came to Emory to talk about his work with the Black Muslims. I asked him if there were any teaching jobs at Clark College. He said there were, so I went there, interviewed and landed not one but two teaching jobs; one at Clark, teaching introductory psychology courses, and one at Georgia State, teaching introductory psychology to student nurses and night students.

This was at the dawn of desegregation, an interesting time to be in the South. Clark was mostly black; Georgia State College mostly white, but both were beginning the slow process of desegregation. For three years I went back and forth between the two schools teaching psychology. In my second year there, I decided I was going to go into medicine. I applied, and was accepted, at the Medical College of Georgia, in Augusta.

These were very busy years. I was teaching at both schools and also catching up on my pre-med requirements: physics and organic chemistry and all the other things I needed. It still wasn't clear to me that I was going to be a psychiatrist. I just thought I was going to be an MD, and didn't think much further about it. I wanted to learn about these other areas: for example, pediatrics, family practice, surgery and dermatology.

The next seven years are a blur. There was med school plus interning at San Francisco General Hospital and working at the Alaska Native Medical Center, ANMC, in Anchorage, as a sort of junior-grade psychiatrist. From there I went to

Vancouver where I began a residency in psychiatry as a student specialist, at the University of British Columbia, UBC.

I got married during those years. To Karen. It's not a relationship I remember with great fondness; I usually try not to think about it at all. But I did get married and we stuck it out for five years before we called it quits.

I met Karen while attending med school. She was a nursing student and we met at an encounter group weekend. T-Groups were the rage those days—where you confront people and relate to them on deeper levels on the beach, with or without your clothes on. We did get a bit carried away with all that.

I was in my last year, finishing medical school. Karen still had about two years to go. We fell for each other, at least so I thought at the time. In retrospect, I think my anxiety fed into the relationship. I had got an internship at the hospital in San Francisco, in the summer of 1969, and I was nervous about moving there on my own. I wanted somebody to go with me, Karen seemed to fill the bill. She would be my support system.

I did my internship at the San Francisco General Hospital. Then I began looking around for a residency, all the while looking over my shoulder, watching the draft board, which wanted to draft me and send me to Viet Nam. Fortunately I met a friend of a friend, Chuck, from Alaska, and the two of us designed a job. I applied, was accepted and was soon off to Alaska to become a general medical officer and inexperienced psychotherapist, working with and for Chuck at the ANMC. While I was working there, Karen finished nursing school in Anchorage.

At the time I had only my master's in psychology, my MD and my personal therapy experience under my belt. I did the physicals, worked in emergency, admitted patients and worried about psychotropic medications, with Chuck overseeing all my work. I did that for two years, from 1971 to 1973, when I left to begin the psychiatric residency in Vancouver, British Columbia.

This was a challenging period in my life and career. Frontier mental health, Alaska style, was a rugged and protean business. The Alaskan Native Americans—including many strong women—with whom I was privileged to work were mostly warm, generous, kind, friendly and appreciative. Individual psychotherapy, however, was an effort, with strangers trying to discover each other through the white man's medium. Group therapy was more syntonic and helpful; the room was often filled with long moments of rich, comfortable silence. The flow of oil had precipitated enormous change in the area. Native villages experienced the further breakup of their traditions, cohesiveness and town structures. Alcoholics and schizophrenics, never particularly popular within the villages, were pressured to move to Anchorage or Fairbanks, where, maybe, someone would look after them. It was a time of political unrest, and confusion and frustration among the native population over their circumstances. Depression and grief seemed endemic. Even now, Alaska is difficult to write about. Heartbreak, helplessness, trans-cultural loneliness commingled, at the time, with despair over the crumbling edifice of my marriage. The cold was too close to my frostbitten soul.

Karen was loyal, kind and funny, but we were incompatible and we weren't happy. We made it through those years by keeping busy—me going through various career pathways, and Karen getting back on the ladder to her nursing degree. We hoped that we might rekindle the erotic excitement that had bound us together initially; however, by the last couple of years we were together, that hope shifted to inertia. They were empty, and mercifully childless, years. Our five-year marriage ended in 1975, after we moved to Vancouver.

Today Karen teaches nursing in a medical center. In retrospect, we were two people who did not have a lot in common, except superficially: we were both from white Anglo-Saxon Presbyterian backgrounds. I liked women, and so did she.

We were still together, in 1974, when I began my residency at West 1, the psychiatry ward at the University of British Columbia's Health Sciences Department, and where I met Betsy—the woman who would knock me off my feet and change my life. Yet again.

12 Betsy

I FIRST LAID EYES ON ELIZABETH ANN LASOR at a very ho-hum party given for the new psychiatric residents, which included me and the staff working in West 1 of the University of British Columbia's Health Sciences Psychiatric Centre. Ward parties generally fall into one of two categories: wild and crazy or dull and deadly. Held at a supervisor's house, this one was headed into the latter category.

Karen attended the party with me, and we were sitting on straight-backed chairs arranged around the walls of this elegant Kerrisdale mansion in south Vancouver. We struggled with the polite and restrained gaiety practiced by the nurses, doctors, social workers and their mates, all of whom seemed more comfortable with respectful discourse than open, candid repartee with unpredictable outcomes. We were bored and longed to leave.

Suddenly at about 10 p.m., a great-looking woman in a flowered jeans skirt stood up, snatched the hand of her date, and announced in a husky stage whisper that could be heard across the street, "C'mon, Tony! I think it's time you and I quietly tiptoed out of here!" Then she and her blushing escort escaped the evening's ennui and disappeared into the night.

"Who on earth was that?" Karen asked.

"I don't know," I replied. Any expert in the language of Don't-Know would have quickly determined what is so obvious to me today—that I also wanted to know, "Who on earth was that?"

That intriguing person was Elizabeth Ann LaSor. Betsy. I had, in fact, seen her before that night, because Betsy was an assistant professor of psychiatric nursing and her office was just around the corner from West 1, where I was working. Her nursing students rotated through my ward, as well. You tend to run into the nurses and nursing professors, so we would exchange brief pleasantries, but the night of the ward party was the first real sense I'd had of her as a strong force.

Over the next couple of years, I would see her occasionally around the Health Sciences Psychiatric Hospital. We would say Hi, or gossip a bit about the department. She was kind of a mother figure for the young nursing students—all of whom were having their first and probably quite anxious rotation through psychiatry, working with the very sickest in-patients in the ward. She had a sense of whimsy and humor that fell somewhere between loving excitement and hating boredom. Occasionally she would do something to lighten things up for her students, like the time she called an emergency meeting of her nursing students. They fluttered into her office, anxious and curious. She closed the blinds and locked the door, then put on a porno tape she had received from one of the drug detail men connected to the hospital.

Once, during those two years, I tried to fix her up with a practice partner from Vancouver's Jericho Tennis Club who told me he liked strong women and wanted to meet somebody new. Somehow, he found his way to an open house that Betsy was hosting but apparently failed to make much of an impression on her. He shrugged when recounting his frustration at not being able to buttonhole her long enough to talk to. "I don't know . . . she'd be charging up the stairs with someone and then heading back downstairs with someone else, and a plate of dip or something. Boy, she sure was busy!"

Typical Betsy behavior, as I later learned.

———

Like most people born in 1936, Betsy was deeply influenced by the Great Depression, probably as much by her parents' memories of it as by her own recall. Those were the years when people saved clothing, cleaned their plates and threw nothing out. This legacy was to manifest in later years, like the time Betsy lost a Christmas ham sent to her by her brother Fred. She had left it outside in a bucket of water to leach the salt out of it. About a week later, our children were coming home from school when they discovered a vaguely familiar, if somewhat bedraggled, hambone with a few attached meat scraps in the street rain-gutter below our house. Obviously, an animal had found it. The kids brought it back into the house, and it was only after much protest and derision from her husband and children that Betsy decided against salvaging the hambone in the dishwasher.

Betsy was a lonely child, living on a farm on the outskirts of Easton, Pennsylvania, with only her two brothers—one a year older, the other five years younger—as playmates. Her father, Dr. William S. LaSor, was a low-paid professor of religion at nearby Presbyterian Lafayette College. He was a loving but critical father, not given to expressions of pride in his children. Betsy once described him as an Old Testament theologian with a bull-headed personality.

It was hard for Betsy. She knew he loved her but needed his approval. She would have loved it if he had noticed her accomplishments and given her a few compliments. She would get bits and pieces, fragmentary fashion, but never an unqualified endorsement of her worth or her value. He was a bright man, with two Ph.D.s. Likely he was more absorbed in his work than in his personal relationships. Beneath Betsy's sauciness and whimsy was a little girl looking for her dad's approval.

Betsy enjoyed a less complicated and almost certainly less conflicted relationship with her mum. Betsy's mother, also named Betsy, grew up somewhere between a traditional role for a woman and a more feminist identity. Somewhere between domesticity and a more assertive, professional person. Vulnerable to periodic depression, she would treat it with a shot of this or that. Betsy loved her mother, but identified more with her dad, wanting early on to be a professional person.

Betsy grew up with remarkable equanimity. For example, she once experienced the ignominy of a birthday party where not one neighbor child showed up. This could have been horribly deflating for a child, but Betsy accepted her mother's explanation that the problem lay in having a birthday on December 26th. It was impossible for children to attend on this day! Her friends also lived a distance away; her life, by default, promoted self-initiated play. Betsy kept herself busy with a paper route, read lots of books and had fun making up games with her brothers.

She was an early junk collector, enjoying trips through the town dump as a child, often on her way home from elementary school. In later life she became a serious junk collector, inspired by finding treasures like an unopened packet of condoms in her early forays. "I have no idea what they are, Mother. But they look perfectly good!" As she grew older, her finds expanded to things like an antique oak filing cabinet, and a rancher's old boot discovered out on the barren east Texas prairie. "I don't know—it might make a terrific planter!"

She was a treasure collector, an archivist specializing in the lost and abandoned, the lonely and neglected, the overlooked and undervalued. She could see through dust and scratches, wrappers and veneer to the true beauty that lay beneath. When it came to people, she could smell bullshit one part per million at a thousand yards. Many of the treasures she enjoyed searching for were already inside her, well hidden but very much present. She was a treasure herself, one with shaky self-esteem; she could see the beauty in objects and in others far more easily than she could appreciate them in herself.

In 1948, Betsy's father took his family west, to Pasadena, California, where he had been offered an Old Testament professorship at the newly formed Fuller Theological Seminary. Its conservative orientation at that time fit his no-nonsense approach to the Bible, to morality and to the twentieth century. The move to southern California was not a happy one for Betsy, and she wrote in her diary:

I had a terrible time adjusting and never really did adequately, finding myself in trouble frequently. My [older] brother found it much easier and became a studious, model student and a very difficult one to follow in school. I have always felt my greatest inferiority to be in keeping up intellectually and socially with my older brother.

This was an ongoing theme, this sense of not being able to keep up with her older brother. In later years, with the insight of a student of psychology, she reflected on how her own feelings of inferiority might have been influenced by her relationship with her father:

My father enjoyed having a daughter but had little understanding of how to communicate and relate to a girl, having had a family background that offered him little experience to learn this.

So she overcompensated for her private inferiority by affecting a tomboy manner and assuming a public mask of confidence.

My scholastic record showed my unhappiness and I had difficulties feeling self-confident in my social adjustments except for church groups. I retained much of my tomboy mannerisms, excelling in sports and outdoor activities to keep from dealing with the pressures of social graces and boy/girl relationships.

Socially, I developed a personality that was inwardly shy, not being sure if I could measure up to phantom standards, and outwardly very sociably gregarious in groups to cover my discomfort . . . with men, with whom I felt so inadequate: Adler would call this feeling one of incompletion or imperfection . . . I felt that I had to have a man who could help me adequately compete with my father and brother.

After high school, Betsy entered nurses' training at the local City College, getting both her Associate of Arts and her Registered Nurse degrees within three years. She had a social life, some dates, all of which were centered around church functions. There, she wrote, she was "gregarious, comfortable and charming."

And so, with the strength of the ugly duckling that had yet to find its place in the tempting and exciting world so loved and so assiduously sought, she would survive and eventually prevail. She intuitively understood the irony in G. K. Chesterton's observation that "there are people who hope for eternity—yet when they have a rainy Sunday afternoon, they don't know what to do with it." Like her father, whose approval she could never seem to adequately capture, Betsy hoped for and also believed in eternity. But she knew what to do with her rainy Sunday afternoons, whether it was sewing, trying out a new recipe or making blackberry brandy for Christmas from her foolproof recipe.[1] And later, loving.

After city college, she worked as an emergency room nurse. Then more nursing school, followed by a rich and emancipating eighteen months in Europe, first as a *sygeplejerske* (soo-ply-eska), or nurse, in Denmark, and then in psychiatrist Dr. Maxwell Jones' innovative therapeutic community in England.

Returning to the United States, more energized, more focused and more differentiated from her family than ever, she enrolled in the Graduate School of Nursing at UCLA, where she earned her master's degree with a specialty in psychiatric nursing. From that fulcrum, she began teaching psychiatric nursing at San Diego State University. She was living in nearby La Jolla, in March 1971, when a postcard arrived.

Dear Betsy:

Lee tells me you're bored with your job. Do you want a good hard one? If so, write to me at home.

Best regards, Muriel

It was from an influential nursing professor and teacher who had just left the UCLA School of Nursing to return to her native Canada. Dr. Muriel Uprichard, a tough and feisty academic, had just been named dean of the School of Nursing at UBC. She was a fierce mother hen and before leaving UCLA began aggressively recruiting the nursing professors she wanted for her UBC faculty nest, many of them UCLA graduates.

In the summer of 1971, Betsy uprooted from southern California and headed north to Canada in a loaded, red and only slightly battered 1968 Toyota Corolla. She was full of enthusiasm, energy and thirst for new adventure. Lucky for me it was an adventure that would coincide with my own.

I returned to a West 1 event twenty-seven months after that first ward party. By then, Karen and I had separated and I was again a bachelor. This was a much livelier ward party organized around a progressive dinner, that is, the dinner was to take place in three stages, at three different homes.

Betsy was there, and spunkier than ever. She and I were somehow chosen to lead the dancing at the third stage of the dinner. Betsy wore an outrageous and wonderful blue denim maxi-skirt decorated with buttons, campaign pins, military decorations, patches and more. The skirt crackled with electric energy and unique creativity, prompting me to ask her about a particular medal that was mid-station between her knees. "Betsy, what's that medal below there?" She responded with an unwavering gaze and two challenging words, in her gravelly alto. "Below what?" Won my heart.

The next morning I went salmon fishing with the husband of one of our dinner hostesses, but I couldn't take my mind off Betsy. I knew I had to see her again. Thus began a courtship in that summer of 1976, our first year together. In her scrapbook, Betsy chronicles those months:

The month of June was heavenly. The sun shone and there were parties, bicycle rides and getting to know one another in two short weeks. We had great fun with the Freemans – visited the Lazersons and had a romantic dinner at Orestes. You covered my eyes to put a rose on my plate and the waiter got tears in his eyes. He said later that he hadn't seen anything so nice in a long time. Neither had I.

Then I was off to Texas. A month away when I thought you'd have a great time "playing." There were still many ladies lusting after your body. My biggest surprise was to receive a letter one week later from you. You had gotten my address and surprised me and indeed made me think about you a lot.

August was a cold, rainy month in which we got reacquainted. The sun shone at times and we rode our bicycles. Your family arrived en masse so I met almost everyone. They were lively and fun and we saw some of Vancouver with them. You went away this time to fish in Campbell River with your folks.

September was lovely and your garden really gave forth. There were tomatoes, zucchini, onions, peas, apples and butter squash. We canned and cooked and baked. The beginning of our blackberry marathon was in Sept. We really stripped False Creek of blackberries.

Jay [a new boarder] moved into my house in Sept. and you two hit it off well.

Here Betsy's insecurity resurfaced as she continued,

Between Jay and Carol [another boarder], I sometimes wondered who you came to visit. The 'old country kitchen' buzzed with activity and good smells. We ate and laughed and loved.

I had no idea that, even as we were getting to know each other that summer, Betsy was blithely overriding advice she had earlier passed on to her brother Fred: "Never go to bed with someone crazier than you."

Betsy bought a stucco home on West 14th Avenue, across the street from Lord Byng High School. She paid for it by taking on three mortgages, but needed help making the monthly mortgage payments. In the tradition of collecting castoffs and hand-me-downs, combined with a spirit of enlightened self-interest, she took in wounded, often divorced and vulnerable men and started a tongue-in-cheek boarding home that she informally christened Betsy LaSor's Home for Recycled Men.

There were women there too, including a nurse and a schoolteacher, but mostly there were men who reported innocently for recycling, refurbishing and general healing. A chemist, a nuclear physicist, a BC Tel engineer and a high school teacher all experienced Betsy's healing touch, her haircuts and her by now well-honed instincts. She tended their various matrimonial wounds and separated them from a small amount of their monthly income. The arrangement also gave Betsy a valued observer's window into a world that fascinated, intrigued and simultaneously dismayed her, a world about which she never ceased to enjoy learning.

She was fascinated by men. Could not get enough of them. Identified with them. At times envied them, yet always knew where she stopped and they started. She never stopped laughing at men's foibles. She had seen too many of us in her emergency rooms, in the U.S. and abroad, in various stages of disrepair, drunkenness, unconsciousness and other even more unseemly stages of vulnerability. She was not fooled by our façades, our talk or our charm.

I remembered her telling, in gleeful fascination, an anecdote about a testosterone showdown between Jay, our friend and her boarder, and a party guest at a Christmas open house at her home. Jay and his opponent had squared off over a point of conversation and, like a pair of verbal if inarticulate bulls, challenged each other with a crescendo of ever louder "Oh, yeah?" They pawed their metaphorical turf and snorted. In retelling the story, Betsy would play the part of both guy-bulls, astounding listeners with her ability to recreate aggressive, macho discourse. This, combined with high whimsy, underscored her keen understanding of low male psychology. No man could hear Betsy's viewpoint without guffawing—not if he had a sense of humor.

I would become the last of Betsy LaSor's recycled men, and the one she decided to keep. Why? I wasn't as strong as her, nor nearly as tough. Perhaps some combination of my kindness and sense of humor, and being in the same business, mental health. And maybe I got just a little bit lucky. I had already struck out in my first marriage; it's possible the nurse in her perceived a wounded, needy and also somewhat horny patient, looking for a healing opportunity. She already had a proprietary interest in me when I moved in at the beginning of January 1977.

We had been seeing more and more of each other since that memorable ward party the previous summer; and me moving in as a 'renter' seemed to give us both some breathing space as the texture of our relationship began to change from friends to boyfriend/girlfriend to landlord/tenant to something even more important, if slightly scarier.

In addition to the newly acquired financial commitments incurred in moving in with Betsy, there were learning experiences. She was her father's daughter, but she was remarkably tolerant. Probably there just wasn't enough time in the day to do everything if she was going to have some fun. The moral high ground was the first thing to go.

For the first four days of that January I slept downstairs in a sort of mudroom in Betsy LaSor's Home for Recycled Men. Hanging onto my independence by my fingernails, I commuted up two flights of stairs each night with my quilt, to sleep with the landlady. The absurdity and humor of the situation struck us both—Betsy before me, I am quite sure. On day five, I left my downstairs room and was sleeping with this wonderful woman, like a regular couple, from the beginning of the evening. I stopped my nightly commute, stopped paying monthly rent and began paying the mortgage.

Ever practical, Betsy did walk the talk with her primary theory about women-and-men relationships: a woman should pick the best man available—best for her, that is; then she should give that man her best shot, holding back not at all, pulling no punches. In other words, don't take care of the guy or flatter or mollycoddle him but really sock it to him. Either the guy could take it or he couldn't. If he withered, whimpered or otherwise weaseled out, why then the woman should cut her losses and let him go. But if he could absorb a punch, weather a challenge to his character or his potency and enjoy and respect a woman who would stand up to him unafraid, and if he stayed around for more, then maybe he was a finalist. Or at least worth spending more time on. Put him on the shortlist. Maybe have another look. She called it, "Training."

I am the better for having been trained by Betsy Ann LaSor. Much better. Self-absorption slowly gave way to selflessness, kindness, alertness and attentiveness, on a good day. "Look around you, David. My Gosh! Gee whiz!" she would say when I'd foolishly and nearsightedly asked her what I could do to "help out." All that plus the courage to love more openly and creatively, with less hemming and hawing, less holding back. She taught me that and gave me that.

Her system showed no pity, only respect for the "Trainee." Once, early on in our relationship, I asked why I was the one who seemed to be making all the apologies. Her answer was simple. "Oh, I don't know, honey," she responded with a warm smile. "Probably it's because you're the one making most of the mistakes." I had walked right into that one, leading with my chin. She was never one to sugarcoat a response that might hurt the other person in a relationship. Instead she would counter with appropriate wit. She hated bombast and pretense.

Persistence and vulnerability were qualities that Betsy and I shared. Though neither of us were quitters, her persistence was a quiet phenomenon. On the other hand, her vulnerability was typically a tougher and more often in-your-face variety than mine. The quality that maintains the balance of these forms of strength in women, that helps maintain practical, honest equilibrium, is integrity. Integrity certainly was there in this woman.

By the time Betsy died, she had faced a lifetime of challenge and disappointment with men: a critical father;

difficult, even homicidal and suicidal partners—an earlier boyfriend had killed himself; and sixteen years of working with dependent and vulnerable patients, culminating with her psychiatric specialty. She could walk a tightrope in relationships because she totally accepted most people, especially those who were honest and sincere. However, when someone close to her crossed over her threshold of tolerable behavior, that person would receive a Betsy LaSor "Training Experience."

And they would be the better for it—although they probably wouldn't recognize it for a while.

MY WALLA WALLA SWEET

My (you know what) for you is
an onion. One layer peeled off finds
more and better of the same
underneath. And underneath
that layer – even more!
What an incredible fruit.
No wonder it makes me cry . . . .

        Your greengrocer,
        David
        February 4, 1980

13 And Baby Makes Three

IN 1977 I BEGAN A WONDERFUL and challenging period of my life: living with Betsy LaSor. As our relationship deepened, I found myself falling more deeply in love with her than I had known was possible between two people. As I grew closer to her, I experienced two fears: that she would get pregnant, a carry-over from my dating days when sex was just about having fun. And that she wouldn't. I was now ready for a family. I was pretty sure. I had found the woman that I wanted to be the mother of my children.

In September of that year, we learned that Betsy was pregnant but, while I was overjoyed at the news and Betsy was ready for the next stage of our relationship, I was too overwhelmed with excitement and anxiety about that forthcoming event to deal with marriage as well. Not exactly a pair of rookies us; my beautiful, absolutely-glowing-in-her-pregnancy partner was almost forty-one, and I was thirty-eight.

Betsy wrote her parents:

Dear Mother and Daddy,

I have been meaning to write you for some time but the beginning of school had done its usual job of flattening me. That's really no excuse, however, and I do have some great news to share with you.

David and I will become parents on or about April 6! We are really happy. We went today to have genetic counseling for the amniocentesis I will have on October 11. I don't think there will be any problem but we want to be sure and my Dr. is quite insistent. So far we have only told a few people until after the amniocentesis in case I have to abort. It's hard not to tell people. [Brother] Fred knows because he was here right after I found out. He suggested we tell you and we thought that it was important to share this happy, and yet anxious, time with you.

I'm sure you are probably wondering about marriage plans. That is something David wants to wait on and I'd like to have now. The security aspect is not a threat and so I've decided to allow David his time. I feel sure everything will work out in time. Fred felt you needed to be reassured about David. I think I have been amiss in regard to this.

David is very sincere about our relationship. He's happy and content – as am I – and very supportive and helpful to me. His previous marriage was a painful and depressing experience for him and he is slowly getting away from this experience and more comfortable with his commitment to our relationship. I do not think you should worry that he is exploiting or using me.

Once Fred was reassured about this and got to know David he really felt good about our relationship. That was when he told me I should share this with you. I guess I'll close.

Let me/us hear from you. It's a really happy time for me –
I'm not sure if I've ever been happier.

Love to all! B & D

Betsy took a maternity break before our baby was born, typing, editing and publishing psychiatric nursing papers furiously in a sort of academic nesting ritual. Her practicality winning out over her enthusiasm, she cancelled the plans that would have seen us going to Africa for Christmas 1977. Instead, we made plans to marry at my brother Doug's Utah home as soon as we could get away over the Christmas holidays. We wanted to be a family in the eyes of society as well as in our own.

Our wedding was a cozy, lively and festive New Year's Eve affair with family and a few close friends attending. The traditional references to love's ending: "Until death do us part," sailed over my head as quickly as the words came out of my mouth.

Betsy, resplendent in her fifth month of pregnancy and gowned lovingly in her favorite grandmother's silk wedding dress by her attending girlfriends, from the UCLA nursing school, announced at the end of her vows, "I pledge to you today my faithfulness, my loyalty, my respect and my love for the length of my lifetime." I responded, "I don't know where we'll be in twenty or thirty or forty years, yet if the first eighteen months with you are any indication of where we're going, I think that I had better fasten my seat belt. I also plan to be around and hope you will."

We returned to Canada soon after the wedding and charged into a major home renovation. With seventy-nine cumulative childless years between us, we seemed to be trying to make up for lost time; the nesting instinct in overdrive. Betsy was relentless in her efforts to clear the deck for her new family, and this included giving notice to all remaining tenants.

One morning, one of the last tenants of the earlier boarding-home arrangement was all packed and ready to go with garment bags, cardboard boxes and a sizable variety of suitcases, when Betsy remarked to the tenant, who'd lived there for at least four years:

"Well, it looks like you're ready to go. I want to look through your boxes now, then."

The tenant, astonished, said, "Excuse me?"

Betsy persisted: "I need to look through your things, just to be sure everything is okay."

Not surprisingly in my mind, the tenant responded, "Well, that just pisses me right off!"

Betsy didn't say a word. Relaxed and calm, she just headed for his boxes.

I could not believe my eyes. Or ears. I don't think the tenant could either. I felt a flush of embarrassment and sympathy for the tenant, and didn't know whether to be ashamed, embarrassed or proud of Betsy. I realized by the end of that spring day that I was all three.

Betsy told me if I had a problem with what she did, the problem was my own. For her there was nothing to it. She ran her boarding home in a style consistent with that of the tough-love captain of an eighteenth century privateer. You could not, and should not, trust everyone in this world, and what was the point in pretending you could? The tenant had an honest reputation but, in her view, this was immaterial. You checked. Her actions lay somewhere between tough, rough and strong, and they were an eye-opener for me. I told myself to get over it and get on with life. Loyalty to family and friends was what counted and Betsy had loyalty to spare.

I was reminded of my friend Maggie's belief that when it came to placing a value on being agreeable or being loyal, being loyal won out hands down. Amongst all her wisdom, this was one of Betsy's finest lessons. We had not established our family yet but, with Betsy ahead of me along the blunt and honest path, we were well under way.

Betsy sailed through the balance of her second trimester and quickly into her third, sleeping a lot in the afternoons, being sick from the smell of green beans and complaining of feeling "bilious." She made new maternity dresses and jeans by adding panels to old but comfortable outfits. She glowed: I have a sepia-toned Polaroid of her as a beautiful nude reclining on the downstairs couch in a softly lit room, looking for all the world like the pregnant model for a French Impressionist painting.

As the time neared for our baby to be born, we went to childbirth classes and exchanged stories and anxieties with other, younger couples. In April 1978, it looked like the baby was coming and I took her to the Vancouver General Hospital. But Dr. Thomas, Betsy's doctor, sent us home. No labor today. Come back when you have something more promising. But nothing happened. Then Betsy's doctor asked us to return on the morning of April 19th for an induction. This was it. Here we go. Betsy, in labor and delivery, remained calm and relaxed. I, by contrast, was almost unmanageably excited. I received much teasing then and later about how I was so busy monitoring her contractions I forgot to pay adequate attention to her, the star and center of the whole experience.

At 4:50 p.m., our beautiful, squalling, pink-toned son, with tinges of strawberry blonde hair, was born. Betsy complained about feeling faint as her skin turned a pale, greenish-yellow and her blood pressure dropped briefly. I hollered into the open hospital hallways to anyone who could assist. Dr. Thomas returned quickly, dressing me down for such an un-doctorly display of fear and anxiety.

Betsy and our baby arrived home in three days. She had now completed, she told me, the goals she'd stated in a silent vow to herself on first arriving at UBC. She had 1) become an assistant professor in nursing, 2) married and 3) become a mother. The baby she once imagined she would call Benjamin was named Andrew William Daniel Kirkpatrick, after my uncle, her father and my best friend, respectively.

With UBC's generous maternity leave program, she was able to take another year off, and spent that time bonding with Andy, breast-feeding and singing to her tiny much-loved son. Together they played games like "How big is Andrew?" Then, her hands rising together with her voice:

"Sooooo**OOOOOOOO**oooooobig!"

She would bathe with him, sing to him, flirt with him. She loved being a mother and sharing children's clothing with her friends on the UBC Nursing Faculty. She was fun-loving, intuitive and warm-hearted, a natural. These were times of deep contentment.

We wanted to remain in Vancouver and I tried to establish a group practice here, but those I would have chosen to partner with were scattering to the winds. For awhile, I worked in an already established group practice, but it was a huge partnership and not much of a collaborative environment, so I suggested to Betsy that we move to the States and find a group that we could join. Betsy, always up for an adventure, said, "Fine, if you want to." But she was as ready for a change as I was.

We moved to Ashland, Oregon. I see, now, that my attraction to this place was that it was very like Yellow Springs, the small town where I had grown up. One of the main features was that, like Yellow Springs, Ashland was not only a small college town, but it also had an annual Shakespeare Festival. Betsy too had lived in a small Midwestern community, so for both of us it was kind of like coming home. It had been ten years since she had lived in the States and eight years for me.

In the early fall of 1981, we rented out our Vancouver home and headed south down the I-5. I planned to join a mental health group practice in Ashland, hoping that Betsy would one day join me there, a persistent professional dream that had not crystallized during our time together in Vancouver.

These were tight times for us financially. Everyone thinks that psychiatrists earn lots of money, but let me tell you that isn't always the case. Not that year, not this book! For the first two months Betsy, Andy and I lived in a trailer park in an Airstream trailer while I worked to build up a small psychiatric practice and we could afford a proper home. Betsy and Andy visited the pond in the local park, fed the ducks and geese, and waited for me to come home from my hard-scrabble day working within a new mental health community.

That period lasted a year and a half, from September 1981 to March 1983. It had been easier in Canada where psychiatrists received government reimbursement; such a thing did not exist in the States. Throughout those dark and scary months, Betsy supported me and never once said, "I told you so." My Christmas present to her, in 1981, was a wooden letter opener, the only gift

I could afford, plus a certificate for a full massage from me that she was reluctant to redeem. She, like many strong women, was a better giver than a receiver.

In the midst of this, we adopted our daughter, Mindy. We'd been trying to have another child, but hadn't been successful. When we settled in Oregon, we regrouped, looked at each other, and said, "Let's adopt."

Eighteen months after we resettled in Oregon came the long awaited phone call from a social worker who specialized in adoption for Oregon's Division of Children's and Family Services. She told us that a beautiful six-month-old baby girl with "special medical needs" was awaiting adoption in Salem. When we asked what the special medical needs were, we were told that she had been born five weeks early and had suffered through a bout of neonatal jaundice. She had been left with sleep apnea, which caused her to sometimes stop breathing while she was asleep, as well as have occasional seizures. Because of her medical needs, she had been in the care of a nursing specialist rather than a regular foster mother.

We learned later that her parents were both young kids from northern Oregon who had met while both were spending time in a mental hospital (she a patient, he a maintenance worker), that her birth mother was bright, willful and determined and that her birth father was shy, speaking in a soft voice with a downward gaze; we learned that this may have been related to the fact that he had grown up in an abusive family.

Mindy's high-tech medical problems were reflected in a paper trail of medical warnings about her apnea, but the parents were neither stupid nor selfish. After having their daughter home for Christmas 1982, they put her interests ahead of their own emotional needs and relinquished her to the official adoption processes. All we had to do was say yes, and we couldn't say it fast enough. Medical needs? She'll outgrow them!

On a cool and gray spring morning, Betsy, Andy, then just seven weeks short of his fifth birthday, and I climbed into our well-traveled Fairmont station wagon and began the four-hour drive to suburban Portland, where we were introduced to Catherine Caroline, or CC, as everyone at her pediatric foster nursing care home called her. (To us, she was, then and always, Mindy.)

CC was the only baby girl who had lived at this special home in the past eighteen months. She was darling, with light copper skin and dark brown eyes, and she had become a pet with all the nurses there, in particular with Pat White, her caregiver and pediatric nurse specialist. Pat told us, "CC has a complicated history and you should know about it before you adopt her." "Oh that's fine," we said. "We know all about it. Neonatal jaundice, sleep apnea? We can handle it!" We were full of confidence, innocence and ignorance.

Betsy was in love. She held this new baby, gently positioning her in her windup swing. We all beamed as she swung and smiled to the steady tick-tock, tick-tock. Thus ended our initial visit with Mindy.

The next morning we rubbed sleep from our eyes and set out again for Mindy's care home, this time with the intention of bringing her home with us. Before we could do this though, a primitive, proprietary dance unfolded between Betsy and Pat, two strong-willed nurses. Pat knew Mindy had to leave and she wanted to share the baby with Betsy and her family, but she wasn't quite ready to surrender her. Betsy, on the other hand, wanted to hold Mindy and made no bones about it. As this brief, almost comic, but quite tense, Solomonesque tug-of-war unfolded. with

Mindy caught in the middle, I found myself both embarrassed by Betsy's unashamed and two-fisted behavior, and delighted by her determination.

Eventually, of course, Betsy prevailed, the tension eased and we said our good-byes. After briefly holding Mindy myself, I wondered how hard it must have been for Pat to relinquish the little one she had mothered for most of the first six months of her life. Mindy's birth mother had visited occasionally, but Pat had been the only real mother this little being had known. I wondered what it was like for Mindy, to lose her second mother in six months.

Betsy bundled our new baby up and, after dropping Andrew off with friends for the morning, the three of us drove to a Portland health clinic where Mindy would get her sendoff exam. "Looks okay, but she's a little floppy," concluded the examining pediatric nurse. "But, of course, she's on those sedating medicines for her seizures." Just in case Mindy stopped breathing at night, Betsy and I were given a primer in cardiopulmonary resuscitation, or CPR. It had been a while since either of us had received this kind of instruction. I remember being embarrassed but proud yet again as Betsy chewed out the pediatric respiratory specialist for keeping us waiting. I think by now I was getting used to having somewhat conflicting emotions when it came to Betsy!

When we stopped at our friend's home to pick up Andrew, we learned that he had worried that we had forsaken him, traded him in for the new little girl in his family. I recognized this to be a natural combination of attachment, displacement and abandonment anxieties. When he was reassured that this was not the case, that we were not trading him in, he wondered then if maybe we were "just borrowing her?" Andy had no idea what he was getting into. Nor, for that matter, did his mother and father.

14   Living, Loving, Learning

MY ORIGINAL PROFESSIONAL partnership had not worked out. Internal disputes had developed between the two partners and a third person, and the practice had become an uncomfortable place in which to work. I said to Betsy, "Let's start our own partnership." In the summer of 1983—just as Mindy was taking her first tottering steps—Betsy and I launched ourselves onto the long road to creating our own multi-disciplinary mental health clinic.

We bought an old Victorian building, fixed it up, moved in and invited some of the colleagues we had come to respect in the first two years in Oregon to join us. Esther, Peter and Nola were the first; several more would join us within the year. The house itself was listed on the town's historic registry as the Colonel Silsby House. We called it 111 3rd Street—that's what we put on our cards. It was a good place, with a great working group.

By then Betsy was ready to come back to work; with Mindy just at the toddler stage, she only worked half-time.

But we were working together, something I had wanted for some time. Betsy worked as a psychiatric nurse practitioner, a high level of nursing sophistication, but was also a psychiatric specialist, doing counseling. We would see couples together, and families. Several of the other counselors saw children. It was a wonderful group, and those were good days.

Things were also improving with our new daughter's medical health. We officially renamed 'CC' Amanda Lydia Pearl Kirkpatrick after our grandmothers. Mindy, for short. Because of her sleep apnea, she came equipped with a tiny Velcro strap to sound the alarm should she stop breathing, and I remember Betsy and me racing to her nursery one evening upon hearing that high-pitched alarm. After first crashing into each other in the doorway of our bedroom, we hurried across the hallway—to find Mindy playing with her detached electrical leads, a happy smile lighting up her face. When she was nine months old, the doctors removed the alarm, having concluded that it was no longer necessary. We replaced it with more practical and reliable warning systems that we had begun to learn about.

As we weaned Mindy off Phenobarbital, both she and her personality grew stronger, more dramatic—sometimes so theatrical that Betsy would call her Sarah Bernhardt, after the acclaimed French actress of the nineteenth and twentieth centuries. In other ways, Mindy resembled Grandma Kirkpatrick, with her combination of strength, anxiety and uncertainty. In her restless and very alert ways, she seemed more like my mother. She also had some of the same characteristics as her brother: intelligence, uncertainty about herself, lovability. But mostly she was and would be her own person.

We were excited, exhausted and happy as our dreams began to slide into place. And then, in 1985, Betsy was diagnosed with colon cancer, and we began the long years of fighting this evil presence that had latched on to her body.

I wrote about Betsy's bouts with cancer in the introduction to this book, about how she recovered from that first bout. With renewed appreciation of each other, we continued with our life.

In the fall of 1987, we bought a seventy-two-year-old wooden Craftsman's bungalow on Ashland's Scenic Drive, did some modest renovations and added an above-ground pool that we bought from Betsy's Aunt Mer and Uncle Jimmy, over in Cave Junction, for $500. I bought some two-by-six rough-cut cedar decking to wrap around three sides of the pool, and to build an additional picnic deck down by our second-hand hot tub. Betsy put her gardening instincts and passions to work, planting rose bushes, daffodils, lilies and ground cover. From our new old home we could now easily walk to breakfast in Ashland's plaza and, on other days, to work.

We began to relax together and apart even more than we had before.

Once again I appreciated her strength and support that allowed me, encouraged me, to stand on my own two feet, to be the best David I ever imagined but usually never dared dreamed I could be. This meant learning not to be afraid to differ with others. Being honest, being open, being out there, being myself.

Since the day we began seeing each other in that summer of 1976, Betsy had been like the song "Wind Beneath My Wings."[1] I look back to our time together in Ashland and see myself growing and emancipating from her, getting closer to her and also less dependent on her, less inclined to expect her to make all the decisions for the family, becoming less passive and more proactive. Betsy expected as much from me and I was up to the bargain, anchored by her calm, usually un-anxious background strength.

The only fly in the ointment was that Mindy, while no longer experiencing sleep apnea, was developing behavioral problems. Around the age of three or four, she became very difficult to discipline. She began having terrible temper tantrums, yelling, screaming. She was a very difficult child to raise. We blamed ourselves while trying to do everything right. Andy had been such an easy child and Betsy was a terrific parent: warm and loving, while setting firm behavioral limits for the kids.

Betsy definitely set the standard for parenting in our family. Once, when Andrew was two and a half, he took a dunking in our hot tub and charged into the house seeking his mother's comfort, soaking wet head to toes and bawling with a child's fear and rage at a world that had, however briefly, betrayed him. He heard his mother's simple greeting: "Well, Andrew! Good for you! Having an adventure in deep water so early in your life." And then she briefly held and comforted him. My son and I both learned from that one. I learned that if a parent intervenes too quickly, they can undermine the child's confidence, and ability to take responsibility for his or her own mistakes. Withhold too long, though, and that parent risks becoming an insensitive and unkind or uncaring person. But a competent, strong woman has good timing. She recognizes, quickly and intuitively, the right point at which to intervene and will move in aggressively.

In addition to timing, the gift or gifts from this one strong woman to her children and partner, and from all strong women to their children and loved ones, also include courage, integrity, determination, warmth, tenderness, intimacy and toughness. Courage, for example, is not just shared directly between a strong woman and her kids, but modeled and frequently illustrated. The children learn those nonverbal lessons of courage by watching their mother or aunt or sister going about her daily routine, encountering and solving large and small problems.

Similarly, a strong woman's sense of integrity is there for her children to see and identify with and, eventually, to emulate. Children and teenagers, and often older individuals as well, learn the distinction between the unnecessary roughness that society rightly condemns and the much healthier toughness that helps make for satisfying, rewarding and effective social transactions.

And within our family, there was so much love. During that busy summer, Andy went off to summer camp and, while there, received mail with the following outpouring of love from his mom:

Hi Poopsie,

You've been gone a week! Wow!—It seems longer & we miss you! I'm sending you a small plastic lined bag for your toothbrush, comb, etc . . . You know how I like to worry about you . . . Must go. Love you & miss you lots.

Have fun.

Love, Mom

Much later when Betsy was becoming seriously ill, I noted in my journal:

Tuesday, March 13, 1990

[Discouraged about his Little League tryouts], and still about a foot shorter than his mother, Andy collapses next to the dining table into Betsy's comforting arms as she comforts and soothes, warmly overriding her own current discomfort, "I know, Andy . . . it's all right. And I'm sorry, too!" I'm touched by what has happened and what Andy and his mother share.

Despite the new and frightening health problems assaulting Betsy's body and spirit, only one problem was important to her at that moment: her hurting twelve-year-old, who had just stumbled in his all-important Little League tryout.

In later years, Mindy was able to draw from the model Betsy set, but in her childhood Mindy was hell on wheels. In the same falling-into-the-hot-tub situation described about Andy, her rage probably would have overwhelmed her ability to accept comfort. She would not respond to limits, did not respect boundaries. Her recalcitrance butted heads with Betsy's strength, and the conflict between them became an ongoing source of noise and tension in the house. On one occasion, an indignant stranger in DJ's, an Ashland video store, sharply accosted Betsy for leaving "that *terrified* child in the van! You really should pay more attention to her." A quick inspection by Betsy revealed two-year-old Mindy screeching and throwing every single layer of her clothing out the side window of our camper van. Betsy returned to the store, quietly informing the self-righteous passerby, "That, ma'am, is an *angry* child. And yes, she is mine. She is having a temper tantrum. Thank you for your opinion."

We went for family counseling. I worried and wondered about any medical conditions that might be affecting Mindy.

There were, however, many brighter moments, often involving animals.

Mindy and southern Oregon horses were a natural marriage that was inaugurated when her mother took her to an Ashland stable for her first equine encounter. This was a decision Betsy made in one of her many intuitive-mother moments, and I knew better than to ask why. She knew what she was doing. She wouldn't talk much before taking Mindy to a horse event but, upon returning home, she would recount what fun or adventures she and her daughter had enjoyed.

She noticed the first or second time that, while some of Mindy's shy or uncertain three- and four-year-old friends cried when first placed on the saddle of a gentle, twenty-year-old mare, Mindy seemed to cry more often when taken off. The bond between some horses and some girls or women is powerful beyond the reach of most boys and men. Perhaps tough or strong girls and women, as well as would-be tough or strong girls and women, recognize a partner in their four-legged, 1,500-pound friend, something that understands what it's like to be big and strong, though not always respected by its masters or seniors.

After enrolling Mindy in a Montessori preschool and believing things could only get better, we learned that she had dyslexia, in her case manifesting in an extreme difficulty in learning to read and write, which would make it difficult for her to make progress in a traditional classroom. Betsy as the mother of a child with dyslexia? No big deal! An opportunity to learn, to help, to make a difference. This was her operative attitude, motivation and drive. Fight back! Learn! And stop feeling sorry for yourself, David. Or Andrew. Or Mindy. There are things to do, so up and at 'em!

We watched with a mixture of despair and resignation as Mindy continued to develop a personality as difficult and demanding on a rough day as it was warm and charming on a good one. Other children, and often their parents, often saw her as whiny and provocative. Shortly after she led her five-year-old classmates off the Montessori property in a mutinous hike, the following conversation was overheard at her grandparents' residence:

Guest: "And Mindy, such a pretty dress! And how was your week?"

Mindy: "Well, I got kicked out of Montessori School!"

Guest: "Oh."

Mindy completed kindergarten in a more conventional setting before starting first grade at Briscoe Elementary, in Ashland. The teachers there seemed to take a special liking to her, and she began to make a better adjustment to school. Both Betsy and I helped out in her classroom in small ways, and we would relax as we watched her at recess, her wiry body running like a small gazelle. Maybe these bumps in Mindy's early developmental pathways were beginning to smooth out.

And so, our lives moved onward. In spite of her counseling practice, Betsy found time to be with Mindy, snuggling with her for naps or teaching her sewing and stitchery. We all took summer trips in our camper, north to British Columbia to visit old Canadian friends, south to southern California to stay with Betsy's family and mine. Road songs, Raffi tapes, alphabet games, and Twenty Questions, usually initiated by Betsy, lightened the travel monotony and helped remind us that we were truly and mostly a blessed and united family.

Andrew, Mindy and I are the beneficiaries today of Betsy's particular, strong woman's wisdom and strength. She would teach each of us, sometimes in tandem, about taking responsibility for our respective lives. And with those lessons, we would learn much about living life fully. The lesson from Betsy's strong woman's portfolio was that she had much to teach but was in no way responsible for our lives. That was our responsibility, as well as our challenge and our gift from her.

As our family progressed, so did our mental health clinic. 111 3rd Street began to flourish. At one point, ten other quite competent mental health professionals worked alongside us. Betsy was very busy developing her own psychotherapy practice, teaching group process to the local college nursing students and continuing to develop her career as a psychiatric nurse practitioner, counseling southern Oregonians from a wide variety of backgrounds. She seemed to have a special emotional wavelength with both professional women and adolescent girls, drawing on the memories, difficulties, conflicts and triumphs within her own life. She had a fierce pride in her profession. "I am not a nurse-educator," she would say. "I'm not a community consultant, a facilitator or a counselor. *I am a nurse!* When on earth will people get that straight?"

Most nurses are pretty savvy about the way the world works after fifteen or twenty years on the front lines in hospitals and outpatient clinics. Shrewd and world-wise, most of them have pretty much seen it all, including the worst of men in the role that men like the least, but the one that reveals them at their most helpless: sick and dependent. The smart and tough medical-surgical nurses often quit just before they get cynical or burnt out and seek another career, and some of the best of these go into psychiatric nursing. They have had enough of blood and guts but not enough of gutsy people facing bloody situations in their lives. Then they are able to put those same nurturing and caretaking instincts back to work on a more sublime level of interaction with others in acute need.

A good psychiatric nurse works in her own operating room or counseling office with her own set of scalpels or interpersonal tools. And the best will experience their patients as both objects with predictable features and as subjects with feelings. Body and soul. (I'm not sure if female nurses accomplish this better than male nurses. I have watched male and female doctors and nurses in action, and the best of both sexes are able to maintain the warm detachment necessary for solid clinical care.)

I was attracted to Betsy for many reasons, including her ability to combine subjective feeling with objective concern. She was able to look into me deeply and, when the times called for it, look right through me. It felt good to be loved and cared for, watched over like a vulnerable crop, with kindness and caring, though simultaneously with objective and completely unsentimental stewardship. She was proud of me and of our relationship. Once, crowing lightly about her husband at a nursing meeting, Betsy noticed other nurses beginning to move in closer to hear better. Suddenly self-conscious about her bragging, she downshifted quickly without missing a gear, smoothly reminding them, "And also . . . well, David is . . . uh . . . a lot of work, you know?"

Even early on, I could feel Betsy's nurturing, sexually comforting and accepting air, her healing chemistry. The possibilities and fantasies of getting the love I wanted, and for which I had searched for almost forty years, was right there in front of me. Before, I had not been ready to appreciate it. Now I could, and now, I thought at some unconscious level, maybe I could return this nurturing and perspicacity. Betsy had helped make me better. I hoped that one day I would return the favor.

Our shared and separate experiences transformed into something darker on a spring day in March 1990.

15 Losing

March 27, 1990:

COURAGE? TELL ME ABOUT IT. *Two hours of GYN/ abdominal surgery for Betsy with Drs. Rote and Six. First report from Dr. Rote is that her colon cancer has returned, and in tears I call my good friend, Maggie the internist. "Oh, David," is all she says or needs to say. Shortly, pathology calls back from Medford that this is a new, primary endometrial carcinoma. Her uterus is full of tumor.*

[Gynecologic Surgeon] Joan Rote tells B in recovery that her cancer is "back," but she's too groggy to process the news except to tell me five words: "I'm going to beat this!"

Cancer had reached out again and blindsided Betsy, hardly four and a half years after she had beaten colon cancer into submission. Such a short time she had had to catch her breath. Both cancers were primary, originating on their own, neither of them metastasizing (spreading) from another site.

My first thoughts were, "We've had our cancer and we beat it. We're not going to get another one; people don't get two cancers." Well, Betsy did.

Blood tests confirmed she could not possibly have the same ovarian cancer that took Gilda Radner, the gifted *Saturday Night Live* star, and so we took the kids off for spring vacation in Death Valley, ignoring the obvious irony of our destination.

I wrote a silent note to Andy in my journal, early on the morning of his twelfth birthday.

Thursday, April 19, 1990
Happy Birthday, Andy; your thirteenth year will be interesting, challenging, maybe very difficult (for all of us). We'll be with you, all of us!

Andy became quieter and attended to his mother's needs more than he talked about his own feelings. He juggled Little League baseball. His schoolwork suffered. Like his father, he managed to push the unfolding tragedy just enough into the background to get through the school day or workday. Weekends were low-key events, in which the four of us would just lie low, sleep in and maybe watch a video at night. Andy liked videos, and there didn't seem to be much else going right in his life in 1990.

I remember less about how Mindy coped when the unwanted news about her mother's new cancer first leaked out of Ashland Hospital's operating room. She was not always able to translate her feelings into words, but was much better than either her brother or her father at not bottling them up—at least with those she trusted. Shortly after her mother's surgery, she snuggled on the lap of our teenage neighbor and told her haltingly that, "Mommy has . . . she has something wrong with her tummy!" And then broke into tears. These were the first sad tears I had known her to shed in all her seven and a half years. I was glad she was able to express her sadness, but worried that our fragile family was so fragmented under the onslaught of Betsy's second cancer that Mindy could not share her feelings with us, at home. More positively, we were given a reminder of how important and comforting a solid big-sister-like friend can be.

I shifted into survival mode, trying to hold the family together. It was a primitive and hapless struggle, and I could hardly see the forest for the sick and wounded trees. As Betsy worsened, the kids fought more. The same boy who had experienced such a difficult and unhappy Little League tryout threw a rock at a playmate and scored a direct hit from seventy-five feet, lacerating her scalp. I received an emergency phone call from Briscoe Elementary School to come "ASAP," and spent some time with a tearfully inconsolable Andy, debriefing the incident while trying to comfort him. I had never seen him hurting so much and so openly.

His sister began unraveling further: bashing, whining, crying and screaming her way through her most difficult moments. But how *do* other girls her age generally behave when their mothers might be dying? It seemed as though I had little time to stop, catch my breath and ask a question like that. I wish I had.

Family therapists make much of their living tuning into how families function during times of crisis. They share their observations and hunches with family members in ways that can be not only comforting but also instructive, often helping the family function more effectively during those times. Our family of four went for family counseling, both in Ashland and in Portland. We were reminded that, while something awful was happening to us, we were not bad people. We needed to slow down, catch our collective breaths and practice being a little nicer to each other. Nice was easier. But how to be less frightened of what our mom and wife and loved one and we ourselves were facing was a tougher problem.

Despite these efforts at counseling, our family still struggled. Mindy's unpredictable and unmanageable emotional roller coasters began to worsen. A small annoyance would escalate when I intervened. When I didn't, it could quickly mushroom into a destructive explosion that probably hurt Mindy and her friendships more than it hurt Andy and me. Weakened by her cancer, Betsy could only watch and listen from her bed or nearby chair, a captive theatergoer in a bad play that neither she nor her loved ones could walk out on.

It was around that point that my second training period with Betsy began as she showed her strength in a highly practical and immediate way by giving it back to me, allowing me to take care of her, nurse her, love her and comfort her. I was able to give back a small amount of what I had gained during those first fourteen years of her continuing seminar in tough love.

What followed, that hot summer of 1990, was one of modern medicine's cruelest blessings: treatment in the form of chemotherapy combined with radiation therapy. Our lives became filled with concerns about low white-blood-cell counts, weight loss, nausea, vomiting and bowel problems. I reminded myself, with equal parts appreciation and bitterness, that only a fool equated health care with health. Betsy's hair fell out but, typically, she used that as an opportunity to inject a bit of "humor in the tumor" by shaping the new hairstyle into a sort of punk haircut.

With her showing no sign of improvement, we opted to stay near home that summer, once trying a camping trip that was a physical ordeal for Betsy as she continued to weaken, lose weight and—most devastating to her high-energy self— her natural vigor. Her get-up-and-go had got up and gone, quietly but no less heartlessly.

On June 26th, I noted in my journal that Betsy had new symptoms, and reminded myself to encourage her to begin psychotherapy with a counselor friend of ours.

[She has] right upper quadrant pain, some pleuritic [chest] component, and we're both scared shitless. She's saying, "Why me?" again, yet does absolutely nothing to offload all that torment and anguish she must be experiencing. I told her tonight to see Virginia or somebody on a regular basis.

We soon learned the source of the new pain. While the treatment appeared to have cleared her pelvis of tumor, there was now evidence that the cancer had spread to her left lung. Good and bad-to-awful news. Betsy and I danced silently around the implications for her brave fight against this beast of a disease. We didn't share the news with the children. The journal continued:

What really hurts is hearing her determination, "David, this thing isn't going to kill me – I've got to watch the kids grow up, and I don't want another woman raising my children." A little earlier, she talked about that very possibility with greater ease. She didn't know how she'd manage in my shoes. I surely do admire her courage, and her poise, if not her stubbornness.

Go for it, Babe!

Determination, courage, poise and stubbornness. Our family was experiencing a strong and determined woman fighting for her life. My discomfort at her show of strength overlapped with my appreciation of Betsy's traits under fire.

And she began a new round of chemo, this time for her lungs.

July 20, 1990

Today's chemotherapy [is] #4 out of 6, we think. Betsy has felt I haven't always been with her the whole time, at least in the afternoon when her IV's begin to run dry, making her nervous, so I'll try to do better today.

We made love the other night with lots of necking and loving tenderness. The closeness with her at this time was just super. I told her all kinds of things about how much she means to me, and I just sort of surrendered.

September 9, 1990

High point of the day was chasing a hit-and-run driver on I-5 at 85 mph, accosting him on the shoulder as Betsy looks straight at him and announces, "You— You are a hit-and-run driver! And we have got your number!" We phone his number to 911, and learn later that day he's in Medford jail.

Why can't we catch cancer that easily?

September 11, 1990

> *Betsy's so tired I can't connect with her. Maybe rub her back a bit and tell her I love her. "I love you too, honey," she'll say, or something like that as she dozes off. It's weird, with her there, I still find myself missing her. Lots.*

Betsy spent more time resting, lying in bed and sleeping. Physically exhausted, she talked little about the personal, but no longer private, hell she was going through. She was irritable at times, but only briefly. In October 1990, my journal entries suggested some of what Mindy—and the rest of the family— was going through:

October 4, 1990

> *Betsy's through with chemotherapy, she says. They want to give her two more Adriamycins, and she says Thanks, but No Thanks. I admire that in her, even though I wish she'd do the two extra treatments. Anyway, it's done.*
>
> *Betsy was crying tonight, "Where did I go wrong as a parent?" (Probably nowhere.)*
>
> *The house is almost painted, the stairwell almost completed and that'll be a relief when through. Bugs the rabbit and Crystal the guinea pig both died in the last two weeks, further destabilizing the household, I think. I did a crude autopsy on the guinea pig with Mindy watching and asking questions: she was probably carrying too many babies —five—and that probably killed her.*

As the family moved through those fall months, we experienced together the evident sunset of Betsy's life. With its own beauty, the colors in our shared lives slowly faded from bright pastels to more somber shades of dark pinks, browns and shadows of darker greens. Betsy worsened in November, and had to return for yet another aggressive abdominal surgery as the ravenous malignancy had resulted in acute bowel obstruction. This surgery was intended to help reroute her twisted bowel. Following that, she began hyperalimentation, receiving all her nutrients and fluid through an intravenous feeding line placed in her right subclavian vein.

November 22, 1990

I slipped into Ashland Community Hospital one morning for a visit as she awakened from a dream, saying only, "David, how remarkable! I was just dreaming!"

We talked, and then I knelt down on the left side of her bed, worked my way around her various tubes, and we began to kiss, oh so tenderly, and I didn't care if anyone came in or not; apparently neither did Betsy. I held her gently and tenderly.

She responded softly but not weakly. And held me gently.

And we held each other.

And we continued for about ten or fifteen minutes of the most wonderful, warmest and most tender kissing I'd ever experienced. And then I kissed Betsy "bye" and floated out of her hospital room, more in love with her than ever. What a woman! I love you, babe!

The children were upbeat and ready for their mother's homecoming from the hospital, very happy that she would be home for Christmas. They had both spent time cleaning up our rambling, newly painted, old frame house beyond what I thought they were capable of, and both were at the doorway—Mindy slightly ahead of her brother—to greet Betsy on her homecoming. With a slight yet mischievous and loving smile on her eight-year-old face, Mindy gently threw herself into her mother's arms, hugging her oh-so-warmly. As she held her mother, it seemed that she was desperately trying to infuse every ounce of strength and fitness from her own fifty-five-pound frame into the body of her frail and exhausted mother. She didn't seem to mind her mother's battered, emaciated condition; she was just quietly thrilled to have her home.

I wrote our annual Christmas letter, explaining that after the final treatments in September, Betsy had experienced a maddening bowel obstruction requiring surgery and a three week hospitalization in November. The diagnosis was massive radiation damage to the small intestine. I said she had been learning to live with a short bowel syndrome, existing on intravenous nutrition and giving her bowel a rest. She was twenty-five percent down from her fighting weight, and exhausted, but was taking a time out on a plateau, without complaint. I added that the family was extremely proud of her. And we were.

It *was* a bowel obstruction, but not primarily because of radiation damage. It was something far worse, but in so writing, I was able to maintain the denial of Betsy's deterioration and quietly collude with her persistent sense of hope. The entire family was staggering between hopeless and helpless.

Christmas was simple, with the children giving their handmade and store-bought gifts to their mother and me before we drove to my brother's home in Medford. Betsy rested on a couch for most of the afternoon, in a new red velour pantsuit the kids and I had bought her. With some help from friends and from me, she had managed to buy a few gifts for the family. I remember looking at her lying on the couch, frail, withdrawn and without much energy. It was a quiet time, not so much a celebration as a time for all of us to slow down and to be together.

Between all the hours I spent caring for Betsy, the kids and I found time, here and there, to go out for dinner or take walks. One night in February 1991, I took both Mindy and Andy on a late night walk behind the house, up on the Ashland Drainage Ditch Trail. Walking in the dark like this, away from our comfort zone, even with flashlights, was a bit scary. I know now, but didn't realize it at a conscious level then, that I was putting all of us through a rehearsal for an event that would prove to be scarier than either the kids or I could imagine. We walked quietly and close together, the evening's silence punctuated only by the children's occasional faintly impatient grievances. We stayed together, a father and two children, but half the time it felt like we were three beleaguered children of a common mother, facing her own destiny.

When things could not get worse, or seemed like they could not, they did. Betsy's sister Suzanne phoned early in February 1991, crying so hard she was out of breath. I could not understand her at first, but then I heard the news that might break the heart of an already badly wounded Betsy. Suzanne told us that their father, recuperating from aortic arch surgery, had stood up from bed that night and fallen over dead. I handed the phone over to Betsy, where she lay resting in her by now pretty much twenty-four-hour-a-day station. PopPop, the name our kids had given to Bill LaSor, Betsy's dad, was gone. Exhausted from chemotherapy, Betsy lay quietly stunned from this latest dreadful news.

Together we decided that I would go to southern California for Bill's funeral service. Betsy wanted me to make a video of her so that she could somehow be there. In that video, she talked directly to her mother, remembering the much earlier days when Gamma, her own grandmother, had died. She recalled with tearful nostalgia, how she and her mother had gone through Gamma's things. Two generations of strong women savoring, sharing and enjoying the legacy and memories of a third as they helped divide up her jewelry and clothing. The memories of this ritual recalled by Betsy on videotape could now be shared with younger generations of LaSors, and be appreciated by friends and family, as they saw fit.

And then shortly after this sad event, we received a call that KC, our beloved beagle, who had seen a few patients with me just that morning, had been hit by a car and killed while returning home by herself. A shaken driver had kindly called us, encouraged by a nearby office worker where he had gone asking for help.

I picked up KC's furry body and, that evening, under the southern Oregon sky, we buried her in our back yard. Mindy, Andy and I held the box and looked at the colors of her softly lush coat. All the times I had fought with her and her stubborn behaviors evaporated. Each of us missed PopPop, but KC was also one of the family. A gift from our friends, the

Lazersons, who owned her mother Sesame, KC had been with us since before Andrew was born, thirteen and a half years ago. Now she was gone. I found myself wondering secretly about possible connections between KC's death and Betsy's precarious position. Did KC sense the seriousness of Betsy's illness and decide to go first? How sensitive are beagles anyway? How much of this was I projecting from my own anxious and bereft position?

Late in February 1991, Betsy's doctor, Tony Hites, visited us one evening with the news that her uterine cancer had spread further than anyone had realized. At the breakfast table one morning soon after that, Andy sat absolutely stunned as I explained to him that his mother didn't have much time left. Frozen, he stared at some invisible point of despair in front of him, unblinking as his body slumped. He would not tell me how he felt and, hurting and frightened for my kids, for my Betsy and for myself, I was too exhausted and frightened to inquire assertively. I was trying to hold my family together with band-aids and bailing wire, but it wasn't enough or even close to it.

I felt uncertain about how to reach out and comfort Andy, but I was twice as bewildered over Mindy, who was only eight and a half, and I could not tell if the message was getting through or if she understood or appreciated what was looking more and more like an impending tragedy.

In March, Betsy's good friend Lee Schmidt, of her UCLA Master's in Nursing class, phoned, supporting her yet reminding her at the same time, "Betsy, you've fought the good fight!" "Yes, I have," Betsy replied. "But I'm angry. For my kids!"

A few days later she received a visit from another nursing friend, Beth Monninger, now Dean of Nursing at Southern Oregon State College. Betsy broached her desire to have a lectureship at SOSC devoted to "the broader issues of nursing in today's world." The college would want seed money from us to get it started, to which we readily agreed. It would offer to nursing students and their more experienced teachers and colleagues an exposure to nursing excellence from a visiting, honored nursing professional. What a wonderful idea for Betsy to think about. She had a weakened body but, obviously, a wonderfully sharp mind still.

It was about this time that an Ashland newspaper listed Betsy as the community's favorite therapist in its annual popularity poll, noting that:

"War in the Persian Gulf has everyone on edge, and when they need some comforting words, our readers chose Betsy LaSor as their favorite. Betsy has been a counselor in Ashland for the last ten years and moved here from British Columbia."

Betsy's off-again on-again self-esteem convinced her that the poll had been rigged because of her illness and that someone was feeling sorry for her; but even so she enjoyed the recognition.

Like the traveler who enjoys the sweet and juicy strawberry while trapped in a desperate, life-threatening situation, Betsy loved in a similarly immediate fashion: reviewing old picture albums with the children, preparing notes for me to transcribe to accompany the jewelry that she wanted to give away to her beloved nieces and a few friends. She dictated a tongue-in-cheek obituary to me, beginning:

"Yesterday, the late, great Betsy LaSor passed away quietly in her sleep . . ." She then dozed off for a few moments.

I called family and friends in Africa, British Columbia, California and Oregon, to offer a chance to come and say goodbye. Mail seemed to arrive at a faster rate as she worsened. She appreciated every last letter, yet one arrived that seemed to mean more to her than almost any other. It came from a woman whose husband Betsy had counseled. Betsy and I had also seen them together in couple's therapy, trying to help the two of them in a busy, high-pressure marriage complicated by professional and family stresses. We were old enough to be their parents, and both of us felt warmly toward them.

> *Dear Betsy,*
>
> *I hope that you will not feel that my writing this letter is inappropriate. I realize that the pain you and your family are enduring is intensely personal and private, and I don't mean to intrude. But I find myself unable to sleep tonight until I write this letter. I really feel the need to tell you how much I like and admire you. Even though we never got to know each other real well it has always seemed that we had a lot in common. I've felt that my therapy with David has always been helped because of his relationship with you, and his understanding of intelligent, independent women. His admiration and love for you has helped me to grow and feel more comfortable with myself. [My husband] and I also benefited greatly from our joint therapy with the two of you.*
>
> *While I don't profess to understand God's timetable, I realize that as humans we don't have a lot of control over our time on this earth. I think that it's important for you to know*

that for me, as well as many others, your time on this earth made a difference. I will continue to pray for you and your family.

> *May God bless you and keep you.*
> *Love,*
> *(Signed)*

A second letter provided the coda for the great number of letters of support Betsy received during the turmoil of the last month of her life, and perhaps for her life itself. It accompanied an antique Royal Crown Cola ("Best by Taste Test") advertising thermometer and was dated March 14, 1991:

> *Dear Betsy,*
>
> *I'm sending you a present which I know is irrelevant now—it's something I found a few months ago and immediately thought of you, then put off sending because of your relapse; now I realize I should have gone on and sent it.*
>
> *When I first saw this, I was reminded of a time when David and I were in Savannah, and we went to a vintage lingerie store, and he bought you some elegant antique underwear. This was the first time I became aware of the part of you that liked wonderful old things—I know I never really knew you very well, only through David and David's love for you. So, I send this utterly useless but nonetheless beautiful old antique to you, to celebrate that part of you that appreciated the things that remain interesting and beautiful even as time passes them by.*
>
> *I think I have always been a little jealous of you for marrying David and to that extent "taking him away"*

from me. I'm sorry if that got in the way of our relationship.
You were always very kind and generous with me, and I
appreciate that. I wish you a more merciful time than you are
having right now, and I admire and appreciate the courage
and tenacity with which you have faced this terrible disease.

Love, Dan

Courage, tenacity and an old Royal Crown thermometer.
With the time allotted her on this earth, Elizabeth Ann LaSor
had made a difference.

She continued to go downhill, losing weight, vomiting,
exhausted and sleeping much of the time, but she didn't protest.
One night, as I lay next to her, I dreamed she was climbing a small
mountain and was halfway up it. I awoke to a loud and dull thump.
She had fallen out of bed, entangled in the intravenous lines that
were wrapped around her like non-poisonous but useless snakes,
neither healing her nor softening her agony.

March 14, 1991:

This is an amazing person I've been living with for
the last 15 years of her life. The letters and phone calls are
pouring in as Betsy spends her last days on this earth.

She was thrilled to see her mother and Sandy, and
uttered a muffled but obvious "Mothhhhher!" on seeing her
mother show up. They hugged each other and wept. Me, too.

Even a strong woman needs her mother at times.

Andy was wonderfully attentive and tender with his
mother. Swabbing out her mouth. Trying to feed her through
a straw that she feebly sucked on. Looking at her with love,
concern and tenderness, and perhaps curiosity.

Family and friends continued to come. Some held her, some cried, some laughed and some did both or all three. Betsy's brother Fred had flown fifteen or twenty hours from Nairobi. As big as a moose, he sat on the side of our bed cradling his much loved and now emaciated sister close to his chest and holding her tired, delicate hands in his huge hams, while tears streamed down his cheeks. Drifting in and out of consciousness, she no longer spoke.

March 16, 1991:

The time is nearing. It's been a warm and really wonderful weekend so far. All this love and caring for B pouring out from so many friends and family . . . We couldn't have done this in a hospital, that's for sure, we all agreed.

I love her so, and the tears come in waves and floods and trickles and moistenings, and then leave me alone to laugh or catch my breath. I'll make it pretty sure, but I'll sure need my friends and family.

Betsy is breathing slowly now, gasping sort of shallowly, with less of a rattle than this afternoon. I'm scared of how I'll do without her. "You are the wind beneath my wings." She seems aware of her surroundings, but barely.

Friends had been to visit and say their goodbyes. When they left, I lay down beside Betsy, talked to her briefly and rubbed her back. There was a night nurse in the room and, shy about her being in the room while I slept with Betsy, I went into the next bedroom and fell asleep. At about 6:10 a.m., the nurse came and gently wakened me, saying quietly, "She's gone." I got up, returned to our bed where she lay, touched her

on her left shoulder and murmured a soft "Goodbye, Honey."
I was so sorry not to have been with her when she left, but
then she took a final breath. I truly believe this was her final
goodbye gift to me. Betsy LaSor: Good to the Last Drop.

Why does it feel like this has never happened to anybody
before in the history of the human race?

Goodbye sweetie. You'll be with me always. I love you.

16 Healing

March 17, 1991:

GRIEF IS A RICH GIFT *that we don't ask for and we don't want, but when we get it, we are older, richer, wiser and, inevitably, sadder.*

In truth, I did not know just how much Betsy meant to me until she was gone, and then it overwhelmed me for the next several years. It wasn't that I didn't love her, it wasn't that I didn't appreciate how important she had been to me, but I don't think we can exist with a full awareness of a person's importance to us and live with any sanity. We talk about taking people for granted but in the human condition, it's necessary to take our partners for granted, a bit, just to live with love.

In the weeks and months that followed Betsy's death, I seemed to do all the crying for the family while the children, especially Mindy, did most of the comforting. I never saw the kids cry. Mindy, of course, was only eight and a half when Betsy died and I do not think she understood what had happened. The day Betsy died, Mindy had spent the night with her big sister surrogate, Carey. She came home at eight o'clock the following morning, learned what had happened, came into the room, looked briefly at Betsy's body, then turned and left. For all she knew, Betsy was just sleeping. I think it took upwards of ten years for Mindy to accept that her mother was gone.

I don't think I appreciated it right away myself. I had seen a lot of people dying and had tried to prepare myself: "Betsy is dying. It's going to be different but similar to many patients that I've seen." But nothing prepared me. Not being a doctor. Not knowing about death. Not having patients die. It levels out some after eighteen years, but the grief process goes on forever.

I was consumed with grief and this meant the kids were often fending for themselves. I hired homemakers and the last one, Deborah, was very good. Deborah was like a substitute mom in all the practical ways: a good cook and housekeeper and a source of some comfort. But homemakers, even Deborah, were good for the tummy but didn't fill the heart. The kids were largely providing their own and each other's comfort.

I can only imagine that for any child to lose his or her mother must be a maelstrom. To lose not just a Mom, but a strong mother, must be an earthquake inside a whirlpool.

Two weeks after Betsy died, I took Andy night skiing. The shadows were beautiful, eerie. He seemed to enjoy himself, but I couldn't take my mind off Betsy and was flooded with memories of our skiing together. And so it would go for many more months, being there for the kids but not as much as I now wish I had been. My mind and heart were with their mother. Andy kept almost all of his feelings about his mother inside. His grief was intensely private, personal and belonged to him and him alone and would not be shared that easily with anyone else, including his grieving dad. He shares more of himself today than in those years, but still plays his cards close to his chest. Bitter? Probably not. Blaming? Not much. Angry maybe some, but many sons—and dads—who lose a strong mom or wife will struggle with at least some disappointment and anger mixed with their sadness.

For Andy it was the first such loss, for Mindy not so. She had been there twice before—placed in foster care by her birth mother over the first six months of her life, then losing her foster-care mother and nurse when she was adopted out to our family —and this experience of loss might have toughened her. But she acted out her sad and angry feelings in a much less than private way, in some ways reminding me of myself as well—though hers was more brusquely honest and open. It culminated in a dramatic explosion of defiant behavior about seven months after her mother's death, one rainy, unforgettably stormy Oregon day on the Briscoe Elementary School grounds. A now nine-year-old Mindy had wanted to take her mother's coin collection to school to share with the other third-graders. I told her I wanted to go with her to tell her teacher, Debi Coleman, about the collection so she could help keep an eye on it, keep it from getting lost. Fatuous, foolish, fatherly fiddle-faddle.

Mindy absolutely refused to let me talk with her teacher. All she wanted was a chance to share her mother with her classmates. She had neither the time nor the interest in fighting with a father hung up on foolish adult details. Complaining, whining and worse all the way to Briscoe in our van, she completely fell apart on a knoll above the school just after we arrived. As the icy October rain began to pour down her neck and back, she half fell and half threw herself onto the muddy prominence, wedged herself in and began sobbing and throwing Betsy's silver dollars every which way as hard as she could. A final act of despair, rage, sadness and grief. And perhaps the most eloquent goodbye to her mother that she was able to express. I tried every emotional tool I could think of, but too close, I could neither coax nor dislodge her from the mud.

At last Mindy's teacher, alerted to the storm of activity on the muddy knoll, began walking slowly but deliberately out into the stinging rain and up the small hill. Debi knelt down slowly and gently next to her distraught student. I backed off and could not hear what the two of them were saying but saw her enfold Mindy briefly and tenderly, then the two of them got up and recovered as many of Betsy's silver dollars as they could before going back down the hill. Inside, Mindy's teacher, acting more sensitively than her dad, made it safe for Mindy to share with her classmates some pieces of the mother she had so recently lost. Whoever observed that it takes a whole village to raise a child should also have given special mention to the village teacher.

I wish I had been there more for them. I know sometimes single parents and their children can become even more closely bonded than two-parent families, but that was not the case for us. We were more like three survivors in a boat trying to make it to shore. I was stronger and older but really probably just as needy and vulnerable as they were. We survived, but I don't think we won any medals. We were just getting by day-to-day, raw and ragged, each of us missing Betsy in our own ways.

I tried to run our office practice, then established for eight years, but the fun had gone out of it without Betsy working with me, so I dissolved the practice and sold the building. I moved into a smaller building where I rented an office from a doctor.

Work was, however, one thing I could still do once I had survived the acute grief. I could still see patients, be there for them and try to help make a slight difference in their lives. It was one area of competence and confidence for me, as opposed to our ragtag life at home. Working at the office, and also at the county mental health clinic in Medford, was a source of respite. I could go there and get away from everything, be somewhere where it was just the clients and me, for a short while.

My parents were a help when they could be and Betsy's wide circle of friends were also a source of comfort, but they were also having a hard time with their loss.

Tuesday evening, March 19, 1991, I wrote in my journal:

What I realize I've learned from B is that one point of life is just to live it without worrying about "the point." That's what she did, rubbing off people, giving of herself, her warmth, strength, humor and wisdom. Going through life with a very light foot on the brake.

She never pulled her punches, and she seemed to have a special commitment to women and expected them to be all that they could be. In the process, she taught men how to be with women. Obvious winners in this were and are Jay, Jack and me . . . probably a bunch of us.

Sometimes the love and appreciation of strong women spawns a sort of fan club in which to share memories, anecdotes and impressions. In so doing, we support each other, give each other courage, comfort and permission to continue to interact with and learn from tough and unapologetically strong women.

Jay and Jack were part of that fan club. In Vancouver, Betsy had been an important figure in both their lives. She had been a strong, supportive friend to Jay, the next-to-last boarder in her "Home for Recycled Men," as he awkwardly managed the transition between his first and second wives. Able to laugh with him at times, at him at other times, and always there to console him when he was hurting, she offered him friendship with a strong woman as well as simultaneously modeling that strength for him.

Betsy had enjoyed collegial work with Jack in their shared teaching responsibilities in the Faculty of Nursing at UBC, but also joined with him in the hijinks and horseplay that helped break the tedium and strain of non-stop academia. On a mostly non-verbal level, they also enjoyed a quality of mutual respect and fond devotion found most often only in the closest of professional and personal friendships.

Both men learned more about living with and being with strong women from their personal and professional relationships and friendships with Betsy, lessons they would take into future relationships, including friendships and marriages with the strong women they would meet one day. At least partly because of their friendship with Betsy and the practice with her that she offered when they would fight and laugh, argue and make up, cuss and discuss the returns of the day, they would function more effectively and competently with these strong women in their respective futures.

Though it would take some time to appreciate all the ways in which I had won, I knew I was a winner, too. Living with the strong woman that was Betsy had helped make me tougher and stronger. And it also helped make me more comfortable and less anxious in the presence of tough women, just from the day-in-day-out practice with her. I was also a winner as I could now, more than ever, appreciate strength in women, and also in men, in ways I had never before experienced.

Betsy had also been a force with "The Group," her special friends from the UCLA Graduate School of Nursing. Each was strong in her own way: Cynthia quietly observant, Henry Etta tough and assertive, Lee reflective and insightful, Mary outspoken in her observations, Betty warm and generous with brassy, southern humor, Sylvia warm and kind to the bone, rarely if ever blowing her own horn. Little, however, seemed to have prepared them for this, the first loss of one of their own.

They dealt with their overlapping sadness and the collective group tragedy by banding together, by being there for each other with the rich and varied repertoire of the tough, durable, strong woman. During the week they spent in southern Oregon to say goodbye to a sister, they laughed, they cried, they held and comforted each other. They might have cursed, but just a bit. They drank wine and told one story after another about Betsy. In so doing, they modeled their separate and individual and collective strengths for the rest of us, shared with and offered inspiration to the non-members of the group, who loved Betsy probably every bit as much. And in so doing, the UCLA women reminded us that Betsy's spirit was very much alive and well, thank you very much! She might have left this earth, but she had not left The Group. No way!

Betsy had loved the poem "Warning" and its pithy and defiant dreams of a somewhat younger woman anticipating a later life as a gloriously unruly, seditious senior. It described Betsy herself, and her dreams for her future, better than I could have, so I read it to The Group, and it was like giving each of them a bit of her.

WARNING

When I am an old woman I shall wear purple
  With a red hat which doesn't go, and doesn't suit me.
And I shall spend my pension on brandy and summer gloves
  And satin sandals, and say we've no money for butter.
I shall sit down on the pavement when I'm tired
  And gobble up samples in shops and press alarm bells
And run my stick along the public railings
  And make up for the sobriety of my youth.

I shall go out in my slippers in the rain
  And pick the flowers in other people's gardens
And learn to spit.
  You can wear terrible shirts and grow more fat
And eat three pounds of sausages at a go
  Or only bread and pickle for a week
And hoard pens and pencils and beermats and things in boxes.

But now we must have clothes that keep us dry
  And pay our rent and not swear in the street
And set a good example for the children.
  We must have friends to dinner and read the papers.
But maybe I ought to practice a little now?
  So people who know me are not too shocked and surprised
When suddenly I am old and start to wear purple.[1]

I thank God that, like the woman in her favorite poem, Betsy had decided to "practice a little now." The whole world would be better if each of us practiced being such an old woman just a little, right now.

———

The night of Betsy's service, Saturday, March 23, 1991, I logged in my journal:

I dreamed last night that Betsy and I were in a boat that was sinking, and so I was bailing or pumping out the bilge water as quickly as I could. I realized after a while that I had to get to my end of the boat to bail more effectively, that the water would drain down to the stern or something like that, and also that it was getting quite dark, and we were in danger of getting lost if we didn't get the boat bailed out and get near some shore or landmark.

My dreams were telling me the obvious: I would have to take charge of our boat now, take our smaller family onward without its previous captain. Dreams don't always offer answers, yet they do shed light when it's "getting quite dark," reflecting our grief back in symbolic form, which is itself comforting. But I still did not know how I would continue without my Betsy's strength.

Within these teaching, relearning and remembering moments, renewal is possible. As Anna Ornstein says in her book, *My Mother's Eyes*, "Renewal is not forgetting; renewal comes from an ever-deeper appreciation of memories that link the past with the present."[2]

But renewal in my case also meant opening myself up to grief. It hurt. A lot.

It takes courage to leave yesterday, to let the previously loved one go, to relax our grasp on her or him, however briefly, in order to be fully alive today as we begin dreaming about tomorrow. And how much more courage is involved when we have lost a strong woman, a robust, vigorous partner? Living with a strong woman is a gift. Losing one is an earthquake. And like most men, I was not very good at grief.

There is a sad and curious phenomenon well-known in medicine as the differential survival rates of bereaved women and men. Women usually live significantly longer following the loss of their spouses than do bereaved males. Without her partner, a woman pushes on for better and for worse. Without his wife, a widowed man is often emotionally and/or physically vulnerable.

And that might help explain the three parts of additional grieving over the loss of a strong woman—beyond the broken heart experienced over the loss of anyone deeply loved—that must be experienced before we can get on with our lives in any meaningful way. First, we miss the strength that we alternately fought and appreciated when they were alive with us in a relationship. And the greater the strength our woman embodied, the bigger the hole in our subsequent lives when she is gone, and the more grief work necessary to function and to go on without her.

Second, the more mixed feelings we experienced about her capability and strength, the longer it will take and the more work we can expect to face in sorting through the complexities and nuances surrounding the lost relationship.

And third, if we have failed to grow along with our strong woman partner as the relationship developed, we may expect an emptiness and a numbness because we failed to do our own work. Conversely, if we have worked on our own personal growth formally (that is, some psychotherapy for ourselves with and/or without her), informally or perhaps a combination of both, we may appropriately expect to be ready in solid, confident ways to continue our lives without our strong partners. Which is not to suggest that we won't miss them or that we can expect to go on happily without them so much as we go on with them within us—a compliment to both partners.

After first knocking me off my feet, reminding me who was in charge and taking me prisoner for two or three months, my grief would then return at unexpected intervals usually widening as time went by. After a few months, a sort of learning-how-to-grieve process began to take over, perhaps similar to the learning an epileptic experiences when anticipating seizures. Lie down. Go into the bathroom—if there is time—to spare the children one more outburst. A sort of learning not to be so surprised by ferocious sneak waves of grief. Yield. Surrender. Then when the wave has passed, come up for air. Get back to what you were doing. Enjoy the fresh air, the sparkling, tingling, oh-so-much-alive body that has been pitched violently about in the stormy sea of grief before being tossed once more upon the quiet shore. And don't hurry—because the more you have loved the more you must grieve to get back on the track of your life. If you have loved lots, you will grieve lots.

The consequences of not doing it, of not going through the necessary grief at the end of a loving relationship, are considerable. It means not being able to move into the future because we are stuck in the past, living in yesterday.

I am reminded of the Saturday afternoon about six weeks after Betsy died, when I was going through her office desk in search of papers or notes to put into the book on her life I was preparing. I had assembled pictures, billets-doux, letters, keys, childhood sketches. It was a good project; it kept me going, kept me wrapped as tightly as I ever would be that first year without her.

Loose but tight enough. Her packrat instincts and fascination and love for out-of-the-way and unusual 'found art' left the reward of an entire treasure trove of our fifteen years together, everything from an old passport to an envelope of hair clippings, on which she had scrawled, "David's first haircut" (by her).

When I couldn't find a certain letter I was seeking in one of her office drawers, I began searching faster and faster. I suddenly found myself frantically pawing the papers like a dog digging furiously for a hidden bone, clawing through the files, throwing papers everywhere, cursing slightly, then mostly crying, then sobbing. How curious, I thought when I had settled down. I realized then that I wasn't looking for Betsy's papers. I was searching for Betsy herself. The same person I had been searching for ever since the day she died, or since I had lost her. And "lost her" just about said it all. The problem was I was not ever going to find her, never see her again, and while I knew that, somehow I could not nor would not let her go either.

But the grieving, and with it the healing, had begun. The wonderful, terrible as well as growth-encouraging irony was that I had never been as alive in my entire life as I was when grieving over Betsy. Weeping, wailing, sobbing, even snorting and laughing while I was simultaneously crying, my entire body wracked by sobs that seemed to originate from somewhere deep within my rib cage, I was alive. Betsy's death had given me a new and fierce experience of life with all its unsettling depth, bothersome breadth and staggering height, as well as more dimensions too mysterious and preternatural for me to get my mind much wrapped around at the time.

Betsy's last gift was now inside me: the ability to go on. It had always been there. I did not appreciate it much until she encouraged me, teased me, cajoled me, forced me, nagged me and made me look at myself. But I knew I needed to go on, and the kids needed for me to go on and not give up. We can not depend on the Betsy Ann LaSors to look after us forever. Sometime, sooner or later, we realize and appreciate that what they had and what they gave to us is also inside us. It was time to dip inside and get to work, to take responsibility like any adult. To start living like a grownup.

What a gift.

As I reread my diaries from those first years when Mindy, Andy and I pushed on without Betsy's direct presence to guide and support us, I feel both proud and embarrassed: proud that we made it through and embarrassed at the uneven, patchy adjustment I made to life without Betsy. I careened between parenting crises, conflicts and devotion to re-entry into the self-nurturing if uncertain social world, something I had not done with anyone but Betsy in fifteen years.

In my psychotherapy sessions with the grief-stricken, it has been my experience that men more than women bounce back from grief and loss in a relationship too quickly— sometimes much, much too quickly.

Women may wait too long, if anything, to begin a new relationship. "One man like John is enough, so stop trying to fix me up, okay, you guys?" Read: "There'll not be another like John, and I thank the Lord I was the one he loved," or alternately "There'll never be another one like that bastard . . . thank God!" In my experience, however, for every woman who waits too long before she begins resocializing or even reflecting on and weighing her options, eight or ten men rebound too quickly. Women mourn and men replace.

In time, I began to think I was ready for new relationships with women. I was not. I began dating and fell in love with four or five women, two or three quite seriously. The thing is, in this grief process, some parts of your body are ahead of others in terms of readiness. Once my heart caught up with those other parts of me, I realized I wasn't in love and the relationship would end. Betsy died in 1991. It would be three years before I was ready, and then just barely ready, to go on without Betsy. Those were long, long, lonely years, and the hardest part then was in pushing myself to go on with the children but without their mother—our mother.

August 27, 1992:

I dream Betsy and I are taking kids on a tour. I'm mostly responsible – I love her and am thrilled to have a chance to tell her again how much she means to me. [On awakening], the loss I experience is studded with the hot burning nettles of disbelief.

I miss you, my sweetheart—I miss you deeply.

On another night I dreamed that as the kids and I were boarding a flight in Vancouver, we ran into Betsy headed in another direction. She greeted us warmly, inquired after us briefly, then excusing herself, turned and headed to another gate. The message from Betsy was clear: it was time for us to move on.

One turning point came on March 15, 1993, almost two years to the day since Betsy had died. I had gone to pick up Mindy at the stables where we boarded her horse, and as she walked over to the car, I could see that she had a small object cupped in her hand. It was a fledgling pigeon that had fallen from its nest in the rafters of the riding arena, smack onto the sawdust and dirt floor. It looked seriously injured and Mindy wanted to take it home to nurse it back to health. Reluctantly, I agreed.

Four days later, I expressed discouragement at "Pidgey's" plight and wondered out loud what we had gotten ourselves into. Pidgey required round-the-clock eyedropper feedings and continuous attention, including frequent adjusting the temperature of the sock bed. "Maybe," Mindy wondered softly, "Maybe– Maybe Pidgey's . . . a gift from Mom, Dad."

How could I abandon this heroic struggle for life inspired by my daughter's larger perspective? The baby squab with all its fragility seemed to mirror the painful but life-giving struggles in which Mindy and I found ourselves enmeshed as we tried to teach each other how to fly, only to crash, pick ourselves up, dust off our feathers and try again. We had done that ever since we met, ten years ago to the month that Pidgey dropped into our lives. Four days later, I noted in my journal:

Baby pigeon died this AM @ 8:20. Mindy took it well but "wants another pigeon."

I was very saddened as this little creature gave out under our eyes. Betsy was gone, PopPop was gone, KC was gone, and now Pidgey was gone too. But I'm not gone, and neither is Mindy nor Andy. Where do we go from here?

Life is an experience.

Shortly after that, with the end of an intense and all too short relationship with a new woman friend, I took a larger step through and beyond my grief for my beloved Betsy and began the hard but exhilarating search for the alive Pidgey within myself. Make me less anxious, I silently prayed, less important and more aware.

17   Moving On

IN LATE SUMMER 1992, my Ashland office partner, Bill Kirkman, suggested that I call Clair Hawes, a woman he knew in Vancouver, adding cryptically, "You might enjoy chatting."

Bill and his wife Caroline, also a psychologist, were part of the Adlerian psychology community, featuring a philosophical approach that emphasized encouragement and respect for the individual, whatever the situation. Clair Hawes was an important part of that community and frequently gave courses in marriage and family counseling, as well as on encouragement. Bill and Caroline had taken courses from her.

To be polite as much as follow through on my curiosity, I called her.

August 25, 1992:

Talked for an hour with Bill's friend Clair Hawes. She's only seven months grieving the death of her husband, Roland.

Clair is fresh, warm and charming, also very focused and working in West Vancouver, in Canada.

An innocent entry, this first mention of Clair Ladner Hawes in my journal. It would be almost a year and a half before Clair and I would meet in person. I pushed her to the back of my mind, unaware of the possibility that within hours of our first talk, her Adlerian convictions, such as the courage to be imperfect, might already be invading my privacy and my future. At the time, I was immersed in grief, riding the wild roller coaster of mood swings from confidence to despair, coupled with dreams of Betsy that felt so good within them and so sad upon awakening.

September 9, 1992:

Clair Hawes phoned on my nadir of 4 days—grief, depression, fatigue—and we talked for a while about grief. Betsy. And Roland.
I was comforted, happy when I fell asleep.

That would be our last conversation for another fifteen months.

Christmas of 1993, I sent Clair a card and note featuring a photo of the kids and me on a fishing holiday on Vancouver Island. I wanted to reconnect and hoped she would respond. She did, sending me a note that ended with an invitation: "Call me anytime."

I was very aware of the saying that women mourn and men replace, but I was quite sure that, while I still mourned Betsy, I had come to terms with her loss and with the certainty that I would never replace her, not now almost three years after her death and not twenty years from now. She would always be a part of me. I also knew that something inside me was different, changed. All parts of me were now ready for a relationship and I was intrigued and eager for a stronger connection, possibly with Clair Hawes, from Canada. I phoned her after the kids were asleep one night and we talked comfortably, setting up a pattern of late night telephone conversations.

Clair's husband, Roland, had died ten months after Betsy, and our shared experience of grief was a natural topic of conversation. But we also talked about psychotherapy practice, Adlerian philosophy, her kids, my kids and other aspects of life like trying to re-enter the social scene after so many years of monogamy and loss. In one of those calls, she shared that she wanted to marry again and had started to date. We shared much talk, much laughter and I enjoyed many single malt Scotches while we conversed.

It was a nice way to relate to someone before the bodies meet. For me it was connecting with a woman on a different level than I was used to and, in some ways I think, a more positive and wholesome way to get to know each other before we met in person. From her side, Clair told me that I was easy to talk with, that I was not judgmental and that I was relaxed. I also was able to make her laugh. She had not talked about her own loss very much, but found it safe to talk about this with me. While we were in some ways acting as therapists for each other, it did not feel like therapy.

This period of phone courtship lasted probably no longer than six or eight weeks, but it was an important time for us. With hindsight, neither of us were ready for anything more than a superficial relationship when we first connected. We were wise to savor the moment until all our parts were more ready. By the end of eight weeks of talking, we were ready for the next stage.

Late one night, Clair became quiet in the midst of one of our phone calls. I asked her what she was thinking and she said quietly, in a rather husky voice, "I think I need to get down to southern Oregon and check this out." We exchanged fantasies of a weekend together. I told her I would love to feed her, nurture her and take care of her. During the next ten to twelve days we exchanged a crescendo of phone calls, together with anticipatory visions and plans leading up to a Valentine's Day weekend together, all interwoven with my day-to-day responsibilities, and the challenges and rewards of single parenting. A high-pitched fever of excitement found me saying to myself: "Let me be at my best: focused, attentive to her needs, kind, responsive, thoughtful and tender. And dear Lord, let me greet her and meet her and trust her with gentle abandon."

Our Valentine's Day weekend went swimmingly from the moment Clair exited the Horizon airliner, on Friday evening. As soon as she saw me hailing her from behind the safety fence, she made a beeline toward me, walking straight across the tarmac until a passenger agent chased her back onto the carpet. She was, and is, lovely. A slender blue-eyed blonde, about five foot five inches tall, with delicate, slender forearms and will-o-the-wisp wrist-bones on a willowy frame. She carried herself with poise and presence, without a hint of self-absorption. I didn't focus on it at the time, but her warmth—her ability to connect in an unhurried and un-anxious way—was evident from the moment she got off the plane. A connoisseur of warmth, I was smitten.

We loved, snuggled, danced, ate and talked that entire idyllic weekend. An agnostic at the time, or so I thought, I surprised myself by getting down on my knees the next morning and saying a prayer of thanks for Clair. There are no atheists in a foxhole, nor perhaps in the fantasies within a single-father's den.

In an effort to avoid potential tension—at least until I knew it was unavoidable—I had arranged for the kids to spend the weekend with friends. They came home Sunday afternoon, though, in time to meet Clair before she had to leave. To my relief, the meeting went well. I knew Clair was a bit anxious about meeting the kids, but they greeted her very casually and it all seemed quite comfortable. It gave me great hope for the future.

Clair invited us to return to British Columbia and share Vancouver's North Shore and the Sunshine Coast with her. It would take some thinking about, and planning, before I could make a move like that. In the meantime, she continued to visit southern Oregon on a regular basis, staying for four to six days at a time, and sometimes longer.

Each time she was away, I could not wait for her to return; and the feeling was apparently mutual. I remember fondly one balmy Friday evening the summer of our first year together. We were driving back to Ashland from the Medford airport when we spontaneously stopped at a rest stop off the highway to hold and kiss each other, briefly slaking our mutual thirst and feeding our starving, ravaged hearts. Then continued on to Ashland.

Less than eighteen months after that memorable Valentine's Day weekend, the kids and I would move to British Columbia. I returned mostly for my new love, Clair Ladner

Hawes, but also for an old one, to work in Canadian health care. I had been sponsored for my return to Canadian psychiatric practice by a solid and seasoned psychiatrist and old friend, Dr. Britt Bright, who had a job for me doing psychotherapy in her private practice office in the Vancouver suburb of Maple Ridge. I would also do hospital psychiatry and community mental health. Clair would be closer, but still a long way away, or so it seemed, with her home and clinic in West Vancouver.

We crossed the border at midnight, July 29, 1995, and I felt like I was coming home. The children, especially Andy, were less enthusiastic about the move. They hated it, and were quite resentful. Mindy was thirteen at the time; Andy was seventeen, a more difficult age for changes, and the move had uprooted him from his friends and life in Ashland.

Mindy continued to struggle with dyslexia and, in hindsight, also Attention Deficit Disorder. She had difficulties with reading and with numbers and, not surprisingly, problems with her temper. These problems continued to surface in the form of temper tantrums in a most public manner. I had my hands full looking after her while trying to develop both an office and a hospital psychiatric practice for myself, working with a community mental health team, all while attempting unsuccessfully to get Andy to return to high school. Fortunately, Britt's steady background presence helped make a positive difference during those first difficult months back in Canada. Working with her was like having a way station, an island of sanity and stability as I tried to get resettled in Canada.

After Mindy's tantrums saw us evicted from our first rental apartment, I bought a house, and Clair would travel out to spend weekends with us, in the process offering homemaking and decorating suggestions. I would have time with Clair, time with my work and some time with the kids. It was a fragmented existence. Neither of the kids ever really settled into their new life in Canada.

Andy was the first one to pack it in, but not before wrecking two of my cars and dropping out of school. I tried to get him back into school in Maple Ridge, but it didn't stick. News that one of his friends in Oregon had drowned was devastating for him on many levels, including a feeling of guilt that if he had been there, it might not have happened. Finally he said, "I'm out of here Dad," and returned to Oregon to live with a friend.

After Andy left, Mindy stayed with me another year. Clair worried that I wasn't ready to move ahead with our relationship, and we continued to maintain separate living arrangements. On the other hand, Clair was there for my family providing, for example, a mother's warmth, wisdom and support when Mindy had her first period, five years to the week after her mother had died. Thank goodness for this, because I was pretty hopeless as a single parent with my volatile teenage daughter who was increasingly flexing her muscles and experimenting with new adult behaviors. I console myself that it would have been difficult for Betsy, as well.

After a year or so of living in Maple Ridge and maintaining a long-distance romance with Clair, I decided it was time to move into Vancouver where we would be living closer together. An old friend from social work I had worked with out at UBC Health Sciences when I was in training there was now head of the Strathcona Mental Health Team, the community health clinic for people living in Vancouver's

Downtown Eastside (DTES). This would have been in 1997. I went for an interview with this friend, and he said, "Yes, I have good memories of you, David. Why don't you join us?" So I signed on with Strathcona, not appreciating the challenge and the rewards of working in the trenches.

Life is etched out in raw and primitive strokes in the Downtown Eastside. It's a struggle for survival, a primitive, sometimes life and death struggle, just to make it from one day to the next. That any of the DTES residents would find work even on a part-time basis, or ever find a partner, is a minor miracle. Couples would come in and see us, but they were few and far between; most individuals in that area are cut off from their families. While many of the patients were brought to us, many times we did outreach, that is, we went to them on the street or visited them in their hotel room, often small dingy rooms where the bathroom is down the hall and there might be just a hot plate to cook on. Because many people released from the mental institutions ended up in this area of the city, we were seeing a high proportion of schizophrenics and people with severe bipolar disorders, and lots of drug users and people with HIV. Frequently we would send them to hospital: involuntary commitments, certifying them on a regular basis.

We probably had the sickest group of patients in Canada but one of the healthiest work teams. The doctors and the nurses working at the Strathcona clinic operated like a M*A*S*H Unit. They were remarkable, and included a comforting number of strong women doctors, nurses, social workers and support staff. Everybody protected everyone else. You never worked alone. It's a very different mental health model than private psychotherapy, which is just me talking with you and without consulting colleagues with any frequency. At Strathcona, I always had someone to talk with. At the drop of a hat you could go next door and get someone if you needed a hand. A very collegial and collaborative model including annual getaways in the form of retreats. I worked there from 1997 up until late 2007, and when I left they presented me with a wonderful album in which they each wrote a haiku about working with me. I was extraordinarily touched and I miss them still.

Mindy and I moved into the Kitsilano neighborhood in Vancouver where I found a great nanny, Emily, and also enrolled Mindy in the Fraser Academy, a special school in the same neighborhood that specialized in learning disorders. We also got Mindy back into horses and spent a lot of time at the Southlands Riding Club. I was working at Strathcona and commuting to Maple Ridge to do hospital psychiatry but, after awhile, I stopped that and started working with a family practitioner friend of mine, Susan Pawlowski, in North Vancouver. It was a very busy two years, working at the Strathcona clinic and also commuting to work in North Vancouver, while also helping Mindy get to school.

Mindy had her horses to enjoy and formed some early relationships out at Southlands, but after a year at the Fraser Academy she returned to Oregon to spend the summer with Verna, a woman she was fond of—one of Andy's former teachers—and she decided to stay. She was fifteen at the time.

So now it was just me and Clair. Her kids had already left home so there were no longer any complications about living together. I moved in with Clair in her home in West

Andy and Mindy, 1983

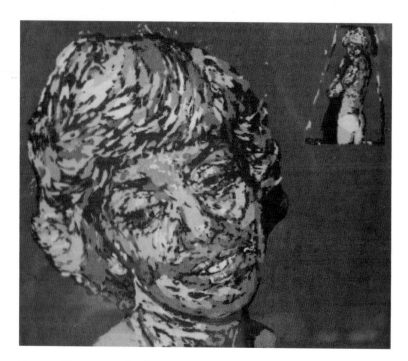

Betsy, silkscreen print by author, 1979

Betsy with girlfriends in Ashland, Oregon, Fall 1990
(l–r) Betsy, Henry Etta, Mary and Betty

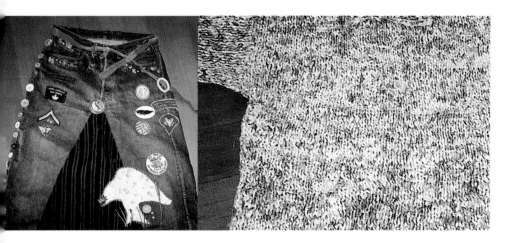

Betsy's recycling creations: denim skirt, detail of crocheted rag sweater

Mindy remembers her Mom

Bryan High School, 25th Reunion, 1982
(l–r) Barbara Bradley, Jeanne Revoir Galliger and Mickey Shook

Bryan High School, Class of 1957 50th Reunion, 2007
Jeanne Galliger and David Kirkpatrick

l–r) Maggie's grandmother, Maggie and Susan, watercolor by author.

Mindy's soapstone carving
of polar bear

Mindy, watercolor by author, 1999

Mindy and her mare Lilly and foal Matrix in rural southern Oregon

David and Clair in Halfmoon Bay,
British Columbia

Clair in Kirkland,
Washington, 2008

Clair, deep relief carving,
Filipino gelutong wood,
by author, 2002

Vancouver and, soon after, Clair suggested, "Why don't you come work with us at Clair Hawes and Associates?" I said, "I'd love to." And I'm still there. I work there Wednesdays and Thursdays doing psychotherapy. For awhile, though, I was working with both populations: those in West Vancouver and those in the Downtown Eastside. Sometimes on the same day, I'd be working in Canada's wealthiest postal code and its poorest postal code, a treat and contrast.

In October of 1997, Clair and I were married. The kids came up for the ceremony. It was a warm and happy time for all, but especially for Clair and me.

18 Clair

I HAD MARRIED ANOTHER STRONG WOMAN. A woman who is who she is, who is tough but not rough, who is honest, open, and not afraid to disagree with me or with anyone. I am a better person today for the opportunity of having loved Dr. Clair Ladner Hawes, my wife of twelve years and partner of over fifteen.

Clair combines moral, psychological, existential and relational strength. In other words, she is a straight-shooter. She is psychologically tough and, like Betsy, can smell bullshit at one part per million. Though she is sometimes anxious, she also lives life pretty much in the here and now, one day at a time. Unafraid, she gives as good as she gets in a relationship, never minces her words and can throw a hard, above-the-belt verbal punch when she is unhappy with a friend, family member or colleague. Her great warmth includes her extraordinary sexual warmth. Clair makes it safe for me to be me; makes it safe for me to surrender when I'm loving her, and makes it more possible for us to be close to each other, because there is no intimacy without surrender. And surrender itself is difficult if not impossible without safety. Giving in without giving up has been a tricky lesson for me to learn over the years. Better late than never.

Who is this strong person whose mind, body and soul I found myself so attracted to? Fortunately, Clair is with me as I write this book so I've been able to ask her directly about some of the events and people that helped shape the person she has become.

Like Betsy, Clair had grown up fond of her professional father, although their relationship was closer and less complicated than the relationship between Betsy and her father. Clair told me her father "had a chair in the living room that nobody else sat in," but that he was an involved parent with her and her siblings.

We would practice our speeches for high school public speaking contests, and he would coach us. He was supportive and would always stand behind us.

Once a teacher made a snide comment about our family. When my father heard this, he had the school principal on the phone immediately. He never doubted the truthfulness of what his children shared with him.

Clair's Mum was a quieter background presence in her life, not as strong as her father, but always present and reliable. Clair describes her mother as "a warm and loving parent who welcomed all of our friends into our home and always had time for us, even though there were five kids."

Strength is transmitted through intergenerational family lines, often quietly and invisibly. Clair had acquired some of her impressive strength from her dad and his family.

The Ladner women were a wide mix of intelligence, courage and, at times, vulnerability. Historically, their collective character had seen them through transmigration adventures and crises. In 1847, for example, they were part of the group emigrating to California through the Donner Pass, infamous because it was there that the Donner party was trapped and forced to spend the winter. Only half survived. The Ladners were fortunate to have made it through the pass just before snow blocked the route.

Married or unmarried, the Ladner women were family matriarchs, intelligent and hard working. They found partnerships either through marriage or, in the case of Clair's aunts Edna and Dorothy Ladner, companionship with each other through teamwork and shared living arrangements.

Dorothy May Ladner, the youngest of the four Ladner children and the younger of the two girls, graduated from UBC with a bachelor of applied science in nursing. She served as a medical nurse in the RCAF during World War II, and then worked as a public health nurse throughout British Columbia. In 1968, three years after receiving a master's degree in public health from the University of Pittsburgh, she became supervisor of public health nurses for BC's Northern Interior Unit, headquartered in Prince George and covering a territory that included Vanderhoof, McBride and Valemont. The job required her to travel long distances in all weather, and took considerable courage and enterprise. She enjoyed outdoor living in the North, particularly camping and boating on Ootsa Lake. Dorothy Ladner was also keenly interested in the welfare of children and was involved in the planning and development of the Variety Club's Children's Treatment Centre in Surrey, BC.

She became the second executive director of the centre, holding that position from February 1971 until August 1974. She died peacefully in hospital on January 19, 1996.

Edna Ladner, on the other hand, attended neither college nor post-graduate education but worked from age twenty-four to fifty-eight with Canada Customs and Excise as a Values and Classification Officer, succeeding in that job by her wits and intelligence. As she broke glass ceilings, she modeled courage and persistence for her niece Clair.

With these strong models, and with parents who believed in her and supported her strengths, it is not surprising that Clair developed into a strong person. She also occupied an important position among her siblings. She was neither the oldest nor the youngest. She had an older and a younger brother, and two younger sisters. In many ways, Clair fits the description provided by family psychologist, theorist and researcher Toman, of the dynamics of the oldest sister sibling position:

"The oldest sister of sisters is a caretaker and order-giver. She likes to be in charge, and derives her leadership position from another person in authority, often an older man or a man in a high position, like her father. She can remain unquestionably devoted to an older man of authority for long periods of her life. Material wealth and goods are less important to her than responsibility and power. She may seem intimidating to men who want to court her. It is hard for her to give in ..." [1]

Clair combined this natural learning with hard work, persistence, integrity, determination and courage. She explained:

I adopted the role of the good girl. I would support and do housework for my overwhelmed mother, who had a higher threshold of disorder which I could not stand! And I was the one allowed to go through my father's papers in his home office with him, deciding what to throw out and what to keep.

Clair was not only responsible; she had a mind of her own.

Some time during this sixth grade year, I was bored with the content and with my fellow students. I decided to stay home, telling my parents that I was tired and not ready to go to school. The unspoken rule in our house was that if any of us did not go to school, we would stay in our bedrooms. Fortunately, I had the choice bedroom on the main floor. It had been the room of my Aunt Clair who stayed with us for many months, but with my mother having another baby, she found other accommodation.

I was taken to our family physician who seemed to tune in to my need to not be at school. He told my parents that when I was ready, I would return on my own accord. They were satisfied with this recommendation. I had many books to read. Like many families at this time, we did not have a television. As a result, I spent all those weeks reading, including my father's Readers' Digest condensed books. It was a wonderful escape.

Mr. Evans was not concerned with the work I was missing, and evidently thought it was not necessary to send work home with my brothers.

When my father arrived home from work he would immediately come into the bedroom and sit on the edge of the bed and talk with me.

When spring arrived, I decided to go back to school so I could play skipping the rope and hop scotch.

She was very close to her brothers, who both died tragically: Edward in a logging accident, in 1963, when he was twenty-one years of age; Hugh while bodysurfing in Hawaii, in 1992. Losing them was painful on many levels.

I remember Edward and Hugh coming back from the bus stop after a Sea Cadets meeting, fighting, cursing. Mum tried to intervene. I listened from another room, curious what Mum would do. I was amazed they would each use the word 'asshole' in front of her!

Hugh died only forty days after Clair lost her husband, Roland, a loss that was especially heartbreaking. She and Hugh had always been close, and he had been an important source of support for her through Roland's last days.

[I remember] when Roland was ill from cancer, Thanksgiving weekend, he was rushed to Lions Gate Hospital with the additional (although erroneous) diagnosis of a heart attack. The Thanksgiving turkey somehow didn't get cooked. At 11 p.m. Hugh was still there waiting for me. He drove me down to the water and hand-in-hand we walked along the seawall. Then we went to the White Spot drive-in for chocolate milkshakes. He was there for me 100 percent! And he was the only one with whom I ever discussed the fact that Roland was dying.

From the age of eight, Clair knew she wanted to be a psychologist, practicing within the context of her family but also searching outside for knowledge. One time, for example, a psychiatrist came to talk to her Girl Guides group and Clair took advantage of the opportunity to question him about psychology, receiving an early lesson in professional status wars: "He told me abruptly he was a psychiatrist and didn't know anything about psychology."

Mostly though, she practiced negotiation among family members during times of disagreement, like the time when her sister Joan was born. At the time, her brother Hugh had a crush on a girl named Juanita, and so insisted the baby be called Juanita. Clair confesses she "manipulated" the interactions, steering her siblings away from 'Juanita,' a name that might have caused her sister undue notice in coming years, and toward the more conventional 'Joan.'

In this way she honed her powers of perception and her problem-solving skills early in her life. These family interactions would help form the solid core of her experience as a UBC graduate majoring in psychology, English and geography. Immediately after graduation she returned to take a fifth year in secondary teacher education, then married in 1964 and with her husband, an educational administrator, moved to the Queen Charlotte Islands, where Roland took a position as principal of the kindergarten to grade ten school, and Clair taught the Haida Gwaii children.

After that, she returned to school in Vancouver for her MA in counseling psychology and opened a counseling practice in Maple Ridge, founding the Maple Ridge Family Education Centre, supporting couples, families and children. Later Clair entered graduate school at the University of Arizona, earning her Ph.D. in counseling psychology; her doctoral dissertation focused on special aspects of couple's counseling. Roland also went to school in Arizona, earning a second master's degree, this time in counseling psychology.

After returning to Canada, Clair and Roland established a small counseling center in West Vancouver that grew much larger as their clientele and colleagues increased. Known as

Clair Hawes and Associates since 1986 until Clair's recent retirement, the center enjoys six busy workdays each week with eighteen psychologists, psychiatric nurses, clinical counselors and at least one psychiatrist seeing individuals, couples, families and a good many children and teenagers.

Until her retirement, Clair led an extraordinarily active life. When not seeing clients in her counseling office, she traveled internationally, teaching within the Adlerian psychology community. In Israel, in the summer of 2004, she shared her teaching specialty with the Israeli Adlerian community, interviewing couples in front of thirty-five professional psychologists and counselors, explaining her strategic thinking as she proceeded, then answering her audience's questions as they worked to sharpen their own couples' counseling skills. For me, being in her physical and emotional presence there and experiencing her poise and courage was like being around a rock star. As the reader can undoubtedly tell, I am very proud of Clair.

I had learned about closeness with Betsy—including the secret that there is no intimacy without surrender—but in ways of which I was often unaware and did not appreciate or enjoy until I met Clair. Clair makes it safe to surrender—to my delight—though I am pretty sure Betsy first gave me that gift. Raising children, while experiencing practice pressures and financial worries, and learning to live with the strong woman I loved so deeply—these were probably all factors that kept my learning about closeness with Betsy on a more latent level. My fantasy now is that Betsy has handed me over to Clair with a smile and a shrug, suggesting to her warmly and supportively, "He's yours now, Clair! With my best wishes. And good luck!" And I imagine Roland watching approvingly.

19 Strength in Madness

CLAIR ALSO HAD AN AUNT on her mother's side, her Aunt Clair. Unlike the Ladner aunts, Edna and Dorothy, and my own aunts, Agnes and Isabel, who were able to draw upon inner resources of strength and stability to balance the more vulnerable parts of their character, Aunt Clair Lambe enjoyed no opposite or complementary personality to help balance out her weaker sides. She carried on her slightly stooped shoulders a more suspicious, insecure and destructive partner, paranoid schizophrenia, a companion that would hamper and restrict her for most of her last fifty years. It is a condition that can strike anyone: a disturbance of emotion, thought and behavior, it is most of all a disorder of trust and comfort, making it difficult for those who have it to love and allow themselves to be loved.

Many mental patients have been short-changed when social courage was handed out. They may fear other people and avoid social situations; co-existing with that cautious, avoidant position, fighting it to a draw, requires a different sort of courage. It requires an existential persistence to make do and meet our own needs as best we can with what personal attributes and personality strengths we *do* enjoy. More than praiseworthy, it is a struggle that we can only applaud, a triumph of will over shyness, reticence and the temptation to withdraw from one's community. It is in this willingness to fight the fight on the other's terms, with the mental illness frequently calling the shots, that Aunt Clair and a number of my Strathcona and West Vancouver patients have captured my respect. At times, they take my breath away.

I recall a Sunday, in 1998, when I arrived at the Pentecostal seniors' residence, where Aunt Clair had been living for the past eight years. I asked permission to give her a hug. Immediately she fell into my arms, responding, "Yes! And a kiss, too!" A wet, warm, tender kiss. There were almost thirty years separating us, yet for the extraordinary warmth I experienced with her, it could as easily have been thirty days.

Aunt Clair was tall for a woman of her age (eighty-three) and era, almost five foot eight inches, and she carried her fleshy, 160-pound body with a cheerful diffidence, like someone who was never quite sure of herself but, by God, she was not going to quit trying. She walked or waltzed with a light and gentle grace. Her blue eyes, surrounded by a series of deep parallel wrinkles, never quite looked at you straight on, but neither did they wander away for long. What she carried inside that somewhat uncomfortable body of hers, however, was a lot more interesting, starting with her soft-spoken voice that stopped just short of a rasp.

On that particular morning, all the motifs were Dutch. We drove to the Dutch Pancake House, on Granville Street, and we talked like a couple of magpies about everything, including her graduation from Vancouver General as a registered nurse in 1940, and her wartime assignments with the Royal Canadian Army Medical Corps in England, Belgium and Holland, where she witnessed the end of World War II in Nijmegen, the Netherlands' oldest city. She also recounted an affair in the Netherlands during her time with the Canadian Army. He was a Canadian Army officer and hailed from the upper crust Shaughnessy section of south Vancouver. After about three years, he had informed her that there was "another woman," and that this other woman was three months pregnant. Aunt Clair was devastated, but continued the affair until the end of the war separated them. "I ran away from that whole experience," she recalled.

After three years working in the Vancouver General Hospital's operating rooms, she took a bachelor's degree in nursing at McGill in 1949, then went on to Columbia University, where she received a master's degree in 1952, also in nursing. She was very proud of these achievements, but functioned poorly in the years to come. She was hospitalized at Essondale (British Columbia's dark and gloomy psychiatric hospital) for some time, then lived on British Columbia's Sunshine Coast, followed by many years in Vancouver living by herself and attending occasional daycare programs for chronic schizophrenics. For the last half-century there had not been a man in her life until she met her new Dutch friend, Willem.

On this morning, as we sat over brunch, Aunt Clair went on to discuss her struggles with her Dutch friend. He was brusque and critical. His room was a mess, and he was in danger of being evicted again because of this. He was also determined and had been pursuing her for four years, calling her regularly four to six times a day, like Dutch clockwork. A couple of years earlier, while considering whether or not to have sex with him, she had visited a somewhat concrete GP who advised her to "use a condom." This had prompted Willem to protest, "I'm not usin' no rubbers!" A twelve-to-fifteen-month impasse had ensued. Recently, she had returned to her physician, who performed a blood test. "I don't know what it was. He's supposed to know what to order."

Willem had a similar test. The stage was now set for . . . something. Living with paranoid schizophrenia is sometimes like having another being at your side, second-guessing you, contradicting your words, crashing the parties of your life. And because of this, one of the largest challenges for the paranoid schizophrenic is establishing and maintaining an important relationship with another, struggling to find room enough in the relationship for the three of you. Three's a crowd—or can be. This was at least part of Aunt Clair's dilemma in wanting to reach out to Willem. or hoping and wanting him to reach out to her sometimes. How to make room.

It was four months later, mid-January 1999, after I had delivered Clair to the airport for a lecture trip to South Africa, that I stopped off to deliver some knitting wool to Aunt Clair. I asked a kitchen aide if she had seen her and was directed "over there . . . she's just getting up from the dinner table right now." Aunt Clair greeted me warmly and invited me up to her room. The wool and I followed her pace, walking slowly up the steps to the second floor and into her tidy but extremely crowded room, decorated with a tea kettle, hanging clothes, two small chairs and her primitive-but-colorful acrylic sketches adorning every wall.

I gave her the wool skeins, and it was then that we talked of her newest quandary. Someone had been coming into her room when she was out and inserting tufts of wool into the vinyl mesh of the tapestry project with which she was going to tell the story of her life. "Messing with it!" she objected. I examined the work; only two clumps of wool poked through the mesh. Both in the ochre and burnt umber colors of fall, they fit the leaf work pattern that she had sketched on the vinyl backing.

"What do you think I should do, David?" she wondered out loud.

Aunt Clair, along with my wife Clair, and I had talked about this before, and so I thought I was ready to support Aunt Clair. I would rely on two of the principles of mental health I knew best. First, do not argue with a person's delusions; they are not only sacred but almost always necessary for the person's continuity, comfort and security. And second, just because you're paranoid, doesn't mean they're not out to get you.

"Leave it," I gently suggested.

"Leave it? . . . just leave it . . . like that?" she softly gasped.

"That's right. Just leave it. Look at it this way: people have been messing with you all your life. Now here's a perfect statement of that. Build around it. Fight it. Go with it. Bring the messiness, the intrusions . . . everything into your tapestry. That way it'll be much more . . . (I fought for the right words) . . . real . . . authentic . . . you know . . . you!"

"Well, sure . . . why not?" she wondered out loud, in both amazement and agreement. "Why sure!" She had accepted a suggestion, whereas stronger intervention would probably have been rejected. A psychiatrist must be cautious about treating family. Another lesson in parenting a parent.

I held and patted her hand gently. This was a woman dear to my heart, who combined the warmth of my Grandmother Kirkpatrick, the intelligence of my mother, the savvy shrewdness of another nurse I had deeply loved, the fragile vulnerability of an old girlfriend of mine who had also been schizophrenic and the bloodlines of the woman I love today, my Clair.

On Sunday evening, October 3, 1999, Clair and I headed back to her Aunt Clair's. She had called the previous day in a tearful panic about her rug-hooking project. On arriving, we learned of her worst fears. "It – it . . . uh . . . h-m-m-m (grunting noises with labored breathing, her oxygen canister having run out again) . . . uh . . . it's just . . . not getting done."

"Well . . . what is it you are doing here? Is there a story you want to tell?" I wondered.

"Well," she grunted, "Hm-m-m-m . . . I Love You Truly . . . to say that to . . . uh . . . "

She paused, embarrassed that the intended recipient of her hooked rug, her namesake and my partner, was standing right next to us. "And . . . uh . . . also . . . someone's still hooking pieces in here . . . I don't know who!"

As the three of us headed outside to Clair's car, I suggested we hide either her yarn or the unfinished rug mesh, and she agreed. We found a restaurant on Broadway that was noisy with background rock music, but its sunny patio was a warm, quiet place to take in the beautiful Vancouver fall day. We ordered one warm, delicious apple strudel with soft ice cream, and three forks, attacking the strudel from north, east and southwest, washing it down with perfect coffee.

I asked Aunt Clair what was on her mind. Her simple answer snapped me to attention. "Uh . . . what a beautiful day it is. Here. Right now. With you and Clair."

We talked more about love. Giving it and receiving it. I shared what I had learned from Tom Malone—that ninety-five times out of 100, being loved is usually a much cleaner, simpler experience, much less vulnerable to distortion and confusion than is the loving experience.[1] And I reminded her that being an artist takes courage, sharing with her my own periodically hurt feelings interwoven with my own creative processes, and how those hurt feelings were essentially my problems and mine alone. Anxiety, self absorption, low self-esteem. Do I want to light a candle or curse the darkness? Paint, David, paint!

"Hook rugs, Aunt Clair! Sculpt, dance, write, but only because you enjoy it!" She seemed reassured. "That makes sense to me," she said. But mostly she seemed to be enjoying the lovely, balmy Indian-summer Vancouver day, together with her niece and her niece's husband.

Afterwards I realized that once again I had started out as a teacher, hitting the brakes just before I crashed into arrogance. Parenting seniors—especially strong women with or without mental illness—is a tricky affair and one must never overstep, parenting prematurely or presumptuously. And so I went home as a student of what had happened and what was important, truly important in life: good coffee and warm apple strudel, love, sunshine and family.

On December 26, 1999, my daughter Mindy was in town for the holidays and together we drove into Vancouver to pick up aunts Edna Ladner and Clair Lambe, as well as Willem, whom Aunt Clair was increasingly lukewarm about, but still, a friend is a friend and at eighty-five years of age new friends do not grow on trees. Two days earlier, Edna had been angry that we had hired new weekend help for her in order to spell off her caregiver, Imme, who was in danger of burning out under Edna's cantankerous confusion. She had threatened to boycott our Christmas dinner but seemed to have forgotten her threat and rode willingly with Mindy and me back over the Lions Gate Bridge to our home. There Clair's steaming turkey dinner and a seven-dish sideboard awaited the extended family.

Aunts Clair and Edna were seated together, with Willem on Aunt Clair's right side to help her with her bib and her shaky eating hand. I sat on Aunt Edna's left. The dinner conversation began wholesomely enough between Clair's two maiden aunts, who had known each other since their teen years in an Anglican Church Girls' Auxiliary.

Aunt Edna: "Well, Clair! It's nice to see you. What have you been up to?'

Aunt Clair: "Well, I've tried a writing project . . ."

Aunt Edna: "Oh . . . ? Really!"

Aunt Clair: ". . . telling the story of my life. But somebody keeps stealing my manuscript, and . . . "

Aunt Edna: "Stealing it? Really!"

Aunt Clair: "Yes – stealing it! And I'm becoming most irritated about it!"

Aunt Edna blithely continued listening on a concrete wavelength, completely missing the flavor of Aunt Clair's paranoid experience, but by this point Aunt Clair was no longer listening to Aunt Edna. They talked on, almost like two monologues.

Aunt Clair: ". . . and so I don't . . .uh . . . really work much on the story of my life anymore . . ."

Aunt Edna: "Where I live, there's also a second lock on the inside door, I think, and . . ."

Aunt Clair: ". . . it's most annoying! . . ."

Aunt Edna: " . . . you know – there are security systems nowadays that . . ."

Aunt Clair: (suddenly raising her voice) "Willem, get your elbows off the table!!"

Aunt Edna: (trailing off, talking to no one in particular) "It's just too bad people aren't more secure these days. And . . . "

Aunt Clair: "Could someone pass me a . . . uh . . . could I have a glass of water?"

I found myself quietly admiring Aunt Clair as well as enjoying the irony of the moment. She had experienced fifty years of a low-grade but persistent form of paranoid schizophrenia and was now also experiencing what was quite possibly early Alzheimer's disease. She required bottled oxygen for pulmonary disease from smoking like a chimney, but she was still 'out there,' in some ways more than Aunt Edna, who herself had been fighting another type of dementia for a short time. Aunt Clair was doing more for herself. She was socializing with courage. Fighting with and loving a boyfriend. And even wrestling with sexuality questions: what to do with Willem and how and when. And where. Aunt Edna, on the other hand, was concerned with her personal safety.

Comparing Aunt Clair to Aunt Edna is like comparing apples to oranges, and probably unfair to both. Nevertheless, while Aunt Clair did less professionally in the last forty years of her life than did Aunt Edna, she took more chances in her later years, especially in relationships.

On Tuesday evening, July 10, 2001, Clair's cousin Kenneth phoned Clair and me separately with the news that Aunt Clair had suffered a massive stroke earlier in the day. As far as he could tell, she "was not feeling any pain but neither was she expected to live." Clair stopped off to visit and had a brief but satisfying visit with her namesake aunt. "She wasn't quite there but maybe we connected anyway," she shared with me.

Another call from Kenneth the following day confirmed the inevitable. Aunt Clair had died sometime overnight. She left specific instructions that no services were to be held in her honor, but she had not left any proscriptions against having a few belts of a good single malt Scotch and sharing a few stories about her with each other. I do miss my times with Aunt Clair, which is almost the same thing as missing her, which I also do.

Strength and toughness include responding to what we must face without dodging or ducking, but with daring. Aunt Clair and her personal and private as well as public struggles with schizophrenia help remind us that it may take *real* courage to move forward while burdened with insecurity, self-doubt, worry. And suspicion.

20   Strength in Age

TIME MOVES ON, and the nature of our relationship with the strong girls and women in our life changes, from the maturing relationship with our life partner to the reversal that happens when mothers, aunts and daughters get older. In some cases, we must become the more responsible partner in the relationship; as we get older, others assume greater responsibility for us. Life moves on. With these transitions come changes in caretaking roles and expectations, sometimes slowly and faintly, sometimes more dramatically as crisis forces the reversal.

I am reminded of a particular phone call to my mother, in about 1997. Recently widowed, and increasingly fragile and vulnerable by herself, she moved at age eighty-eight to her final residence, the health center of the Rogue Valley Manor, located on the high desert of southern Oregon, where she would sit quietly and unobtrusively near the nursing station. Mother started her tenth decade calmly watching and studying fellow residents, nurses and other staff in the nursing center, and friends and family members visiting loved ones. She did not miss much. Once, on a visit to her, I saw a hapless male Manor resident, at least eighty-five years old himself, mistakenly take her platform walker and begin to totter away with it. Mother yanked it back so fast, from her sitting position, that he didn't seem to quite know that he no longer had possession of his prize and continued doddering away.

I called her at the residence one night, at about 9:30. It was a late hour for her and she was tired. I could hear this in her voice, quite hoarse and gruff, when she came to the phone.

"Hello?"

"Hi, Mom."

Silence.

"Hi, Mother. This is David . . ."

"Oh, yes. Of course it is, honey. Oh, I love you so . . . I was just going to bed. . ."

"Well, Clair's out of town and . . ."

Silence.

"You remember Clair, Mom?"

Silence.

"The woman I married. . ."

"Well, yes, sure. Of course. But I didn't– didn't know you married her . . ."

I had an awful sense of unreality. Maybe I was talking to the wrong woman.

"Excuse me . . . what is your name?" I blurted out. There. The words were out of my mouth. Out into the disbelieving open.

"Elizabeth Kirkpatrick!" she barked softly and sharply as if I'd just asked her if night followed day. Which I had.

In two seconds, we had gone back fifty-five years, and a son who should have known better was properly scolded by a mother. I regretted my words. But how do you say goodbye to one who's starting to leave before they're gone?

"Well, listen, Mother. Good to talk with you. Uh . . . I'll give a hug to a pillow tonight, and pretend it's you."

"Sweet dreams!" she half whispered, half commanded.

Once again it was time to go, and I hung the phone up on the cradle gently, sheepishly and a little sadly.

On a visit to her in July 1999, from a distance I spotted my mother sitting near a corner by herself in the Manor's health care center. To see if I could get her attention, I sat at the Manor's well-used upright piano and stumbled through Bach's *Prelude in C Major*. She glanced up briefly, looked around, but didn't put the experience together and continued sitting. I stopped my awkward musical efforts and went to greet and kiss her. She seemed genuinely surprised.

Our visit was brief yet went well. At ninety-one, my mother was still headstrong, with her own sense of impulsivity, an only somewhat subdued dowager queen. A college graduate for almost thirty years by that time, she wore her formal education, and experience in numerous schools of hard knocks, with a quiet grace, betrayed ever so slightly by a gleam in her eye, hinting at a sense of mischief that had never fully abandoned her.

She died in February 2001. I wrote in my journal that night:

Elizabeth Ann Cowan Kirkpatrick:
July 25, 1908–February 23, 2001
Relief. Slowly descending sadness. Real. Not real. She was one in a million. Strathcona folks are warm, supportive, loving, respectful. Doug sounds tired and sad and lonely.

Clair there for me. Mom'll be cremated, her ashes to rest next to Dad's body in the Somonauk United Presbyterian Church cemetery in DeKalb County.

Three weeks later, at her memorial service, I read a poem I'd written for her. I called it The Agony of De Feet, a private joke we had shared because she always complained about how her feet hurt.

TO MOM: THE THRILL OF VICTORY – THE AGONY OF DE FEET

I remember well those weary, worn-out feet –
her Final Years –
With weathered, sounded, tired, tattered, battered, beaten
feet, perhaps reflecting weary fears.

With bunions, corns and twisted toes.
Those gnarled feet supported her so many years,
So many times, so many ways. Who knows?

Who knew? Her Girls. Her Boys. (Were two of each).
But did her grasp exceed her reach?

Only rarely, or so it seems. She was a peach.

And keeping up with
looking after, under,
over Dad.

Left her mostly glad, sometimes sad,
(and only, on occasion, slightly) mad.

So now she's resting – sleeping? – napping 'neath the dew.
And today at last, the memories of those feet are resting too.

A well deserved break finally
Next to her Loved One, David E.

Now, no feet, new feet,
Pristine, pink and neat feet
With which she starts perhaps anew.
And terse and tender, ten-toed dreams on which to walk
ahead at David's side,
Perhaps another plan or goal or hope or two.
Now rest, content that pair; and side-by-side, no longer any
need to hide.

Sleep well, Our Mom and Aunt and Omi too.
You've earned your rest. (Your feet have too).
Sleep well.
Please do.

My mother was strong and proud to the end.

Women like my mother, like Clair's mother, like any of the strong women we know, have a difficult time accepting the loss of physical and mental strength that comes with aging. Especially frustrating is having to relinquish control and decision-making to others. For a woman who has been used to taking care of others and making her own decisions, who has been active in her work and/ or community and accorded respect for her accomplishments, it's incredibly galling to see this respect diminish, to be patronized by younger or healthier beings who take the liberty of referring to her as "dear" or "honey," or who assume she is stripped of any intellectual or physical capacity.

Recently there was a crisis in Clair's family. Her mother left the North Vancouver retirement center, where she had recently taken up residence, to go for a walk and had become lost. Wisely, she trudged slowly with her platform walker over to the Shell station at the corner of Capilano and Marine Drive to ask for help. The station manager phoned the RCMP, and the constable, who quickly arrived at the station, learned from her that she was "Mary Ladner. My husband was Judge Ladner . . . ."

The alert officer put the database together and phoned Clair's sister, Joan, who went to pick up Mary and drive her back to her residence. It was there that we all rendezvoused. Going inside (where the door exit code was clearly marked), we accompanied Clair's much-cared-for mother to the elevator and up to the second floor. There, several worried nurses greeted us, explained their anxiety about their missing charge, and suggested that Mary might wear an alarm bracelet that would trigger an alarm, should she leave for an early evening hike again.

I interrupted gently, suggesting all of these thoughts were important but might better be shared in the light of day. We then walked a slightly embarrassed and contrite Mary back to her room, while one of the nurses followed. Before we left her, Clair's mom confessed, "Well yes, I was lost. But I'm the only one who made it happen. I did it—no one else."

A lesson in the importance of maintaining this sense of self, self-worth, self-esteem and pride, and that balancing pride with practicality can be a delicate exercise.

The following poem, written by Bonnie Paetkau, a bright and creative, extremely well-educated and competent volunteer worker at St. Mary's Hospital in Sechelt, British Columbia, serves as a reminder that within every old woman lie many stories. And, by extrapolation, within every old, tough and strong woman, probably quite a few more.

OLD WOMAN

Old woman
    sitting there
tell me about your life.
    I who breeze through your room
know that in the dim past
    you traveled through a busy time,
were needed.
    Old woman
in a wheelchair,
    tell me about your passions.
Did you bake bread, champion causes?
    how much did you love someone,
when your body was agile and strong,
    beautiful? . . .

Call me an optimist . . . but . . . do you think
    about those busy years,
or are you as you seem,
    locked into an empty space,
waiting for a chance to leave it and join
    your spirit?

Old woman,
    thank you
for being there to remind me
    that life is short and to be lived,
every moment touched and tasted,
    while mind and body are still
together . . .[1]

21 Growing Strength – Mindy

AS THE STRONG WOMEN in our lives grow older and on occasion lose some of their strength, the girls we raised—with varying degrees of competence and success—become older and often stronger. So it has been with my daughter, Mindy.

Mindy did not march gently into life but rather kicking and screaming. As a child with learning disabilities and issues around abandonment, she seemed filled with anger and had little sense of boundaries. Betsy's death, when she was not yet nine years old, sent her into further turmoil. In future years, when she struggled with being a strong, tough girl and then with becoming a stronger, tougher woman, she would draw upon the memories of those first eight years of her life with Betsy—years of loving and being loved while battling with this strong woman who was both her mother and role model.

When she was eight and a half, nine, ten and eleven, and missing her mother, Mindy most often would return to her horse, comforting herself and soothing her grief with the equine emollient she knew best then. Unfortunately, at that time I was in too much turmoil to give her as much of the love and guidance as she needed. And then there were her teen years. I've done a lot of thinking about how I might have made that transition easier for my daughter.

As a young girl moves from her pre-teen years into the stormy and unpredictable years of her early adolescence, complete with major hormonal changes, menstrual periods and many other exciting and unsettling body changes, she has her hands (and body) full. She also experiences new possibilities within her community, an increased sense of competence and confidence (or at least the potential for them), and greater power and options with which to manipulate and change her social and physical environment. As she begins to move forward, the world around her is dynamically impacted too.

Flexing her muscles and experimenting with new adult behaviors in a trial-and-error fashion may be more unsettling for a teenaged girl's dad than for her mom. In Mindy's case, her mother was gone, and her father was flying on his own as a single parent without Betsy's strong womanly support for him, and her motherly, feminine empathy for what Mindy was experiencing. Mindy was new at this business of becoming a woman, and a two-fisted one at that, and I was utterly inexperienced as a single parent. Each of us could only hope to learn from our own missteps and from each other.

What makes this stage so terribly important is that what stands to be lost is the focus of the relationship itself. In other words, in any positive and healthy working relationship—whether between a tough daughter and her dad, or a strong woman and her partner—it is vital to have a certain balance between being together and being apart. In addition, being able to focus on one's self plus being able to focus on the partnership *at the same time* is crucial for the effective functioning of the individual and the relationship. And when a tough, strong girl or woman asserts herself to her mother, father, partner or special friend, it is all the more important for that significant other to tune in and focus more than ever on what might be occurring. Because the tough girl or woman has something she needs to share, and wants to be heard.

I am reminded of the magical, balmy southern Oregon summer evening, in 2000, when, following a dinner with my daughter and her roommate, which they had obviously knocked themselves out preparing, Mindy took Clair and myself for a horseback ride up into the hilly pear orchards. She saddled up Lilly, the recalcitrant mare she had been fighting with since Lilly gave birth to Matrix, now a four-month-old thoroughbred stud colt. To Clair and me, who were not totally comfortable in the saddle, Mindy demonstrated how she handled difficult horses. As Lilly backed into her, Mindy delivered a quick and sharp blow to the horse's massive right hip. "This is my space, okay, Dad and Clair? If she tries to take it, I punch her back." A faster learner than I, Lilly understood immediately and moved her hindquarters back into her space.

After we crossed West Valley View Road, Mindy and Lilly led Clair and me, seated on two much gentler mares, higher up into the pear orchards. She watched over us as needed, then continued upward. At ten o'clock that night, the temperature was a dry eighty to eighty-five degrees Fahrenheit, a balmy evening wrapped in soft velvet. As we rode higher, the lights of nearby Phoenix and Medford began to twinkle, offset by the pink and rosy remainders of a late sunset. Distant sounds of I-5 traffic receded into the background. Giant Orchard-Rite wind machines reached up to the sky, their monster windmill blades resting quietly, no longer needed now that summer had come to protect the vulnerable pear blossoms and young fruit from freezing temperatures.

Mindy offered a free-floating narrative about the taste of the pears in this orchard and of the skunk family that lived under one of the fruit storage buildings among the pear-packing boxes. "There they are right now!" She told us how much she was falling in love with Matrix, and the different relationships and struggles she experienced with her many horse friends. Maggie. Lilly. Matrix. Skye. Blue. Dragon. Summer. Clair and I were silent. Riding down the hill on our return, Mindy taught us how to shift our weight backwards to make it easier on our sure-footed mares. "Lean forward uphill, backward downhill, okay, Dad? That's it, Clair," she encouraged.

It was an idyllic, intimate evening with the wrangler of my choice. Clair had not ridden in thirty-five years and I only once recently, with Mindy a year earlier. I was feeling warmly appreciative and quite close to our equestrian hostess. Back at the stables, Mindy helped us off of our nags, then quickly and efficiently un-tacked them.

Something special began to happen that evening, that month or year. Mindy was growing from a tough daughter to a strong young woman, now teaching us about important things such as horses, nature and more. At first, I missed the rest of the transition: that Mindy was also moving to an early hint of what maybe one day would be a strong mother to her father and stepmother, a new, just-starting-out teacher of her parents.

Three days after that horse ride I had dropped by her stables to say goodbye before returning to Canada. She and her horse Maggie pulled over to the fence and we looked at each other, all too briefly. I extended my hand upward to her as she brushed a strand of hair back and wiped some sweat off her copper cheeks. Squinting into the sun and looking up at her gazing patiently down at me, I told her how proud of her I was and that I loved her.

"I love you too, Dad." She paused for a few seconds. Then, pulling on her left rein and nudging Maggie gently with her right heel, the two of them began their turn back to the riding arena. She quickly went into a full canter, becoming smaller by the second as she picked up speed and moved into the distance. Her mother and grandmothers would have been proud of her. I know I was.

Today I consider Mindy to be strong, in no small part because of her resilience. Resilience—so fundamental to living a full life—is variously framed in terms of attributes like 'the ability to endure,' to be 'self-righting,' to 'problem-solve,' to be 'hardy' and to 'thrive, mature and increase competence in the face of adverse circumstances.' It is about bouncing back from adversity whether chronic or sudden. It is dynamic in nature: increasing, for example, in response to new self-perceived competencies, possibly decreasing in response to calamity.

Those who have resilience have a greater sense of control over their destiny; they are more optimistic in outlook, more forward-looking and goal pursuing. They have drive and initiative. They are resourceful. They have higher levels of self-esteem and self-efficacy.[1]

Most of us carry around a certain amount of latent strength within us, though it often lies untested until challenged. Then, facing a crisis or simply prolonged experiences of hardship, we get in touch with it, discovering our courage, integrity, kindness, resilience, toughness and problem-solving skills. Many strong girls and women have been given this gift of hardship, awakening their strengths, sometimes quickly and rudely, but more often over a prolonged period of time. Up to a lifetime. And each new challenge allows them the opportunity to practice these learned and sharpened strengths, leading to greater strength, to becoming comfortable with newer, even more difficult challenges. It is this process that is embodied in the Chinese character for crisis, symbolizing both a time of danger and a time of opportunity.

Many of the women in Vancouver's Downtown Eastside embody resilient strength. They live in deplorable conditions, often living on the street and prey to violence. But they persevere. They pick themselves up and continue. They learn how to work the system in that community: where to get food, where to get medical help, which police to trust. Their survival is testament to their persistence, courage and tenacity under some of North America's most difficult circumstances. Tenacity is a huge part of resilience.

And courage. Courage is being able to sit down and have coffee with your counsellor, after you've spent a week on the street surviving assaults, drug dealers, johns, arrests, whatever you've been through, just surviving by your wiles and wits. Now *that* is forward-looking behavior!

Strength is measured not just by how much an individual has accomplished and achieved in life, but to what extent they have survived against the odds: medical issues, physical illness, family backgrounds, childhood trauma. If you get through that, you've really accomplished something!

In our family, my personal metaphor for resilience is Mindy. There are some who know her who might say she is not strong because she is prone to crises. She can have a very bad temper and has experienced several bad relationships and bad breakups. But she is tenacious. She is a scrappy survivor. She is resourceful. Mindy lost three mothers in her formative years but when she finds herself needing a mother she reaches out to the women she knows: aunts, grandparents, big sister types, sometimes Clair. She finds substitutes who can fill some of the emptiness and need in her life. She works hard and puts a lot of energy into whatever she takes on. Often those things she takes on are not in her best interests, but she keeps trying, bouncing back from calamity and landing again on her feet.

For those reasons, I count her as one of the most resilient people I know, and I have faith that she will continue gaining strength and a better sense of herself as she continues to mature. Mindy returned to school to become a Certified Nursing Assistant. With her Aunt Terrie's and Uncle Doug's help and support, she studied her daily lessons while looking after her young daughter, Lydia Clair. Yes, Mindy is also a single mother.

Most strong women do not gain their strength on a smooth growth curve, but in an up-and-down jagged fashion. And the teenage girl becoming a woman lives much of her life right at the crossroads, the defining moments of development, creating a great sense of drama for her—and usually also for those who share her life at that vital time. She appreciates, perhaps even enjoys, a moment of truth or a step forward.

On a sour day, the turning points become times of crisis for all involved. Change rarely occurs in a vacuum; growth and development, never.

A father with a strong daughter—or with a daughter becoming stronger, a gift and a challenge—must tune into her needs, emotions, motives and conflicts, whether expressed verbally, non-verbally or a combination of the two. He may be tempted to turn away from her strength and demands, finding them off-putting. But both he and his tough daughter stand to move forward more quickly, more comfortably and more surely in life and love, the more attention he pays to her and the more he responds to her in as many and as appropriate ways as possible.

As I look back over the more than twenty-five years we have shared together, it seems clear that Mindy has never tolerated my inattention, and so, whether by design or by default, she was pretty much guaranteed to get a response from me. By design is better. And, while the squeaky wheel gets the grease, a proactive dad beats a passive, avoidant father hands down.

I reflected on her growing resilience and courage—no doubt enhanced by her partnership with her mare Maggie—and independence, and thought of the following story she had written when she was about eleven. I found it one time when going through my files, and it reached out to me, the words embracing me fiercely from the page.

One day in a far off land there was a mysterious forest. The trees and flowers were beautiful. There were rivers and waterfalls. This forest was untouched.

There was a girl who lived on the other side of the forest. One day she was walking and she wanted to go into the forest, but no one ever went in there because they said strange things happened in there. But the girl didn't care; she wanted to know what was in there.

As she walked into the forest, she saw all of the beautiful trees and flowers. There were animals everywhere. The girl saw tracks in the grass. She thought they looked like horse prints. They were different.

She had never seen horse tracks that glowed before. She had a blanket and laid it on the grass under a tree. She heard hooves clicking on the stones. She looked up and saw an amazing thing. She couldn't believe her eyes, standing in front of her was a horse. Not just any old horse. The horse was an opal color and had what seemed to be glitter on her. The horse looked like it was floating with every step it took.

The girl got up and slowly approached the horse and the horse knelt down. The girl got on and they rode off.

The girl was never seen again.

The End
  by Mindy Kirkpatrick

22　Strong Women, and What Makes Them That Way

I HAVE BEEN WEANED, trained and taught by a number of strong girls and women since my earliest years. All of them have played an overarching role in raising me, teaching me, and eventually making me stronger. You've met them all in this book, beginning with my mother and her Aunt Isabel, then Grandma Kirkpatrick, then Jeanne Revoir, my third grade love, and Gerry Partee and Zaiga Folkmanis, childhood friends who died. You've met the strong women who taught me, like my second grade teacher, Mrs. Esterline, probably the first person to identify that I had Attention Deficit Disorder, and Teresa Grote, my tough but warm sixth-grade teacher who taught with few smiles but so much caring integrity. In college, I learned from Jo the generosity and depth of a strong woman's love. And in graduate school, from Maggie, the benefits of friendship with a strong woman.

And Betsy, my beloved wife and mentor in strength, whose death encouraged me to reflect about strong women and brought their existence to the forefront of my consciousness. Realizing what influence and impact Betsy had on me made me think about all the women in my life who had so influenced my development. Losing Betsy made me ache for the kind of deep sharing that can only come from a meeting between two works in progress, and that would not happen for me again until Clair.

Through the women in my life, and through the hundreds of other women I have been privileged to know over the past thirty-five years in my psychotherapy practice, I have come to have a greater understanding of what it means to be a strong woman and what accounts for their strength. I've also come to have a better understanding of what makes a strong woman so attractive to someone like myself, and how to address some of the challenges inherent in a relationship with a strong woman.

I learned that strong women tend to have different attributes:

- Like Grandma Kirkpatrick, they know their minds. They have a good sense of who they are and what they value. They are often warm.
- Like my mother, they are caring but firm.
- Like Aunt Isabel and Betsy and Clair, they have drive and initiative, and a strong sense of their ability to affect the world around them. They resist others' attempts to control them.
- Like Betsy, they are proactive and forward looking. They take care of business and, nine days out of ten, their need for approval is medium low.
- Like many of the women in my practice in Vancouver's Downtown Eastside, they are resilient in the face of immense obstacles. They persevere and draw upon

available resources. They gain confidence and competence through success in the school of hard knocks.

- Like my young friend Zaiga, they have a sense of hope and vision, and tend to be positive and optimistic. And caring.
- Like Gerry, they respond to urgent circumstances quickly without deliberating. They do what needs to be done.
- Like my third grade sweetheart, Jeanne, they have a strong sense of inner control and the ability to problem solve. They see options, they are resourceful, confident and proactive.
- They take responsibility for their actions.
- They are like good doctors, that is, they know when to move independently and when to ask for a second opinion. And sometimes, like Maggie, they *are* good doctors.
- They are tough, like Aunt Isabel, but usually not rough like my grade four teacher, Mrs. Finley.
- Like my wife, Clair, when presented with an unpleasant task, they do what they need to do to get the job done.
- Like Mindy, they persist without self-pity.
- They endure.

Strong women are not the same as strong men. They, for instance, are often more practical, more down-to-earth than are their male counterparts. I am not just talking about the day-to-day differences between Marge and Homer Simpson. Throughout history, men have dreamed and fantasized, written poetry, operated with their feet (usually) on the ground and their heads (often) in the clouds. They have started, fought and finished nearly *every* war this planet has experienced. All the while, their women partners and the mothers of their children have been home nursing and feeding the babies; searching for, finding and cooking the food; doing the laundry; protecting their families; and running the family business often in the absence of their partners.

Women's strengths are more diverse than men's. Men do a few things really well. Women do many things really well. There are many more women who have piloted an airplane, flown into space, fought in combat, supervised a police force or driven a school bus (as did my late Aunt Gertrude, in her late teens and early twenties) than there are men who have nursed or raised a baby or kept a household running smoothly. There are many more women who have plowed a field of corn, participated in a pole-vaulting contest, conducted a seventy-five-member symphony orchestra or surgically removed an appendix under emergency conditions than there are men who have taken the primary responsibility for the final stages of their mother's or father's lives, helping to make them comfortable in their last days while balancing a countless number of practical, ethical, medical, economic and strategic factors.

Women have an existential strength that does not need the level of reinforcement that most men seem to need and seek. Not that they do not want to be appreciated, but rather there is not the same gnawing, aching hunger for appreciation and approval, the same emptiness that cries out for attention, as there is so frequently in men. Strong women do the job that needs to be done and then push ahead to the next chore, knowing who they are and what they have done, with or without feedback and appreciation. Appreciation is a bonus, not the *sine qua non*, in their daily lives.

One afternoon in my psychotherapy office on Vancouver's North Shore, a patient and I discussed courage and strength as we sifted the sands of the human condition. She reflected, "I love men, but I'm realizing how much stronger women are in crises."

My mind drifted two miles across Vancouver's Burrard Inlet, from my office to a drug-using street poet who was hustling for survival in Vancouver's Downtown Eastside, the site of Canada's poorest postal code. One frosty fall morning I found her magic marker words written on the grimy cement block near the Strathcona Community Mental Health Team. They sang out her strength and courage, her refusal to back down or back out of a harsh and demanding existence, and her determination to continue her search for meaning in her difficult life:

> *I'm just a girl from around da way*
> *My alias Dynamite Bitch 2nd*
> *I gonna say I'm a pretty*
> *hustler trying to*
> *make it last But my*
> *Dope disappear to Fast*
> *Leaving wit no extra cash*
> *I've got spend my*
> *stash cause I keep coming short n shorter*
> *until I got nothing*
> *left except a few*
> *dollars and 1 lik or*
> *2*
> *But somehow I know*
> *I'm gonna make it through*
> *cuz I'm 2 true playa.*

I know dis game well
Plus I can always smell
when da chedda is near
Feeling like I got nothing
2 Fear I start 2 chase
da cheese
I'm getting
nothing but a tease.
But hey it's a habit
You can't blame me
trying 2 grab
it![1]

These two women—the suburban patient and her urban soul-sister, unknown to each other but joined by their persistent refusal to give up—pursue their respective existences, each determined not to yield, defer or surrender. Some might question whether Dynamite Bitch 2nd and her drug-using lifestyle best represent a woman's strength. Philosophers and psychotherapists might praise her existential courage, her gutsy and relentless search for importance in her life. Other street people might admire her physical strength, and would probably sum her up more quickly and in simpler terms; they might call her one tough bitch—a compliment for many, including Elizabeth Wurtzel in her witty, at times confusing book *Bitch: In Praise of Difficult Women.*[2] We might question Dynamite Bitch's choices, her associates, her dreary life, but not her refusal to give up or her defiant answers to those who challenge her worth. Her ability to "smell when da chedda [street money] is near" suggests her survival strengths.

Women are usually more emotionally and psychologically driven, restless, searching and proactive individuals than are men. They are interested in making a good thing better, in becoming stronger themselves through transforming growth experiences and opportunities, including counseling and psychotherapy; they are often driven in this direction by one more crisis or trauma. In my psychotherapy practice in West Vancouver, I have heard this dialogue between women and their partners replayed with some variation, again and again:

Man: I'm not going for therapy, Marge. I'm not sick.

Woman: Well, I am going for therapy, John. Because I'm not well. And I want more out of life!

This difference helps to explain why seventy to eighty percent of my West Vancouver patients are hard-working and often over-functioning women who are searching for more wellness, more meaning in their lives. They come to my office, almost always on their own initiative, often with a warm and understanding nudge from their family practitioners. When their partners or other men do come for therapy, they are often encouraged by others, but they are often convinced that counseling or psychotherapy is for sissies or weaklings. "But it's not for me—I'm not sick! So can we make it quick, Doc?" they add, almost apologetically. Men avoid counseling because they know they're "not sick!" Women pursue psychotherapy, appreciating that they are not well, at least not as well as they envision themselves becoming.

Of course 'making a good thing better' is a more intangible concept among the patients I served in Vancouver's Downtown Eastside. On Skid Row, endless life-and-death battles with schizophrenia, bipolar (manic-depressive) illness and major depression—often antedated by experiences with horrific families of origin—are all too frequently interwoven with malignant drug-addiction problems. Patients with AIDS, HIV and Hepatitis A, B and C necessarily spend much more time in a battle to stay alive, fighting off and occasionally escaping sickness, than they do seeking wellness. Survival in Vancouver's Downtown Eastside is a pitiless, pounding battle, and a person's priorities there have more to do with getting one square meal a day or finding a warm and safe place to sleep at night than with going for counseling 'to make a good thing better.'

Despite their often primitive free-for-alls in their endeavors to stay alive and to salvage a scrap of human dignity, the female residents of Vancouver's Downtown Eastside often seem to have more in common with their North Shore counterparts than they do differences. One hot July afternoon, a hardy and hard-hitting tattooed woman shared her anguish, her exhaustion and her deep concerns for her physically ill partner with her nurse and me.

Patient: I am . . . just so tired and . . .

David: You're exhausted . . .

Patient: If you'd just shut up and let me finish, please? *. . . I am worried about my partner and all the medical problems and stuff and . . . with all this heat and everything . . . (She begins crying)*

The nurse offered her a box of Kleenex. The patient continued crying, wiped away her tears and went on:

My Wellbutrin [anti-depressant] was stopped, you know, and . . . I don't know . . . but yeah, if you . . . wanted to restart it, I could 'get down' [agree] with that!

This forty-something woman was too tough and uncompromising for the nurse and me to discuss hospitalization with her or even a halfway respite-house for a short time-out. She needed and appreciated her anti-depressant medication being restarted. But her conflicts and her worries over her much-loved partner, and her salty tears, were no more and no less heartfelt and human than those of the many people I have been privileged to comfort in my psychotherapy practice across Burrard Inlet. Her heart was no bigger or smaller than those belonging to her West Vancouver sisters. The inner demons in Canada's poorest and wealthiest postal neighborhoods differ in quality and quantity. But both groups of women experience the same needs and conflicts about nurturance, love, respect, mutuality within relationships, dependency and interdependency, comfort, security, peace of mind and contentment.

Finally, women seem to be more comfortable living in *and enjoying* the here and now than do men. They are more grounded, and more easily accept being wherever they happen to be in whatever situation they find themselves. Philosophers and other observers of the human condition suggest that most happiness and contentment in life comes down to our capacity to be right here, right now, whether we are scaling a mountain, making love, meditating or just being with friends.

This does not mean that these women are superhuman. They struggle with issues such as self-esteem and indecision, frequently err on the side of giving, can be brusque and dismissive, and sometimes their toughness can shade into roughness. But, overall, we feel safe with them. We trust them with our feelings and look to them for support and guidance.

Now then, how did so many women get to be so strong?

From my observations and from the literature, I would say the things that make a strong woman or girl fall into the following categories: genetics, modeling, birth order and the presence in their lives of what are sometimes called 'protective factors.' These are not mutually exclusive conditions.

First, some are born as strong girls or, more accurately, they are *conceived* as strong girl-embryos, carrying two X-chromosomes. One or both of *their* parents were made of resistant, stubborn, robust DNA, inherited in turn from their parents and grandparents. Varying amounts of this resilient genetic material were passed down to their daughters. These kids are 'naturals,' and with only a small encouragement in subsequent years will not only survive but also prevail. Most of the natural strong women in my life also grew up with other strong women models: my mother with her Aunt Isabel; Clair with her Aunts Clair, Dorothy and Edna; and Mindy with Betsy.

While it might be argued that mothers and relatives provide opportunities for learned strength through modeling, more than through biologically inherited strength, I would counter that there is truth to the saying that a person 'comes from solid stock.' The woman with an Aunt Isabel or an Aunt Dorothy in her lineage is more likely to come into the world equipped with a temperament and inner resources that support a positive and confident approach to life. If they are then lucky enough to be nurtured by a family that is also affectionate and caring, warm and cohesive, a family that provides support in times of stress and sets high standards and expectations for their children, what better recipe can there be for strength?

Strength and dignity are her clothing, and she laughs at the time to come. She opens her mouth with wisdom, and the teaching of kindness is on her tongue.[3]

History is full of strong women, and genetically strong women—and men—have probably been with us as long as people have existed. During expeditions from 1959 to 1976, anthropologists Mary and Louis S.B. Leakey discovered a series of hominid fossils in the Olduvai Gorge of northern Tanzania. When combined with more recent discoveries, the Leakeys' findings suggest that the genus Homo ('true human') coexisted in East Africa with other similar forms from one to three million years ago. The most famous archetypal and metaphoric grandmother of these fossils lived north of the Olduvai in Ethiopia's Afar Triangle, part of Africa's Great Rift Valley. Lucy, known by her fossil name *Australopithecus afarensis*, was discovered in 1973 by a research team led by anthropologists Donald Johanson and Maurice Taieb. Her partial skeleton plus the remains of twelve other individual australopithecines became known as the First Family.

Apparently a young woman at the time of her death, Lucy nevertheless has proven strong enough to survive in skeletal fashion for an estimated 3,200,000 years. She also survives within our minds and imaginations as a symbol of the spirit and durability of the human experience. In 2000 the remains of another female, older than Lucy by about 5,000 generations, were discovered in northeastern Ethiopia scarcely 2.5 miles from Lucy's resting place. Known as Selam, 'peace' in Amharic, she died at about age three, but it is clear she walked upright and had a mixture of ape and human attributes. Together, Lucy and Selam remind us of the utter uncertainty and vulnerability our resilient ancestral mothers faced in the enduring struggle for survival that would lead to our own existence today.

Professor of genetics Bryan Sykes has looked at more recent and more intimate connections with strong women through the prism of mitochondrial DNA, genetic material passed down only from mothers to their daughters and sons, and only from those daughters down to the next generation, and so forth. In his book, *The Seven Daughters of Eve*, he describes his surprising genetic research findings that all of us are connected to each other through only a small number of mitochondrial mothers. More specifically, almost all those of European ancestry are descended from just seven common ancestral mothers who lived as long as 1,800 generations ago, or between 11,000 and 45,000 years ago, and those seven daughters had one common ancestral mother or 'Mitochondrial Eve' who lived in Africa about 150,000 years ago. How's that for genetic matriarchal strength?

Sykes is quick to caution us against idealizing or sentimentalizing these clan mothers and does not focus on the necessary strength and persistence of their lineage—specifically their daughters, their daughters' daughters and so on—that allowed for the existence of himself and his family. Rather, he steps back, imagining, and appreciating: "A thousand rows back Tara herself, the ancestral mother of my clan . . . [I] feel the pull on my own stomach . . . sense our deep umbilical connection . . . looking at my brothers and sisters . . . a feeling of closeness and intimacy with others in the same clan."[4] Within genetics lies procreation, survival, maturation, bonding, procreation again in the next generation, and continuation of the species, all documented through a woman's mitochondrial DNA that helps remind us how closely connected we all are.

The second pathway to strength is journeyed by those women and girls who were raised by strong moms and/or dads, parents who modeled courage, vigor, persistence and physical strength. When strong genes and strong upbringing are combined, the chances for the offspring to be strong probably increase exponentially. The outcome brings forth children who are and will become resilient and flexible and are capable of learning both in and out of the classroom. Supported by strong and healthy parents, they stand to become good book learners as well as on-the-job learners.

Strong mothers have an enormous impact on children. Whether nurturing youth or modeling strength for them, strong women feed young minds and bodies; they also provide relationship templates that influence the young people with whom they come in contact. The stronger the available female or male model, the more powerful the cathexis, or memory bonds, that will influence children across the spectrum of their mental and emotional health, affecting their adult decisions, partnership choices, dependency issues and conflicts, achievement and competence areas, child-bearing decisions, family, marriage, work, play, education and more, probably for the rest of their lives. I continue to feel the influence of my mother and grandmother. I saw strong parenting up close and personal by observing Betsy with our two children, and now I watch and learn from Clair.

Third, there is birth order. Betsy, Clair, Maggie, Jeanne, Gerry Lee, Zaiga and my sister-cousin Susan were all first-born girls. Maggie, Jeanne, Gerry Lee and Zaiga were also the first-born child of either sex.

The oldest girl born into a family almost always experiences unusual pressures as well as opportunities to become stronger. Extra amounts of responsibility, dependability and accountability will be expected of the first-born, versus that traditionally hoped for and expected of her brothers and younger sisters. Being the oldest girl in a family is a mixed blessing, often a thankless assignment of multiple tasks, expectations and responsibilities, taken for granted all too often by her parents and resented by her younger siblings. She may appreciate her responsible role while resenting it at the same time. If she slacks off, she is "... not being the good big sister we expected of you." On other days, when her bossiness spills over onto younger sibs, she hears about it from them, from her parents and, all too often, from both. A first-born girl who also happens to be the first born *of either sex* in her family can expect an extra load of impossible expectations: take care of your brothers and sisters, and sometimes Dad and/or Mom too, and be cheerful about it while you're at it!

In a recent study published in *Political Psychology* (Vol. 22), Blema Steinberg reported that first-born women, like first-born men, are over-represented among political leaders and, more specifically, that first-born women are also overrepresented among *female* political leaders.[5] Other studies have found that first-born females have the most positive attitudes toward women as managers among all birth orders, and that the first-born of both sexes[6] were less vulnerable to loneliness after a social loss[7] and more likely to be chosen for positions of leadership (and for popularity).[8]

On the other hand, first-born women may also be more vulnerable. Psychologist Nicholas Skinner found them to have higher degrees of hypochondria than their other siblings, a fact that is possibly explained in terms of parental treatment; that is, inexperienced first-time parents may model greater concern and anxiety about the health of their girls.[9] A study by Frank H. Farley showed first-born women to have a slightly greater need for approval than did last-born females.[10]

There are often covert expectations and fantasies regarding formal role-assignments of first-borns. For both parents and children, the expectations are often that the first-born will do more than his or her share of a) nurturing and taking care of others, b) looking over and after others within the family, and c) parenting both their own parents and their siblings. The family's hopes and fantasies are understood as: he or she will take care of us and one day, perhaps, be the mother or the father, the nurturing figure that one or more of us never had, or enjoyed only in part. If the first-born is a girl, these fantasies and implicit or explicit expectations are frequently magnified.

The first-born girl in a family usually assumes a disproportionately large share of responsibility. Gerry Lee Partee, with five younger brothers, undoubtedly learned a great deal in her all-too-short life about nurturing and taking care of others. Not surprising, then, that she reached into the water without hesitation to save her friend.

Even if the girl is not the oldest of the siblings but is still the oldest of the girls, like my cousin Sue, she often finds herself the family caretaker. This may help to explain why Sue returned to the family home when she could have had a softer berth with the Clifton family. Like other first-born girls, she may have experienced a host of complex feelings about her role.

One thing seems quite certain: in the process of taking on all this responsibility she became more resilient. With this caretaking background, it is little surprise then to find that strong women are frequently the ones who after a death, when there is grief in a household, see to it that meals get cooked, clothes are laundered and—should there be any leftover energy—that the children and men get looked after.

But not all women are first-born, and not all women are born into families that provide strong modeling and support. Some girls are born into poverty, into families filled with discord, drugs or drunkenness. Girls grow up in tough, crime-filled neighborhoods, or are raised in milieus where no one talks about the need for higher education or supports drive or ambition. Yet one study by Emmy Werner and Ruth Smith followed a group of these 'at-risk' children for thirty-two years, and discovered that even children in these circumstances can turn out as resilient adults.[11]

Inspired by their findings, other researchers began to focus on the kinds of things that accounted for strength in adversity. They found that children born into high-risk situations can gain strength given the presence of conditions that provide opportunities for support and for gaining a sense of competency: the protective factors mentioned above. My daughter serves as an excellent example. Born with dyslexia and a sleep apnea that left her with seizures, Mindy would lose three mothers in her first eight-and-a-half years. These setbacks exponentially increased the likelihood that she would not be able to recover well from future calamity in her life. In her youth and teen years, this seemed to be the case. But she has, like the song says, continued to "pick herself up, dust herself off, and start all over again." Each time she does this successfully, it is further proof, for her, that she is indeed a strong and capable person.

I would attribute much of Mindy's determination and perseverance to having Betsy as a mother and role model in her early years. But there were other elements working in her favor. She was able to attend a school where her needs were met, she had the opportunity to spend time with horses—a pastime and passion that let her dwell on beings other than herself, and where she excelled—and she has had the support of both family and other caring adults.

Having known and been influenced by strong women, it is hard to settle for less. While Grandma Kirkpatrick's tough and anxious ways probably helped mold my father into the anxious person that he was, her anxious pushiness was also part of the strength that she modeled. She provided my father with a template of desirability that saw him absorbing some of her strength as well as being attracted to another strong woman, my mother. With my mother as my model, I have been unconsciously drawn again and again to strong girls and women, starting with Jeanne, my third grade sweetheart. Thus do destiny and fortune impact us in determining the people we find ourselves attracted to and involved with, often many years after those first formative experiences.

23 Drawn to Strength

I KNOW NOW THAT WHEN CLAIR and I first met in person, that Valentine Day's weekend in Oregon in 1994, I had come to a point in my life when I was desperately seeking a good, strong woman. Betsy was gone, but she lived on within me and, unbeknownst to me, I was still searching for her: a tough woman with strength to spare. Where was she? Who was she? What I know now is that I was not just seeking a good woman, I was seeking a good, strong woman. Having experienced the soul-enriching benefits of living with and loving a strong woman like Betsy, I could never be satisfied with anything or anyone less. Although I dated several women in the years after Betsy died, I knew in each case that something was missing. I knew when I first corresponded with Clair that that something *was* there. I also knew enough from living with Betsy to know that I could not take on this kind of relationship lightly; I would need a measure of inward strength myself before I could be a good match for Clair, before I could interest her and fulfill her in the way I sensed she would fulfill me. I waited until I felt stronger, and I'm glad I did. I'm only lucky that Betsy had been willing to take me on when I was less strong, and I'm fortunate that living with her helped make me stronger.

Why are more vulnerable, less strong people attracted to stronger women? First, some of these individuals are dependent, needy individuals wanting to lean on the stronger would-be partner, just as I had sometimes been with Betsy. Sometimes this is the result of memories of strong mothers, fathers, aunts, uncles and siblings, and of longings for one or more of those people and, with these longings, a desire to re-experience one or more of these relationships. An example of this can be seen in the weaker, more dependent man attracted to a stronger woman who, he fantasizes or imagines, will take care of him. Should his fantasies be realized and the strong woman willing to fulfill this role, a relationship begins to take shape, but one fraught with dependency problems: for example, if the weaker man sits back and begins to coast through the relationship, rather than working on his own personal growth.

Related to this first group are those individuals who fear growing up, who fear moving beyond the dependency of childhood and becoming all they could be. In its most extreme form, these individuals experience success anxiety or sharp conflicts about being successful. If such a person approaches life and success with one foot on the gas and the other on the brake, what better person to have in their garage but . . . a strong mechanic? Again, the most positive possibilities of this relationship are directly related to the weaker individual's willingness to take long-term responsibility for his or her success conflicts, to address them straightforwardly.

Strength is valued not just by dependent people but by other less strong people who greatly respect and appreciate strength in a woman partner. Why and in what ways is a less strong person drawn to the strong woman? Fate oversees many of the pathways leading us to short- or long-term—but almost always memorable—experiences with a strong girl or woman. In reality, there are probably four or five of these important connecting, bonding and matchmaking trails.

First, people love challenges, and the oh-so-alive experience of being pushed to live up to our very highest potential, our outer limits. To be pushed to our highest potential by a strong woman is to be truly challenged and to experience joy. In searching for our inner strength, it is often more comfortable and less anxiety producing—if less straight-forward—to seek it outside rather than inside ourselves.

Second, family therapist Carl Whitaker also suggests that individuals with strong mothers, fathers or sisters are often attracted to strong women; the two most common examples here would likely be men and women who are drawn to female partners reminiscent of one of their parents.

A third category of those attracted to strong women would include those men and women drawn to the *challenge* represented by a relationship with a strong woman, while at the same time, consciously or unconsciously, expecting to subdue her and, thereby, maintain their own fragile sense of strength. Almost every strong woman has met this person, a saboteur in sheep's clothing, usually a man who seems eager to cooperate—until the dénouement in which he maneuvers to undermine his partner, thereby improving his position. Or so it seems to him.

The fourth group of individuals drawn to strong women includes those men and women struggling with deep-seated feelings of ambivalence about living with a strong partner, though they have been conditioned by strong women relatives, teachers and peers to expect women to be strong. Often first attracted to the strong woman by other qualities—her warmth, physical beauty or vitality—they then experience two fears: 1) that their partner will be a strong person who will dominate their lives, 2) that their partner will *not* be the strong person or mother figure upon whom they had hoped and fantasized they could depend.

A fifth group of individuals who end up with strong women—though perhaps never having asked for the experience—are those who find themselves in context with them. For example, what eight- or ten-year-old student asks for a strong teacher? Or strong women relatives, that are neither sought out nor can be avoided? But because of them, their lives will be different, at times significantly and forever altered. Because of them they are and will be inspired and encouraged to be stronger and more alive.

Most of us not-as-strong beings find ourselves scrutinizing a fairly large group of people when seeking possible partners, but strong women usually have fewer people from whom to choose. This is true in part because most strong and emotionally healthy women prefer to be involved with other strong individuals—in friendship, in family and in intimate relationships—for the simple reason that most humans are attracted to parts of themselves. Like attracts like. Just as the skilled tennis player's best game emerges when playing against an equally talented player, the strong woman finds herself reified when in the presence of other strong, competent people.

There is a sense of affinity, an awareness or feeling that she is with her own people. The emotional and intimate experience of this is appreciated as mutuality, a sharing and communication between souls, a sense that goes above, beyond and beneath its verbal and physical expression. She sees and appreciates herself within another. This other strong or almost-as-strong person is one whom she realizes she will not usually have to take care of and will not have to feel responsible for.

The odds of a strong woman finding this other equally healthy, hearty, strong, tough person with whom to form a partnership are somewhat steep, and the stronger the woman, the steeper the odds.

Great-aunt Isabel, for example, never married, but not because she wasn't interested in marriage or in having a romantic partner. A journal entry, written while traveling overseas with her sister, Jean, suggests she may have had opportunities to review her spinster status. In this case, she found herself in a situation with a "canny Scotsman." One suspects she was intrigued by the man. But her dislike for the direction the discussion took, and her inability to suffer fools ended the interchange quickly.

Kelso, Scotland
May 9, 1893

We started northward, again to meet strangers who are really not strangers. At Kelso, there was no one to meet us, but one of the porters, with a meek gentle manner, accosting us inquiring if I was Miss Cowan, and if so Willie Wilson had bidden him see to our luggage and to send us by bus to 121

Roxburgh Street. As usual, our bulky American trunks were the subject of comment. One of them falling while being lifted up to the bus was the occasion of our observing that "canny Scot" was not so canny as he looked. Jean heard one of them swearing at [the] trunk for having enough in it to fill three trunks. The same old fellow entered into conversation with us while I was waiting for Jean to see about storing our second trunk, asking me if the trunk was mine, how far I had come, where I was from . . .

He was so friendly and so Scotch, I was tempted to return his sociable spirit, so I suppose I was justly punished by what Jean would call some of his Scotch impudence. When he found we were Americans, he turned to a companion, Jimmie, and told him we had come in search of a husband, and as we no doubt had abundance of money, either of us would suit him, Jimmie, very well.

I told him he had no reason for supposing we were not married, but he said he knew I was not for I had no rings on my finger. I thought the conversation had gone far enough so closed it as abruptly as possible, with an uncomfortable feeling that the theory as to the motive of unmarried American women in visiting England is more general than I had ever believed. This is not the only time that it had been broadly hinted to us that there might be various reasons besides the alleged ones for our being here. Like a Dale Twp. oracle, I just said 'Fills'—[Fools] and resolved to beware of over talkative strangers, even though they chance to be canny Scotchmen.[1]

Great-aunt Isabel quite possibly presented as an imposing woman with a generously proportioned "Proceed at your own Risk!" sign swinging from her durable neck. How many other strong women were conflicted and caught between being an authentic, if threatening, stronger self, on the one side, and presenting a less honest but more approachable persona on the other? My great-aunt had strength and a steely will combined with integrity, sinewy fiber and a manner that refused to subside or settle into the background of family or community affairs.

A person with an IQ of 140 might experience moderate difficulty in meeting or finding a compatible intellectual soul mate, but if you add another twenty or thirty points to her IQ, her search becomes considerably more challenging. A strong woman seeking a compatibly strong and competent partner faces a similar challenge, and needs all of the patience, determination and courage she was born with or has developed. She will struggle with compromise in this search for love because, while she values strength that will mirror her own robust personality, she also appreciates kindness, sensitivity, warmth, intelligence and thoughtfulness. If she can find these qualities in someone not as strong as she is, she may consider it a good bargain. For example, both my mother and Grandmother Kirkpatrick chose mates who had these fine qualities, but were perhaps not as strong as them.

Some really strong women find themselves attracted to less strong partners because of their need to nurture or to mother or parent another. The strong woman then often faces a variety of choices in forming lasting partnerships, but when strength is balanced by good mental health and perspective, those choices are apt to be most propitious, positive and promising.

If you are fortunate enough to convince a strong woman in your life that you are the one for her, and you and she set up house together, you will likely find that living with this woman can be a challenge, even if the challenge is rewarding.

24 The Challenge of Loving a Strong Woman

I WAS RECENTLY and forcibly reminded, while climbing North Vancouver's Grouse Grind, of the rewards and challenges experienced by one living in such a partnership. Grouse Mountain is a skier's paradise in winter, but the rest of the year the Grind challenges hikers. It is a demanding 853-meter (2,800 feet) vertical climb through a defiant, twisted mass of rocks, boulders and hills, bordered by stands of Douglas fir and western red cedar, with only occasional wooden steps to help the hiker. It is best not attempted by either the faint-hearted or the out of shape. It stares and sneers, taunting its intended hikers, "You wouldn't dare try to climb me! Would you?" While I try it once or twice a week, Clair climbs the Grind less often, so it was with surprise and delight, in the early summer of 2005, that I noted on the monitor screen at the top of that climb that she had recently posted the third fastest Grouse Grind time that year for women aged sixty to sixty-nine.

I crowed my delight to anyone who would listen, much to her embarrassment and pleasure. Clair's competitive wheels were revving up. Within four days, she would return to the Grind and, after a large drink of water, shoot up that steep, rocky hillside, knocking the previous fastest woman in her age group out of first place by several minutes. Her time was fifty-five minutes, placing her seven minutes and thirty-one seconds ahead of the nearest competitor in her age group.

These days, when we climb the Grind together—largely an abstraction, as I really don't see her after we enter the starting gate—I climb behind her, feeling a mixture of excitement and considerable pride in my jet-propelled partner, while at the same time experiencing a certain amount of loneliness as I push away my poorly covered-over competitive feelings. Sometimes living with a strong woman means not living continuously with her, not being quite as high up the Grind as she is or quite as fast. It means enjoying her strength and wisdom and appreciating her power and her joys, even the mixed feelings of competing with her.

I console myself that men have always had these mixed reactions to women's strengths. But how does one enjoy another person's strength without being swallowed up by it and self-destructing? To live with a strong woman is to risk ambivalence of the strongest sort; those mixed feelings, when not ignored, can be a revitalizing gift.

To be successful in a business, social or marriage contract with a strong woman, the partner—especially the less strong partner—must take responsibility for the challenges they face in the relationship and appreciate the inherent opportunities. They must engage in a continual learning process while on-the-job. With courage and perspective, they may also go for counseling, not because they are sick but because they recognize that they have been given a gift, an invitation to greater wellness. They experience a chance for an extremely rewarding relationship with a strong woman and want to respond in kind by growing, changing and becoming socially, emotionally, professionally and psychologically stronger themselves.

In short, both men and women contemplating or in a relationship with a stronger woman are almost certainly better off not wasting time complaining or resisting, but working harder, celebrating the opportunities to make a good thing better in the companionship of a model of strength. In fact, most will find themselves too busy growing and changing, laughing and having too much fun to protest. During those infrequent intervals when they do feel like complaining, however briefly, they will find themselves too much out of breath to do so.

It is not, however, a task for the faint-hearted. After a mere trial period some individuals will have had enough of the 'joys' of living with a strong girl or woman to last themselves a lifetime. Many will find new, less vigorous partners, then discover themselves mysteriously resenting the new partner for not having enough of what they resented in their previous partner! We often neither know nor appreciate what we have until we lose it. Others will give up on their relationship with a strong woman and pack it in, only to realize in another five or ten years that they have married or committed to yet another strong woman, jumping out of their frying pan memories into the heat of a new yet similar fire. Such behavior—repetition-compulsion—is quite familiar to mental health workers.

Others will stick it out in their partnerships with strong women in a resentful fashion, struggling with depression and quite possibly a variety of other medical, surgical and mental illnesses, disorders and dysfunctions, often related to chronic unhappiness. Overlapping with this group is a no-happier but more content third group that will largely profit from their partnership with a strong woman, their commitment and courage having paid off. Finally, there is a fourth group of voyagers who not only have done well but who also crow about their productive and profitable partnerships, singing quietly and sometimes loudly and happily their joy, appreciation and praise of their strong partners, to anyone who will listen.

There are many, frequently overlapping, reasons why individuals stumble into conflict after entering into a relationship with a strong woman. It's more of a problem for men, because men still struggle with the competitive instincts of their primitive forefathers and must frequently battle against the tendency to assume the right to control. Men's role models—teachers, coaches, dads, uncles, grandfathers, older brothers, sports figures, and political and religious leaders—continue to be relatively macho and testosterone-laden when contrasted with female role models.

Fortunately, these patterns are changing as society develops greater comfort with strong female leaders within our political, religious, educational and social communities. Many more men today express pride in women's accomplishments within their families and communities.

An enlightened partner is genuinely excited when his or her partner moves forward in her life in small or earth-shaking ways. In a healthy couple, one triumph fills two glasses.

The partner cheers his significant other on, with tons of support, visible and genuine, loudly shared and vocalized pride. A friend who is happily remarried to a partner of her own sex reminded me, "We don't have to compete with each other. When she comes home after a great day at work, well, that's a good day for both of us!" In the absence of such mutuality, competition can become truly destructive. The less open-minded and less enlightened partner feels discounted in the face of the partner's achievements, with the relationship often paying a continuing, cumulative price for such grudging behavior.

The unhappy partner may act out, expressing his or her feelings in concrete ways that have the potential to bring a host of other problems to the competition forefront. The angry, frustrated or conflicted partner may turn to alcohol or drugs. He or she may act out sexually, with extramarital dalliances. Not appreciating that his or her own unhappiness arises from a failure to appreciate and enjoy their partner's accomplishments, the unhappy partner may be (at least temporarily) convinced that within the false fabric of an affair "someone finally understands him."

In addition, acting out pulls partners away from each other, widening the fissure within the partnership. Marital acrimony may in turn lead to separation and even tragic divorce, caused not by genuine grievances but by insecurities, jealousies and competitions that were neither appreciated nor addressed during the relationship.

Acting out—the often non-verbal, behavioral expression of unconscious, unrealized, unacceptable or unappreciated feelings or conflicts—may also travel in the reverse direction. The individual acting out his home-partnership conflicts at work, in visible and unhealthy ways. Or acting them out in workaholic or other unhealthy ways in an effort to prop up his self-esteem. Conversely, he may act out by avoiding work. A grumpy man not tuned into his own conflicts and unhappiness with the world may unconsciously or semi-consciously choose not to work, as a way of a) expressing his own frustration with and contempt for his world, b) escaping responsibility and greater participation in that same world, and c) avoiding any insight into those same difficulties that saw him withdraw in the first place, thus helping to seal his doom and perpetuating this unhappy cycle. A marriage involving such a quietly unhappy, frustrated partner is more than likely doomed to twice as much misery.

Dependency conflicts are not infrequent within relationships with strong woman partners, especially in later relationships where the woman has been more successful financially or prestige-wise than her partner has been. The not-so-strong partner does not like depending on her—she owns the house and the yacht—yet he shrinks or recoils when his dependency is threatened by outside forces. He may be afraid of losing her strength, frightened of something that threatens to redefine the relationship or of any development that might see him becoming more independent and, as a result, less dependent on her. Sometimes a man will persist in his dependent child roles as a way of punishing his stronger partner. The fact that change within relationships is usually for the better, that he will be evolving into a stronger, less dependent person, does not occur to most such people when under fire.

On the other hand, some people may over-identify with their partner's attributes, including their strength. In other words, what they lack in themselves they may impute to their partner, sometimes in friendly ways and at other times in hostile fashion. A not-so-strong man may resent his stronger wife or friend and defensively harp on her ways. "She's a ball-buster, that one!" or "This one . . . she's too big for her britches, I'll tell ya!" Sometimes called projective identification, this defense sees the less strong partner focusing on what he is lacking by seeing it in larger, more contemptuous or less flattering forms in her.

This problem of projection arises when a person struggles unsuccessfully with internal conflict (in this case, his conflict around living with a strong woman and her success) and because he is not able to own his conflict, he puts it onto his partner, projecting the problem, thus hindering any further efforts to identify with, own and work on the conflict.

Stereotypes, like other forms and aspects of prejudice, are almost always learned, in part, at home from family role models of influence. Hearing that "a woman's place is in the home!" or the left-handed compliment "Gee . . . she thinks like a man!" may help children organize their developmental world more efficiently—if less accurately—but it leaves lasting impressions and attitudes that they take with them when making friends and later when dating, courting and building partnerships and marriages. More often, these attitudes are not so much learned in verbal interaction with parents and older siblings as they are non-verbally modeled. As such, they are less subject to discussion, refinement and refutation. How Mother stood up to Father, and how Father responded to her spunk and spine (or lack of it) impacts on the children in subtle but powerful ways that will help see them to and through adulthood. Consider this spirited exchange between my exasperated step-daughter, Christy, and her daughter, Brynn, at the breakfast table one summer morning:

> *(A frustrated) Christy: "You know, young lady . . . you're pretty weird!"*
>
> *(An unruffled) Brynn: "I'm pretty. And I'm weird!"*

With a comeback like that four months short of her fourth birthday, one can envision just how strong this young lady will be ten years from now. We would get a glimpse just one year later, in this aside shared quietly with her older brother in the back seat of my car, "Cameron – when I hit you . . . please don't hit me back!"

What can be learned from earlier relationships like these—or from, say, a first marriage? A healthier attitude in a second marriage or partnership would be to learn as much as possible from the first relationship, and to use those memories and experiences as necessary—but not sufficient—building blocks for a mature partnership. Competition with a strong and spirited full-of-life woman can become more harmful to the partnership when the not-so-strong partner is not working on his or her own growth, at least semi-independently.

This includes personal growth opportunities pursued through psychotherapy, which offers one the opportunity to appreciate the breadth and depth of the competition, dependency and rivalry conflicts in living with a strong woman—and puts these conflicts into words that help make life's anguish manageable and, later, actionable. We can learn from our past, build more affirmative and effective tools with which to work on our most important relationships in positive and proactive ways, beginning with "Why was I attracted to her in the first place?" Personal growth may also involve the not-as-strong partner pursuing new and exciting spiritual or religious pathways; taking on and working on important friendships in responsible, wholesome ways; working on physical, emotional and mental health opportunities through exercise, recreation and meditation programs; taking on new hobbies or other pursuits, or returning to new aspects of satisfying old ones; attempting major challenges, including career changes, returning to school or writing a book.

When people pursuing their own personal growth within a formal therapeutic system find themselves exploring other physical, emotional and intellectual pathways of growth and development, it is sometimes just for fun, but it is sometimes with more serious motives. The difference is often moot, but the operative word here is 'fun.' I learned that from Betsy. The desire to play is human, and to play with another risks divine possibilities. Conversely, much conflict within a partnership may arise from a lack of playfulness between the partners. The same males who might enjoy a competitive Friday night poker game with the boys may shirk from enjoying a fun competition with a strong partner. So why can't competition with a partner also be fun? In fact, it can. While many men are hooked on winning, in their obsessions with victory they miss a much higher goal: the value of play with another. This is itself exceeded in importance by only one other possibility on earth: the value, importance and rewards of regular play with a partner. In healthier couples where both partners are pursuing their own individual personal growth, competition can be a delightful feature of a growing partnership or marriage; where individual achievements, as well as competition between those same partners, can be enjoyed they can also be celebrated.

I cite as an example my own experience on a cold January day, scurrying by car from the Horseshoe Bay ferry terminal to meet Clair at West Vancouver's Presto Cuccina for a plate of their delicious Chicken Pesto Penne. In her own car, she had taken a different route from the ferry, and I found myself alternately speeding up and slowing down, wondering if,

a) she was racing me,

b) I was racing her,

c) did I really give a fig?

It turns out I did. When I arrived, I spotted her Mazda MX-7 parked right in front of Cuccina. Damn. "What took you so long?" she greeted me, half teasing, half challenging. I tried ignoring the question, to no avail. She laughed. I smiled and reminded myself that being only mildly competitive with a strong woman makes about as much sense as a touch of pregnancy.

You don't have to be brave to live with a strong woman.

But it helps.

25   Living With a Strong Woman

HOW DOES ONE LIVE comfortably and happily in contentment with a strong woman? Based on personal and professional experience, I think there are at least twelve parts to this never-ending, but neither unsolvable nor impenetrable, mystery.

The first part is existential. Take responsibility for your state of affairs and circumstances, for the position in your life shared with this special and uncommon, but not rare, person. No one put a gun to your head to make you get involved with her, forced you to commit to this challenging and ultimately or eventually rewarding experience. Don't blame her for what you did—you are the one who took this brave and gutsy leap of faith! And while you're at it, give yourself some credit, a silent pat on the back for having done something that many, perhaps most, people would not do. The stronger the woman you have found, the fewer the people in the world who would have braved living with her, would have aimed this high for such a prize. Two pats on the back.

Second, why skimp on your praise or hide your growing light under a bushel basket? You can light a candle or curse your subjective darkness. Write to her: prose, poetry, or why not both? Kiss her feet. Write about her, praising her to your friends and to hers and to your families. Feel the feelings, take pleasure in them and savor them, focus on them and enjoy them. Maybe this represents too much of a stretch for a shy person? Accept the challenge and meet it head on. Expect some ambivalence, not as a mark against this newest, shared adventure of yours but as the human organism's natural resistance to change, then move, jump, walk, step, dance and go with it, and beyond. Praise, appreciation and support, along with admiration and showing your fond affection for your strong partner, are among the most important parts of that process.

Third, watch out for your own need for approval and appreciation. If you are male, this could be especially important, as men often have higher needs for approval, appreciation and acceptance. Ask for approval, even with helpful reminders and hints about why you deserve a stroke or two, but don't harp on this need. And be sure to show appreciation for the appreciation that you do receive! You are in the Big League now. Living with a strong woman you stand a greater chance of bringing yourself up to her level by spending more time in enjoying, appreciating and praising her than by worrying over not getting your fair share of praise.

Fourth, living with a strong woman represents an opportunity for you to become stronger. You do that by giving more and taking less. In moving into a relationship with a tough and durable friend or partner, you have more than likely hit the jackpot! The irony of supporting a strong person—and how we grow from that opening and the chance to get stronger ourselves in giving back to her—is yours to enjoy.

Fifth, do not try to change her—*ever*. This natural but unfortunate instinct surfaces when we sense we might be in over our heads, especially on those days when we realize, "Gee . . . she really is a tough one, eh? What have I got myself into, anyway?" At times like this, remembering your decision to be with this strong person can be comforting. Do not try to change your partner just because she's acting in the tough, strong ways today that drew you to her yesterday! These moments of conflict (and at times confrontation) with a robust and competent partner are also the ones in which people often grow and change. If you want to feel powerless, try changing someone else. If you want to feel powerful, work on changing yourself. You have been given a gift, or more accurately, because of a certain admixture of personality traits and memories and models from your childhood, you have given this gift to yourself. Enjoy her, do not change her or even try (it will not work, anyway). And when you do find yourself trying to change your partner, in frustration, anger, discouragement or temporary despair, step back, take a peek at yourself and reflect on what you are doing. If you are having a good day, don't forget to laugh at yourself. Humor is not only a super medium to connect with another in an intimate fashion, it is also holy and frequently healing.

Sixth, guard your careers and your professions with your lives because your respective professions or careers are an enormous part of your lives; on one level they are who you are. Concentrate on building a long-lasting relationship that is big enough and secure enough for two careers, hers and yours. If she is a homemaker, chances are that she has a second part-time or full-time career, in addition. In other words, she works time-and-a-half on a slow day, and may be on chronic overtime. This over-functioning tendency is not especially healthy, but it can overlap with the strong woman's territory.

There may be room for one or both of you to slow down, which may be difficult for you if you sense that her job is more important or more prestigious, or if you see her work as more valuable than yours. A friend's recent e-mail reminded me of the challenge that living with a strong woman poses to many men, as she reflected:

I think you are right about the power struggles. Two females just have a different kind of energy. I used to say to Bob . . . when he would feel that I somehow outshone him, that we were on the same team so the points counted for both of us. I never have to say that to Barbara.

In other words, watch out for feeling competitive with your robust, solid and tough friend and/or partner and expect to find yourself biting your tongue and putting an entire or partial lid on these shameful, unacceptable feelings of rivalry. But don't continue with unhealthy, secretive behaviors. If you do happen to be feeling competitive with her, do not be afraid to voice these feelings and conflicts. You will earn more of her respect in so doing, will feel better after having ventilated these all-too-human feelings and frailties; you will have done your share in moving your relationship toward a higher, more accepting and probably less competitive level, toward a relationship that is healthy enough and roomy enough for two growing, independent, hard-working people in love with each other.

And do not forget that whatever each of you brings home from your workplace stands to enhance your relationship. Listen to her recount her day, her highs and lows, the triumphs and tragedies. Share your own; it may be a relief for her to hear how someone else's day has gone. Enjoy the contrast in your job descriptions and look for complementarities—ways you help complete each other—points of similarity, points of difference and in-between points. While we are more than our jobs, that same work often represents a large share of our hopes for our lives, many of our dreams of, perhaps, making the world a better place and, finally, a big chunk of what turns us on, whether that job is geology, education, medicine, law, gardening, children or an entrepreneurial pursuit.

Seventh, look around you, and learn. Which of your friends has had the guts, the courage or even the impulse to partner with a strong woman? How did they do it? Why did they do it? And how are they doing today? Learn from them, their ups and downs, and from the strong woman in each of their lives. How is she doing? How is she coping? And how are they doing together? It's okay to compare notes and to want to learn from others who are following parallel pathways, perhaps contemporaries, or maybe family members who have gone before you, an earlier generation or two, aunts, uncles and grandparents.

Eighth, learn from literature, where strong heroines are depicted by female and male writers alike,[1] and where more human and vulnerable women are also presented. Write a short story or an essay yourself. How about writing a poem, a paean to strong women or to all women, and giving it to your partner or to a friend?

Ninth, be prepared to share your strong friend or partner with others, including her family, friends, peers and community and with your shared world as well. She does not belong to you. Although most of the time you probably appreciate this, you may occasionally forget this important truth. Let her go, let her fly, wherever she and her winds decide to go. Family members and friends will likely want some time and space to share with her, desiring some of that same strength for reasons similar to those that drew you to her. She grows from these important connections in her life; the more you let her go, the less you endeavor to keep her to yourself, the stronger your relationship will become, returning strength to each of you individually.

Tenth, while sharing your strong partner with important others in her world, do not forget her children, your kids or the kids that you share together. Play an active role in sharing this woman with these young learners, teaching them by your role model how one lives comfortably, kindly, lovingly and effectively with a strong partner. Anticipate the occasional stumble on the children's part as they grow first into comfort and later appreciation for having grown up with a strong mother. They will be learning how to live with a strong woman partly through trial and error and partly by watching you grow through a similar process, one step backward, two steps forward. They learn from context, and a large part of that context is watching and learning from your risk-taking and willingness to enter into a relationship with someone stronger than you. Learn together, laugh and cry together, but stay together.

The children may not thank you until they are thirty or forty—thankfulness is a learned trait and not usually part of a younger person's emotional repertoire. One of the biggest thank-you notes from your children may not be written on a Hallmark card or even verbalized in a heartfelt fashion. Rather it will be delivered in one of the varied ways in which they pass on to the next generation their acquired strengths and their convictions about the importance of that strength, power and vigor.

Eleventh. Sometimes it helps to get outside of yourself and see the bigger picture. Remember that you and your partner are a team and whatever your partner or friend does reflects positively on you, and what you do is a credit to her as well. It wasn't just you, remember, that chose to be with her. She chose to be with you, also. Look at the bigger picture, and don't forget that on the best days in the best relationships the whole is more, so much more than the sum of the parts!

If you are a man, there is almost certainly a growth opportunity here for you. This is the kind of stuff men have trouble dealing with, seeing the larger picture and appreciating that life is larger than they are. But know that you are important. Your partner is important. In some special, often quiet ways, what the two of you have created is quite different from either of you on your own. When that strong woman stands up to you, it is neither a discredit nor a disservice, but a compliment as well as a complement. She is saying you can take a punch, take a hit, and so she is giving you her very best. This is the finest praise or tribute most of us will receive in our lifetimes. It is almost always given non-verbally, with neither preface nor apology, so do not expect your strong friend or partner to explain or offer a context. Take it, experience it and savor it. It is yours.

Twelfth, and finally, what if you have decided that you can not, will not take it anymore? Get some help and get it quickly. Talk to a friend, a family person you can trust, a rabbi, priest, minister or imam. See your family physician. And if you're tired of the status quo that characterizes your current relationship with your strong partner or friend and would like to get further ahead and grow from this, ask any one of the above people for help in seeing a first-rate counselor or psychotherapist. Expect to feel some resistance about doing this, especially if you're the kind of person who thinks counseling or therapy is only for sick people. It is not. You will be working at making a good thing better, and are already ahead of the power curve in having chosen a strong woman for a partner.

You might not ever catch up to your partner in strength. But remember, the contest is not to catch or compete with your partner nearly as much as it is to be the best, most content and most alive person you can be. In going for counseling you can lessen at least some of the emotional distance between you, as well as learn from this critical relationship. This is a growth opportunity, but it will not happen overnight. Many people have made important, life-altering and life-improving changes in fifteen to thirty counseling sessions, and sometimes less. Be patient. Rome was not built in a day nor were strong partnerships. Remember, also, that not all counseling relationships are life-changing or even positive experiences. You will know within four or five sessions whether you are seeing a psychotherapist who can help. If you are still in serious doubt at that point, cut your losses, get another counselor or therapist. There is a counselor or psychotherapist out there for everyone. You may not always find yours the first time around, but by keeping at it and searching for the best, you will find a winner—that particular professional person who is not only comfortable to be with but also effective and appreciative of the opportunity to act as your research assistant in this important work.

Still stuck with those persistently ambivalent, mixed feelings about living with a strong woman? Don't forget about couple's counseling opportunities, working with individuals who are especially skilled and comfortably competent in working with partners; usually, but not always, at the same time. Sometimes a lot can happen when two people go for help together. You explore what you have to give to her and share with her and what she brings to the relationship, and how those two sets of gifts interplay and interweave, and how they don't. In couple's counseling, neither you nor your partner is the patient or client; your relationship is the focus, the star of the sessions. What feels like a curse today could and will easily transform into a noticeable blessing, maybe not tomorrow, but one day. It just takes some old-fashioned hard work. Whatever you do, do not blame your partner for your difficulties and the strange mixture of speed bumps and goose bumps in this relationship. It's not her fault she is a strong person. It is her gift, right? Don't shoot the messenger.

The sad fact is, however, that most men will not seek out professional counseling. So how do they actually live comfortably or even with any sense of contentment or peace of mind with a strong woman in the very real world? Some will compartmentalize their marriage, building a wall around it that affords them a sense of safety and boundaries. An example of this would be the man who adores his wife but is not comfortable in sharing her with his other worlds, including his professional community, his circle of friends, his extended family. Nor would he share his wife's other worlds. Several zones of safety and comfort are established in this series of parallel universes, but the sad downside of this model is that when people don't get to meet each other, fun is lost and warmth within this marriage is almost certainly sacrificed.

A second model would be the man who stays at home, acting as a homemaker and taking more of the direct responsibility for raising the children. Not to be confused with a weak position, this is the man who chooses to put his strengths into a more domestic world rather than working as a second bread-winner, competing with, sharing with or operating completely independently of his wife. Nothing is lost as long as both partners enjoy themselves in this reversal of traditional roles.

With the children raised, some couples move about quite comfortably in overlapping roles. In the later years of a relationship or in second or third marriages each partner pursues her or his career in an unfettered, highly rewarding fashion, and at the same time manages to find time with each other over a drink or supper.

All twelve of the previous strategies can play an important role in the lives of the partners of strong women, helping them to find highly rewarding ways to develop partly separate, partly together and overlapping lifestyles. My wife has quietly instructed me in her non-verbal, Canadian style as follows: "I like it when you wait on me—sometimes. I do not like it when you wait for me, however. You have your life. I have mine. And when we get together, we have ours to fully enjoy!"

I get more practice with this on the days and weeks when she is traveling abroad, teaching internationally or going to the psychology meetings that mean so much to her. I miss her, though somewhat less so than when we first started dating twelve years ago. And I know that she is more fully herself and more content when she returns home from a rewarding week or so with her colleagues. And I am a better, stronger person for her travels because, living with myself at home, I am growing in directions of my own. For example, these days I appreciate more readily the differences between (neurotic) loneliness and a (healthier) sense of aloneness; I often savor more of the latter and experience less of the former than in days past when she was out of town. The get-togethers when she returns home are rich, rewarding and often much fun. They are filling, stick-to-the-ribs experiences for me and, I suspect, for her as well. She is my partner, beloved and wife. But long before that, she was—and continues to be—a mother, a daughter, an aunt, a sister, a person. A woman.

A strong woman is a panoply of sight, sound, smell and just about all that makes up the human experience. She is a symphony of bass and treble instruments, alto and soprano voices all—on her very best days—exquisitely and harmonically balanced. And we who love or fight or laugh or play or cry with this strong woman are the beneficiaries of this gift, the happy recipients of what Nature herself has given to us and shared with us. And so,

- Take a chance. A love like this and a woman like this are rare indeed!
- Don't try to change her. (Why on earth would you want to?)
- Enjoy her enormous sense of integrity, patience and compassion for the world.

And, finally, if the relationship doesn't work out, count your lucky stars for the number of days you were able to enjoy each other, the number of steps you enjoyed with each other. Savor them. Because of your risk-taking and your courage to love a strong woman, you are probably stronger and wiser.

Any individual struggling with mixed feelings and the challenges of living with a strong woman should recite this meditation, mantra or prayer: "Make me less anxious, less important, more aware." And if he or she is listening carefully during this prayer, the difficulties of living with a woman who is sometimes smarter, faster, sharper, kinder and more understanding than you, might just be soothed by this spiritual, meditative emollient. Finally, remember that being kind is more important than being right. This is not just a meditation but a way to live life, a yardstick by which you can tell how you have done today, a compass during the brightest days and the darkest nights.

Strong girls and women offer priceless gifts. By their examples, they model courage, kindness and love. By their very presence, they teach us the important differences between their toughness and others' roughness. These quiet, unspoken offerings are there for us for all our lives. With their understanding, we learn it is never too late to learn from them, and from all others. All we need do is keep our ears and eyes open and, if we are enjoying an unusually special lesson at the feet of a strong woman, our mouths shut.

As they challenge and confront us, strong girls and women remind us by their words and behavior that they do not have a corner on the market, a monopoly on positions and decisions. In reaching out to us in this way, they compel us, challenge us, to look within ourselves, to peek at our own possibilities and our own strength—however well hidden— to ponder our potential as strong persons. "You too can be strong, competent and productive in this difficult world," they remind us, and then almost parenthetically, "And by the way, what's stopping you?" These lessons and offerings usually come quietly, with neither words nor judgments attached. We are better for their presence yesterday, today and tomorrow.

This is their silent gift.

APPRECIATION

You've disagreed
with me more.
And maybe heard me once
(or twice) a bit better.
But never, ever
do I remember you
differing so much
while listening so well,
and keeping in such close . . .
and quiet touch.

26 Growing Old With a Strong Woman

WHEN CLAIR AND I MARRIED, in 1997, we were both older, both had been married before and both had suffered over the loss of our former partners. We had come to our new partnership with different baggage from when we started out years before. For those reasons alone, our marriage would be different from our former ones.

It would be different for other reasons. Our needs were different from those we had fifteen or twenty years before. We had feathered our nests, had our babies, seen them grow up and have their own children. We had done that.

Falling for Clair would see me leaving Oregon; in fact leaving the United States, the country of my birth where I had lived over four-fifths of my life. It would see me returning to British Columbia, taking out dual citizenship, reestablishing my psychiatric practice and working with a new community psychiatry team, buying a new home and selling an old one. Clair would also relocate several times, selling her family home as we tried a variety of housing options to help meet both her needs and mine. Each of us would find ourselves tossing away our talismans, our security blankets, as we started anew, vulnerable in new territory. Re-nesting.

Clair and I didn't so much have a blended family as enjoy two separate, sometimes interwoven families: Clair's children and grandchildren in British Columbia, my children in southern Oregon. We travel frequently to southern Oregon to visit Andy and Mindy, and all of us meet together every two to three years at Club Med in Mexico.

In most ways, the relationship Clair and I have is typical of mature marriages and relationships when most of the children are launched. Like many other settled partners that have found each other relatively late in life, we spend more time balancing our own and each other's needs rather than worrying too much about what's best for the larger family. There are still challenges, like blending Clair's retirement with my semi-retirement fantasies. There are occasional competitive overtones, sometimes louder than at other times, such as when we compete as psychologist versus psychiatrist, Clair being the owner and boss, until recently, of one of the two clinics in which I practiced. I sometimes miss the days when Betsy and I enjoyed our own mental health clinic that we built in southern Oregon. When, a few years ago, I followed Clair around Israel, where she taught marriage therapy, I was twenty percent envious, eighty percent just plain proud of her. It is never black and white. If a man who marries a strong woman late in life is as content and as happy and as fulfilled as I, then I wish him well and say, "Enjoy your competitive feelings within your relationship, too! Like spice completing a delicious dinner for two."

There are further differences between an earlier and a later partnership with a strong woman. While feelings of competition and envy may spark a slow day, there is more that is good, even enthralling, about what I experience with Clair. With it, comes an awareness that what we have learned from an earlier marriage we may re-experience in our new partnership, and we may enjoy it more. Psychologists term this *latent learning*: a person's ability to learn something that may not be evident right away, a learned attribute or behavior that will not manifest itself openly until later, usually under different conditions.

Grief is a natural, organic part of growing old. We, and our relationships, are better for this. When someone you love dies, and especially when that someone is a strong woman, you don't just stop loving them. But grieving allows us to slow down our loving—just a bit, just one manageable step at a time. It helps us keep connected to our loved ones even while our hearts and souls and minds and bodies are struggling with the absurdity and the enormity of the loss and practicing letting the loved one go.

Betsy was important. And continues to be so. No longer beside me, she lives on within me and within her children. I learned from Betsy a precious secret and that is that loving is its own reward. You get out of anything just what you put in to it, but especially into a relationship with a strong woman! Every human being presents us with the opportunity to love with gusto, abandon, relish and creativity; to take our hesitant feet off the brakes of our relationship and let it fly.

I enjoy this more frequently with Clair these days, as we seem to have more time together than Betsy and I were able to have thirty years ago. Taking Clair a cup of coffee. Picking up her empty cereal bowl. Rubbing her back at night before we nod off.

Or writing her a spontaneous haiku of affection and appreciation. Sometimes I may overdo it, push my limits, and Clair is quick to react with a smile and a gesture or brief word telling me, "That's enough, David. Stop it, okay?"

Marriage is so often a matter of fine-tuning, but we must first take those moments of initiative in order to have something to fine-tune. And being married to a strong woman is all the more an opportunity that beckons us.

What a gift!

Pitching, bitching.

Rolling, strolling.

Yawing, jawing.

Flying, crying.

Leaping, creeping.

Swerving, curving.

Slipping, tripping.

Sliding, striding.

Lurching,

skidding,

veering.

Toward a pathway that is nearing . . .
(and a road that's not worth fearing)—
Pray . . . a lesson most endearing—
that the secret lies both here—and there.
Quite possibly . . . it's everywhere.

"It's her! It's him! It's them!" they cried.

Not so.

The Truth is here.

Inside.

Where the Flame is softly burning.

While the Truth is slowly turning.

Over.

And under.

And in . . .

And out.[1]

Sources

Introduction

1. Fletcher, Joann. *From Warrior Women to Female Pharaohs: Careers for Women in Ancient Egypt.* http://www.bbc.co/uk/history/ancient/egyptians/women_01.
2. Felder, Deborah G. and Diana Rosen. *Fifty Jewish Women Who Changed the World.* New York: Citadel Press, 2003. The story about Deborah appears on page 13.
3. History of Women Warriors Through 19th Century. http://www.fscclub.com/gender/warrior-hist.
4. For more information on matriarchal societies, see http://www.saunalahti.fi/penelope/Feminism/KhasiGaro.
5. Davis-Kimball, Jeannine. *Secrets of the Dead: Amazon Warrior Women.* http://www.pbs.org/wnet/Secrets/previous_season/case_amazon/interview.
6. Saunders, Nicky. "Women as Warriors in History." For full essay, see www.lothene.demon.co.uk/others/women.html.
7. Fanny Mendelssohn Hensel. http://www.wwnorton.com/classical/composers.
8. Phillips, Rick. *Sound Advice.* CBC-AM, January 23, 2005.
9. Will, George F. Labor Since the Overpass. *Newsweek,* August 15, 2005, 54.
10. Parkinson, Colin. Voice of the People. *Vancouver Sun,* December 12, 2006, A8.
11. Ensler, Eve. *Insecure at Last.* New York: Random House, 2006, xx.
12. Mermin, Liz. *The Beauty Academy of Kabul.* Documentary. New York, NY: Noble Enterprise Production, 2006.

13. Barba, Sharon. "A Cycle of Women." *Rising Tides: 20th Century American Women Poets*. New York: Simon and Schuster, 1973. Permission to print by Laura Chester, co-editor of *Rising Tides*.

Chapter 2 Pearl Bernard Kirkpatrick
1. Oberlin College. *Catalogue*, 1905–06.

Chapter 4 Elizabeth Ann Cowan and Isabel Cowan
1. Friedan, Betty. *The Feminine Mystique*. New York: Dell, 1963.
2. Cowan, Constance and Lois Castledine, eds. *Aunt Isabel's Diary*. Copyrighted Washington, D.C., 1984.

Chapter 5 Mom and Dad and Dayton, Ohio
1. Newman, Randy. "Dayton, Ohio 1903." *Sail Away*. Album. Burbank, California: Reprise Records, Warner Brothers Music, 1972.

Chapter 8 The Reunion
1. Girl Drowned. Friend Saved by Brother. Full article in *Dayton Journal Herald*, May 16, 1951.

Chapter 9 Zaiga
1. Konstantin Folkmanis, his wife and three children leave their war-torn roots to start a new life in Yellow Springs, Ohio. Full article in *Dayton Daily News*, 1948.

Chapter 10 Set in Concrete
1. Kirkpatrick, David. Untitled poem. Circa 2000, unpublished.

Chapter 11 Post-Graduate Studies from Atlanta to Anchorage
1. Kirkpatrick, David. Success Conflict 65 Years Later: Contributions and Confusions. *Canadian Journal of Psychiatry*, Vol. 27 August 1982, 405–9.

Chapter 12 Betsy
1. BETSY'S BLACKBERRY LIQUEUR
    2 ½ cups berries
    1 mickey (375 ml.) of rye, scotch or vodka
    1½ – 2 cups sugar
    Turn occasionally. Serve in 2–3 months after straining through cheesecloth.

Chapter 14   Living, Loving, Learning
1. Henley, Larry and Jeff Silbar. "Wind Beneath My Wings." 1982.

Chapter 16   Healing
1. Joseph, Jenny. "Warning." Watsonville, CA: Papier-Mache Press, 1991.
2. Ornstein, Anna. *My Mother's Eyes.* Cincinnati, Ohio: Emmis Books, 2004.

Chapter 18   Clair
1. Walter Toman quoted in *Extraordinary Relationships.* Roberta M. Gilbert. New York: John Wiley & Sons, 1992, 202–3.

Chapter 19   Strength in Madness
1. Malone, Thomas Patrick. I Love You. Essay circa 1968. The full essay is reprinted as Love on pp 9–11 in *The Art of Intimacy,* written by Tom and his son Patrick Thomas Malone. New York: Prentice Hall, 1987. The excerpt reads: "Because being loved allows the other to be what he really is, it is much easier to know when you are loved than it is to know when you are loving. The affirmation of your love is the other person's being, the confirmation of being loved lies in your experience of being yourself. This you can most readily and reliably know. Since it is easier to know when you are loved than when you are loving, the most serious personal distortions of human experience lie in the loving, not the loved experience. Most psychiatric problems arise out of confusion about loving; mistakes about being loved are rare, if they occur at all."

Chapter 20   Strength in Age
1. Paetkau, Bonnie. "Old Woman." Circa 2000, unpublished.

Chapter 21   Growing Strength — Mindy
1. Bancroft, Wendy. "Sustaining: Making the Transition from Welfare to Work." Vancouver: Social Research and Demonstration Corporation, 2004.

Chapter 22   Strong Women, and What Makes Them That Way
1. Poet unknown. Vancouver's Downtown Eastside. Circa 2001, unpublished.
2. Wurtzel, Elizabeth. *Bitch: In Praise of Difficult Women.* New York: Doubleday, 1998.
3. Proverbs 31:25.

4. Sykes, Bryan. *The Seven Daughters of Eve*. New York, London: W.W. Norton, 2001.

5. Steinberg, Blema S. The making of female presidents and prime ministers: The impact of birth order, sex of siblings, and father-daughter dynamics. *Political Psychology*, Vol. 22 (1) March 2001, 89–114.

6. Brenner, O.C. and N.J. Beutell. The effect of birth order and gender on American managers' attitudes towards female managers. *Journal of Social Psychology*, Vol. 129 (1), Feb. 1989, 57–64.

7. Andersson, Lars. Loneliness, birth order and social loss among a group of elderly women. *Journal of Psychosomatic Research*, Vol. 29 (1), 1985, 33–42.

8. Eckstein, Daniel. Leadership, popularity and birth order in women. *Journal of Individual Psychology*, Vol. 34 (1), May 1978, 63–66.

9. Skinner, Nicholas F. Hypochondria in women as a function of birth order. *Psychological Reports*. Vol. 80 (3 pt 2), June 1997, 1344–46.

10. Farley, Frank H. Family structure and approval dependency in college females. *Journal of Marriage and the Family*. Vol. 37 (4), Nov. 1975, 760–62.

11. Werner, Emmy E. and Ruth S. Smith. *Overcoming the Odds: High Risk Children From Birth to Adulthood*. Ithica, NY: Cornell University Press, 1992.

Chapter 23 Drawn to Strength

1. Cowan, Constance and Lois Castledine, eds. *Aunt Isabel's Diary*. Copyrighted Washington, D.C., 1984.

Chapter 25 Living With a Strong Woman

1. For further information on strong women in literature, read *Sisters in the Wilderness* by Charlotte Gray. Toronto: Penguin Books Canada, 1999.

Chapter 26 Growing Old With a Strong Woman

1. Kirkpatrick, David. "Finding the Center." November 2008, unpublished.

Index

About the Author

A psychotherapist and psychiatrist for over thirty years, David Kirkpatrick, MA, MD, was born in Kansas City, Missouri, and grew up in Yellow Springs, Ohio. Following studies, work and specialty training in Ohio, Georgia, California, Alaska and British Columbia, he opened a practice in Ashland, Oregon, and then in Vancouver, BC. He now enjoys a balance between community mental health (including ten years on Vancouver's Downtown Eastside) and a private psychotherapy practice where he uses a family orientation approach with individuals, couples and families in West Vancouver and on BC's Sunshine Coast. Since 1973, David has published numerous health care and humor articles.